yourself ®

the british monarchy
from henry VIII
stewart ross

For over 60 years, more than
40 million people have learnt over
750 subjects the **teach yourself**
way, with impressive results.

be where you want to be
with **teach yourself**

For UK order enquiries: please contact Bookpoint Ltd, 130 Milton Park, Abingdon, Oxon OX14 4SB. Telephone: +44 (0) 1235 827720. Fax: +44 (0) 1235 400454. Lines are open 09.00–18.00, Monday to Saturday, with a 24-hour message answering service. Details about our titles and how to order are available at www.teachyourself.co.uk

For USA order enquiries: please contact McGraw-Hill Customer Services, PO Box 545, Blacklick, OH 43004-0545, USA. Telephone: 1-800-722-4726. Fax: 1-614-755-5645.

For Canada order enquiries: please contact McGraw-Hill Ryerson Ltd, 300 Water St, Whitby, Ontario L1N 9B6, Canada. Telephone: 905 430 5000. Fax: 905 430 5020.

Long renowned as the authoritative source for self-guided learning – with more than 40 million copies sold worldwide – the **teach yourself** series includes over 300 titles in the fields of languages, crafts, hobbies, business, computing and education.

British Library Cataloguing in Publication Data: a catalogue record for this title is available from the British Library.

Library of Congress Catalog Card Number: on file.

First published in UK 2005 by Hodder Education, 338 Euston Road, London, NW1 3BH.

First published in US 2005 by Contemporary Books, a Division of the McGraw-Hill Companies, 1 Prudential Plaza, 130 East Randolph Street, Chicago, IL 60601 USA.

This edition published 2005.

The **teach yourself** name is a registered trade mark of Hodder Headline.

Typeset by Transet Limited, Coventry, England.
Printed in Great Britain for Hodder Education, a division of Hodder Headline, 338 Euston Road, London NW1 3BH, by Cox & Wyman Ltd, Reading, Berkshire.

Hodder Headline's policy is to use papers that are natural, renewable and recyclable products and made from wood grown in sustainable forests. The logging and manufacturing processes are expected to conform to the environmental regulations of the country of origin.

Impression number 10 9 8 7 6 5 4 3 2 1
Year   2010 2009 2008 2007 2006 2005

The state of monarchy is the supremest thing upon earth; for kings are not only God's lieutenants upon earth, and sit upon God's throne, but even by God himself they are called gods.

James I's speech to parliament, March 1610.

That what is called Monarchy always appears to me to be a silly contemptible thing. I compare it to something kept behind a curtain, about which there is a great deal of bustle and fuss, and a wonderful air of seeming solemnity; but when, by an accident, the curtain happens to be opened, and the company see what it is, they burst into laughter.

Tom Paine in *The Rights of Man*, 1791–2.

contents

introduction

This is an extraordinary story. Its theme is survival – for whatever else the British monarchy may or may not have achieved over the past half-millennium, it is at least still there. Very few contemporary thrones with whom it shared a glittering dais in the early sixteenth century have shown similar resilience. Like a snowman in May, the British monarchy lingers on when all logic, precedence, history and experience suggest it should no longer be there.

How may such longevity be explained? Much depends upon one's political viewpoint. Those who favour the crown's continued existence emphasize the wisdom or other talents of the individuals who have occupied the throne; they also suggest, Tigger-like, that monarchy is what the British like best. Opponents of the institution are more likely to grumble about an unholy alliance between the crown and what is still (just) known as 'The Establishment'. They believe that Fortune has had a hand in the matter, too: during the period when monarchies were falling fastest Britain happened to be, in the celebrated words of Sellars and Yeatman in *1066 and All That*, 'top nation'. Its hereditary head of state was, therefore, subliminally (and by some politicians, cynically) associated in the popular imagination with this top-ness. And when this faded, the crown was retained, like an athlete's medals, as a sort of souvenir of former greatness.

Be all that as it may, the British monarchy, in the currently fashionable form of a 'royal family', has survived into the twenty-first century as one of the most gawped-at, photographed, written-about, and newsworthy items in the world. No celebrity, it seems, beats an hereditary celebrity. This, incidentally, introduces another possible reason for the institution's continued existence: pity. When a footballer or fashion model falls from grace, the populace relishes the come-uppance because Nemesis is assumed to have been self-invoked. When something goes awry with the royal family, on the other hand, there are always many to point out that unlike the rest of us, who are supposedly blessed with infinite choices at every turn, the royals have had their onerous, self-denying roles thrust upon them by cruel fate. Hence the pity.

Pliability is a further reason for the monarchy's survival. It is no coincidence that the most obdurate king in our period, Charles I, came closest to bringing down permanently the entire hereditary edifice. Whether out of choice or, more usually, by force of circumstances, the position of the monarch has changed almost beyond recognition over the past 500 years. Indeed, in several aspects there has been a complete volte-face. At the time of Henry VIII, for instance, the most important quality for a successful monarch was longevity. The earlier their death, the more likely they were to be remembered, if at all, as harbingers of unrest. Henry VIII (who reigned for 38 years) glares down from a thousand pub signs, while his sickly son (six years) graces not one; Henry's elder daughter (five years) is remembered simply as 'bloody', but his equally ruthless younger daughter (45 years) is popularly heralded as a virgin queen who presided over a 'golden age'. With modern-day constitutional monarchs a case can be made for the opposite: the longer they occupy the throne, the greater the chance that their subjects will become bored and start to peer behind the royal curtain. Today, early death guarantees immortality; in the past, it guaranteed anonymity.

Monarchs have always been fascinating creatures. The attraction used to be their power and wealth. Ordinary mortals were drawn to them as the fleeing Israelites were to the pillar of fire in the desert – something literally awful: bigger, brighter and more powerful than anything else on the landscape. By some, monarchs were even considered close to God himself. The current lure of royalty is of an altogether different nature. A king or queen inspires neither awe nor fear – only in story books can they still threaten instant decapitation. What attracts us, what makes their most trivial peccadilloes front page news, is their uniqueness. In a meritocratic age of political equality and democratic capitalism, there is nothing else remotely like them. Like the dinosaurs recreated in *Jurassic Park*, they are living links to a vanished past, alluring relics, genuine antiques to set beside cheap modern imitations. They are the real thing, living history, symbols of a reassuring or irritating national continuity.

The most startling change in monarchy has been in the qualities that serve it best. Successful Renaissance monarchs required vigour, intelligence, flair and charisma. The best were near super-human: a general, politician, actor, lover, and leader within one star-studded frame, oozing personality from every gilded pore. And today? The constitutional monarch must be the exact opposite. The justification for their existence is that they are a living symbol, a figurehead fulfilling roles best kept out of the hands of politicians: receivers of oaths of loyalty, the fount of justice, the head of government, and so forth. As a figurehead is inanimate, the ideal modern monarch needs to be as close to inanimate as is humanly possible. Their puppet-like role involves having no opinions, creating no controversy by thought, word or deed, passing no judgement, and expressing support for everything and every one requested by the people's elected representatives. Like dolls, they should speak only when given a prompting squeeze.

Vitality, independence, insight – so necessary to an active ruler – are to the constitutional monarch handicaps. Where once the crown required flamboyance, it now asks for self-effacement; those who had received the nation's service are today its humbled servants. In the sixteenth century, in order to marry the woman of his choice, Henry VIII wrenched the English constitution off its medieval hinges; when in the twentieth century Edward VIII expressed a wish to marry the woman of his choice, it was the constitution that stood firm and the king who had to give way: a tale that had begun with a bang (in more senses than one) had ended with a wimp, if not with a whimper.

This 500-year revolution has been as total as it has been surprising. What follows is a brief examination of how it came about and of the cast of extraordinary characters who played out its strange, eventful drama.

NB The lists of monarchs' children comprise only legitimate offspring and those who lived long enough to be named.

part one

The Tudors, 1509–1603

Introduction

An unlikely combination of lust and luck brought the Tudors to the English throne. The family name was of Welsh origin, and it is among the rugged landscape of Denbigh, North Wales that our strange tale begins. In the late-thirteenth century, after Edward I of England had defeated Prince Llywelyn ap Gruffydd ('Llywelyn the Last'), a number of the prince's followers deftly switched allegiance to the new master and so retained their influence. (The Welsh 'ap' means 'son of', like the Scots 'mac'.) Among them was Tudur Hen (the 'Elder Tudur'). The Hen's descendants became mixed up in the revolt of Owain Glyndwr against Henry IV and one of them, sporting the surprising name of Maredudd (ap Tudur), perpetuated the memory of his unsuccessful hero by christening his son Owain (ap Maredudd ap Tudur). This Owain – 'Owen' to his English friends and acquaintances – later fought in France with his liege lord King Henry V.

Having conquered a large part of France, King Henry married the highly attractive Katherine de Valois, daughter of Charles VI of France, and was declared heir to the French throne. Katherine gave birth to a son, England's future Henry VI, just before Christmas 1421. The following August the boy's father died. When Katherine's father died shortly afterwards, the infant Henry was declared king of both England and France. His mother, the Dowager Queen Katherine, was now one of the most eligible heiresses in all Europe.

In those days noblewomen did not marry for love – at least, they were not supposed to. The secret marriage of Queen Katherine to the handsome but lowly Welsh courtier Owen ap Tudur was a soap-style scandal that might have landed the groom in serious trouble. After much official huffing and puffing, though, the match was accepted. Following Katherine's death, her sons Edmund Earl of Richmond (in Yorkshire) and Jasper Earl of Pembroke were watched over by their half-brother, King Henry VI. Their father, bearing an anglicized version of his surname, was welcomed into the royal household. The Tudors were clearly on the way up, although they had yet to establish a blood link to the English crown.

At this stage we need to rewind a century or so, to the household of Edward III's third son, John of Gaunt, Duke of Lancaster. By his favourite mistress, whom he later married, the duke had numerous offspring, the Beauforts, who were later legitimized by an act of parliament. In 1453 Edmund and Jasper

Tudor, perceived as reliable men, were given joint custody of Gaunt's orphaned ten-year-old great-granddaughter, Margaret Beaufort. Two years later Edmund married the girl.

The earl did not enjoy his child bride for long. He died the following year, leaving the pregnant Margaret to the care of his brother Jasper. Still only 14, she gave birth to a son in 1456. The boy, who was baptized Henry after his king, inherited the earldom of Richmond from his father. Thirty years later he seized the throne as the first Tudor monarch, Henry VII.

Henry VII

As there were many others with stronger claims, the Beaufort blood, although royal, was unlikely to have brought Henry the crown on its own. His path to the throne was gradually cleared by an orgy of noble bloodletting that goes by the rather poetic but historically inaccurate name of the Wars of Roses (1455–85). Coalitions of grand families, loosely gathering around the houses of Lancaster and York, fought a series of costly campaigns that slowly whittled away the male descendants of John of Gaunt until only Henry Tudor was left.

Meanwhile, the Yorkist cause had been undermined by the unprincipled behaviour of Duke Richard. Following the death of the first Yorkist king, Edward IV, the duke removed and almost certainly killed his brother's young sons (Edward V and Richard of York, the Princes in the Tower) and seized the throne for himself as Richard III. Such skulduggery split the Yorkists and played into the hands of Henry Tudor, then sheltering in Brittany. He invaded England in 1485, defeated and slew Richard III at Bosworth, and claimed the crown by right of inheritance and the judgement of God in battle. To make good his position, he promptly married Elizabeth, the sister of the Princes in the Tower, thereby uniting the red rose of Lancaster and the white of York to form the variegated Tudor flower.

Henry, an astute and cautious man, devoted his reign to securing the inheritance he had been so fortunate to obtain. This involved executing the one remaining significant Yorkist threat, Edward, Earl of Warwick, building up the power of the crown, and establishing good relations with important foreign powers. The latter development was assisted by marriage: Henry's daughter Margaret married James IV of Scotland and his eldest son Arthur married a Spanish princess, Catherine of Aragon.

Arthur's name had been carefully chosen. His accession, it was hoped, would herald a new and glorious Arthurian age. The plan did not work out as the feeble 15-year-old Arthur died less than five months after his wedding. His earnest Spanish widow was held ready for the new heir, Prince Henry.

The English monarchy

The throne that Henry was destined to inherit was an ancient and noble institution reaching back to the Anglo-Saxon 'bretwaldas' (all-Britain-rulers) of the ninth century. Since the Norman conquest of 1066 the English crown had been passed down in an irregular yet unbroken succession to the Tudors. Along the way it had extended its sway over Wales and, in theory, Ireland. From time to time it had also laid claim to Scotland and France. The Scots had resisted English imperialism with ferocity and in Henry's time were still defending a dogged independence. Of the French empire carved out by Henry V, only the heavily defended port of Calais remained in English hands.

There had always been an element of election in the title 'King of England', and Henry VII's insistence that he held the crown partly as a result of God's judgement at Bosworth suggested the concept was not yet wholly outmoded. To a very real extent, a medieval monarch was 'primus inter pares' – first among equals. Once crowned, however, their status changed. The elaborate coronation ceremony gave the king or queen the Church's blessing – henceforward, as 'God's anointed one', they were under the Almighty's protection as well as their subjects'. To harm an anointed monarch was a sacrilegious act. Not that this necessarily ensured their safety: five of Henry VII's nine immediate predecessors had met with violent ends.

The chances of the Tudor kings and queens dying in their beds (which they all did) were increased by the monarchy's increasingly elevated status. For a number of complex reasons, among which were the decline of the authority of the papacy and the development of the nation state, the Renaissance monarch was coming to be seen as the living embodiment of the nation. It was a move that all the astute rulers of western Europe encouraged – the title 'Your Majesty', for instance, dates from the reign of Henry VIII.

The Tudors did not have it all their own way, though. While several continental monarchies were lurching unevenly towards what historians term 'absolute monarchy', their counterparts in England (and Scotland – see p.46 onwards) were reined in by tradition and practical necessity. Power meant the ability to take independent action, untrammelled by either financial or personal considerations. No Tudor ever enjoyed such freedom. It was essential they remain on good terms with at least some of the 'political nation' – that portion of the population with power and influence. Richard III's alienation of the better part of such people had played an important part in his downfall; nor could his successor forget that his Bosworth triumph had been facilitated by his step-father changing sides at the last minute.

Breaking free from the need to work with the political nation was theoretically possible, but only at a price. It would require a large and independent armed force, and that would need serious money. A shortage of cash, more than anything else, prevented the Tudors, like their predecessors and successors, from ever having complete freedom in matters of administration and policy. The wealth that attached to their title – essentially the crown lands and certain other perquisites – was insufficient for more than day-to-day matters. Anything extra, like a war, required taxation, and taxation required the approval of parliament. If the crown were to try to raise tax without parliamentary consent, it risked confrontation with the political nation as represented in the proud assemblies of Commons and Lords. That, in a nutshell, was the English monarchy's Catch 22, and the challenging inheritance of Henry VIII.

10

Henry VIII, 1509–47

Parents: Henry VII and
   Elizabeth of York
Born: 28 June 1491, Greenwich
Died: 28 January 1547, Whitehall
Marriages and children:
1 Catherine of Aragon, 1509
   Child: Mary I, b.1516
2 Anne Boleyn, 1533
   Child: Elizabeth I, b.1533
3 Jane Seymour, 1536
   Child: Edward VI, b.1537
4 Anne of Cleves, 1540
5 Catherine Howard, 1540
6 Catherine Parr, 1543

Henry VIII is a major industry. More has been written about him than any other king in British history. Millions recognize his face as readily as that of the present monarch, his marital adventures are the stuff of popular songs and dramas, his wives are popular heroines, his music is hummed, his palaces visited, his armour stared at with awe, his beds with mischievous longing ... and why?

Very simply, Henry is the first monarch with whom we can closely identify. He is one of us. Before his time the throne had seen its fair share of heroes, fops and bullies, but not one of them comes across today as truly alive. Their achievements appear remote, their biographies academic, their portraits flat, and even their sins strangely cold. In contrast, Henry is warm and tangible – our first modern monarch.

This feeling of modernity is not just the creation of popular mythology. It rests on serious historical foundations. Henry and his servants severed England's links with the Catholic Church of Rome, establishing the Church of England, and thereby putting in place a key foundation stone of the modern nation state. It was as significant as British accession to the European Union would be 450 years later, although Henry's move was of course in the opposite direction. What's more, this move was carried out by traditional means: through parliament. This ensured parliament's continuing interest in all religious matters. Since religion would never be far from the top of the national agenda over the next century and a half, the prominence of parliament itself was sustained.

In short, if we seek a reign during which England ceased to be a medieval state, then that of Henry VIII fulfils most of the criteria.

Flattery and fortune

Henry probably could not remember a time when he had not been flattered and fawned upon. But while enjoying much spoiling in his youth, he also met frequently with death. His spirited, blond mother, 20 at the time of her marriage, passed away in the stony gloom of the Tower of London when Henry, her third child, was but 11 years old. By then she had given birth at least eight times, the final confinement proving terminal.

Queen Elizabeth's last child, the daughter whose birth killed her, herself died about ten days later. By this time four other children had predeceased the exhausted queen. If they were to remain sane, Tudor parents could not afford to expend too much emotional energy on their children; nor could spouses allow themselves to become too closely attached to partners whose lives hung by perilously thin threads. Such observations help deter over-sentimental judgements on Henry's later behaviour. Moreover, matrimonial cynicism was by then a well-established Tudor trait. Towards the end of his life, Henry VII set off in ardent pursuit of Joanna the Mad, the 28-year-old widowed Queen of Castile and sister of his son's widow. He ignored all reports of the woman's insanity, declaring that in the arms of a loving husband and refreshed by clear English air she would surely recover her wits. Although the suit came to nothing, it set an unappetizing precedent for reckless Tudor wooing.

The most politically significant loss Henry met with was that of his elder brother, Arthur, in April 1502. Despite his grand name, the youth had never been up to much. Henry probably already sensed that the pale 16-year-old would not make old bones when he had escorted his bride, the 16-year-old Catherine of Aragon, at her wedding in St Paul's Cathedral the previous November. Perhaps the young Henry had gazed at the chubby, peaches-and-cream Spanish bride with more than fraternal interest?

It turned out as many had predicted: Arthur perished after a brief and apparently lustless marriage, and his widow was swiftly assigned to the younger brother. Several hurdles had to be overcome before the new union could be formalized. Henry had to reach the age of 16, the English and Spanish crowns had to agree terms, and the Church had to give special permission for the Prince of Wales to marry the widow of his deceased brother (a practice it was traditionally not keen on).

Time solved the first problem and the Pope, having assured himself that Catherine remained as pure as the Virgin Mary, saw to the third. The diplomatic wranglings, however, proved less tractable. First the marriage was on, then it was off while the king pursued his distasteful fantasy for Catherine's loopy elder sister.

When the old king's time ran out on 22 April 1509, his son was still unwed. Henry swiftly rectified the situation, marrying the 23-year-old Catherine shortly before his eighteenth birthday and arranging a glorious joint coronation ceremony for them both 13 days later. The queen became pregnant almost immediately.

The outlook for Henry VIII and his Tudor dynasty could hardly have been brighter. Young, gifted and in excellent health, the king could look forward to a long and memorable reign before handing the crown safely on to the son Catherine would certainly bear him. The nightmare of civil war that had tormented the land even after his father's accession would fade with each passing year. The royal coffers were well stocked. Furthermore, the Spanish alliance cemented by marriage linked lowly England to the strongest power in the western world – the mighty Habsburgs: Holy Roman Emperors, rulers of Spain, Austria, countless other European principalities, and a swelling empire in the New World that was rumoured to be awash with silver and gold.

Henry, still a teenager, might be excused a little proud delight at his rich inheritance and bright prospects.

Games and war

Henry appears to have devoted the first few years of his reign to courtly delights, perhaps deliberately creating the image of himself as the ideal Renaissance prince. There were plays and dances, poetry and hunting, jousting, dressing up and love-making. At the climax of it all, on New Year's Day 1511, Queen Catherine was delivered of a son, Prince Henry. (Her first baby, a girl, had been stillborn.) The king's exuberant delight was cut short by the boy's death less than two months later. All of a sudden, life had taken on a rather more serious hue.

In keeping with the new mood, Henry went to war with France. There was nothing unusual in this – it was, after all, precisely what the king's hero and model, Henry V, had done with such success – and Pope Julius II had played into English hands by calling on all good Christian kings to help him in his struggle with France's Francis I. Reading about the exploits of Henry V proved much easier than re-enacting them on the battlefield. Henry VIII was no master strategist and his limited forces had to be content with the seizure of a couple of fortified towns (Thérouanne and Tournai) and victory in a small-scale cavalry skirmish ('The Battle of the Spurs').

Unimpressive though these exploits were by the standards of the European super-powers – the French, Spanish and Austrians – they were announced back home as glorious triumphs of arms. The true glory, though, had gone to Thomas Howard, the elderly Earl of Surrey, whom Henry had left guarding England's northern border against the Scots. Immediately Henry's back was turned, James IV of Scotland (married to Henry's sister, Margaret) assembled a large and dignitary-laden army and crossed into northern England. Surrey out-manoeuvred him on Flodden Field and inflicted on the Scots the most devastating defeat in their entire history (see pp.51–2).

Wolsey and his king

Although not the spectacular success Henry had wished for, the French campaign did at least have one fortunate, if unexpected, outcome: it brought into the king's service a man of consummate administrative skills who was only too happy to take care of the day-to-day running of the kingdom and so leave the young monarch free to attend to less tedious matters. This civil servant *par excellence* was Thomas Wolsey, a churchman of humble origins but gargantuan ambition. By the end of 1515, having proved his organizational skills during the French campaign, he was already the second most powerful man in the country. His impressive array of titles – including Lord Chancellor and Cardinal Archbishop of York – was matched only by his prodigious wealth, exemplified in the majestic cardinalatial residence of Hampton Court.

Powerful though Wolsey might have been, there was never any doubt that he was a royal servant. The poet John Skelton might have mocked the cardinal's pretensions in the famous lines

> Why come ye not to court?
> To which court?
> To the king's court?
> Or to Hampton Court?[1]

but this was simply satirical point-scoring. Apart from the time when Francis I embarrassingly and memorably threw the English king in a brief bout of wrestling when the two monarchs met near Calais in the Field of Cloth of Gold (1520), no one got the better of Henry. He was too domineering, too powerful, too big a personality to fear competition from any commoner.

That said, we must not fall into the trap of over-simplifying Henry as 'bluff King Hal' or the gross old lecher of parody. He did become gross and there was a bluff element to his make-up, yet his true character was more complex. He was majestic and forceful, but at the same time suspicious. With a strongly held religious faith went a flexible conscience that enabled him to convince himself in all sincerity of the wrongness of what he had once believed to be true.

The king's talents were many. He was musical, scholarly and athletic. His body was tall and strong, and in his red-headed youth he exuded an attractive handsomeness. Add to those qualities an unshakable belief in his own rectitude, reinforced by a lifetime of flattery, and a daunting wilfulness, and the result is a veritable titan of a king whom none but the foolish, desperate or saintly dared gainsay.

Annulment

The turning point in Henry's reign came in the mid-1520s, when he was in his thirties. To his intense irritation, things started to go wrong. Wolsey's foreign policy, which at one stage unrealistically suggested that he might become pope and his king the Holy Roman Emperor, produced further highly expensive cross-Channel campaigns of no tangible benefit. The demands for taxation led to a row with parliament and a virtual tax strike in some parts of the country. Blaming his chief minister for so abusing his people, Henry was obliged to back down. After 15 years of lavish spending, the crown was close to bankruptcy. The outlook was far from rosy.

Future prospects were further darkened by the failure of Queen Catherine to provide the Tudor line with a male successor. Thus far she had suffered a number of miscarriages and stillbirths, and only one child, Mary (born in February 1516), had survived the perils of early-modern pregnancy, birth and babyhood. Moreover, having turned 40 in 1525, the queen was beyond the age when she might expect to conceive again.

Henry's frustration was turning to deep anxiety. It was his royal duty to leave the succession in the hands of a son. The alternatives were almost unthinkable. If the crown passed to Mary, the precedents were dire. The last time a queen had ruled, in the twelfth century, the chroniclers had bewailed her lawless reign as a period when 'God and His angels slept'. If not Mary, then who? To see how civil war might stem from a disputed succession one had to look no further back than Henry's own father. Somehow or other Henry had to produce an heir.

One possibility was to legitimize Henry's bastard son, Henry Fitzroy, Duke of Richmond. Far better, however, would be an annulment of the king's marriage to Catherine and remarriage. By 1527 a willing consort was already waiting in the wings: Henry had fallen seriously in love with the black-eyed Anne

Boleyn, the sister of one of his ex-mistresses. All he needed now was the annulment.

The king's great matter

Henry's marriage to Catherine of Aragon, it will be recalled, had required papal dispensation because of her previous union with Henry's brother. Annulment would require Pope Clement VII to reverse that dispensation, an unlikely but not unimaginable move. Two additional factors, however, made it impossible. First, Catherine refused point blank to go along with any talk of annulment. Second, from 1527 onwards the pope was to all intents and purposes prisoner of the Emperor Charles V, Queen Catherine's nephew. (Charles, Holy Roman Emperor and King of Spain, was the son of the mad Joanna fleetingly wooed by Henry VII.) The emperor, and thus the pope, sided unequivocally with the queen.

No matter how Henry huffed and puffed, no matter how many biblical texts he cited, no matter how darkly he threatened, the Pope would not budge. Wolsey, charged with seeing that the king's wish be granted, was the first victim of the 'king's great matter'. Thomas More replaced him as chancellor and only death from natural causes in November 1530 saved Wolsey from execution as a traitor.

All this was taking place against a background of momentous religious upheaval throughout north-west Europe. Inspired by the teachings of a German ex-monk, Martin Luther, a swelling band of religious dissenters – the Protestants – had rejected the Pope's leadership of the Christian Church and established numerous churches of their own. As well as their independence, these bishop-less Protestant churches also developed their own non-Roman Catholic theology.

In the 1520s, Henry, as a god-fearing churchman and an instinctive conservative, had jumped to the pope's defence against burgeoning Protestantism. As a mark of gratitude for a pro-papal book the king had written, the Pope had awarded him and his successors the title 'Defender of the Faith'. ('*Fidelis Defensor*' – 'F. D.' is inscribed on British coins to this day.) It is one of English history's sweeter ironies that the defender of the faith, in order to get the woman he wanted, proceeded to undermine the faith he had been honoured to defend.

For two years after Wolsey's death Henry leaned increasingly heavily on the Church in England. Then, having resisted the king's high-pressure advances for over five years, by Christmas 1532 Anne finally allowed herself to fall pregnant. Time was now of the essence as her baby – earnestly desired by father, mother and the entire political nation to be a boy – had to be born within wedlock.

Reformation and resistance

Two royal servants, one a churchman the other lay, emerged to fill Wolsey's ample shoes. The Protestant-leaning Thomas Cranmer became Archbishop of Canterbury while the astute Thomas Cromwell, secretary of state, became Henry's leading minister. Between them they oversaw an era of unprecedented change, often heralded as a revolution.

In order to marry Anne Boleyn, which Henry did in January 1533, Henry had to renounce the authority of the Pope. A new head had then to be discovered for the leaderless Church. The choice was obvious: an Act of Supremacy (1534) tactfully announced that the king always had been Supreme Head ('under Christ') of the Church of England. To the crown came massive powers of appointment, revenue collection and doctrinal interpretation. Further laws tidied up the situation and switched the succession to the children of Queen Anne.

These momentous changes were not brought about by simple royal diktat – English government did not operate like that. They were mostly done through parliament, and therefore with implicit popular consent. Moreover, although delighted at his new-found supremacy, Henry, an enthusiastic amateur theologian, was willing to colour his reformation with some Protestant tints. These were sharpened when the beliefs of the new Church were defined in articles that, under the influence of Cromwell and Cranmer, included certain of Luther's teachings such as dislike of pilgrimages, monasteries and associated practices. Royal anxiety deepened with Anne's failure to provide him with a son, resulting in her execution for supposed infidelity in May 1536. Like her predecessor Queen Catherine, who herself had died earlier the same year, Anne left Henry with a daughter, Elizabeth.

The king was by no means the only one concerned about the direction of affairs. The royal supremacy had cost the lives of many conservatives who refused to go along with it, most notably Cardinal John Fisher and Sir Thomas More. Far more serious, a few months after Anne's execution Henry faced the 'Pilgrimage of Grace' (1536–7), the most dangerous revolt ever experienced by a Tudor monarch. Angered by changes already made and confused by rumours of more to come, large swathes of the north and east rose up against those they labelled the king's 'wicked councillors'.

Without a proper police force, let alone a standing army, the government was obliged to make concessions. When the revolt flared again, Henry accused the rebels of gross ingratitude and proceeded to take revenge on the previous year's ringleaders as well as the latest ones. The multitude of exemplary executions ensured that Henry faced no further rebellions.

A decade of decline

Only days after the death of Anne Boleyn, Henry married again. He had had his fill of powerful women and for his third bride chose the demure, pale and plain-looking Jane Seymour, sister of one of Henry's less significant courtiers. Mousy and submissive Jane might have been (although the extent of her subservience has been challenged), but she succeeded where her more high-profile predecessors had failed. In October 1537 she gave birth to a son, Prince Edward. Even the death of the child's mother shortly after the difficult birth did little to dampen the royal delight. At last, 28 years after ascending the throne, Henry had done his duty. Barring tragedy, the Tudor dynasty was secure.

The birth of Prince Edward was the last true high point of Henry's reign. The years immediately following the joyful event were taken up with further religious changes, most notably the despoilation of the country's vastly wealthy monasteries and shrines, and the insistence that every church have a copy of the Bible in English (the Roman Catholic version had been in Latin and therefore open only to the well educated). The appearance of holy scripture in their native tongue made everyone a potential priest, a change that would have repercussions for centuries to come.

The impact of the dissolution of the monasteries was equally momentous, although not in a manner that benefited the crown as much as it might have done with more careful stewardship. Most monastic wealth, in the form of land, buildings and treasure, passed swiftly on to a wide range of debtors, entrepreneurs and others in one of the largest redistributions of wealth the country has ever seen. By the end of the reign the crown was resorting to debasement (mixing base metals with the silver of the coinage to make it go further) to boost its revenue. The opportunity for the crown to re-establish its finances on a secure footing and perhaps even do away with the need for parliamentary grants was lost for ever.

Foreign affairs accounted for much of the escalating royal expenditure of Henry's later years. At one time or another forces were deployed in Ireland and against Scotland and France (leading to the capture of Boulogne). At the end of the 1530s, the government reacted to the very real fear of a joint Catholic invasion of Scots, French and Imperial forces by spending a fortune on strengthening south coast defences from Deal in Kent to St Mawes in Cornwall.

Foreign policy, steered by Cromwell, explains Henry's fourth marriage. His bride was Anne, the 24-year-daughter of the Protestant-leaning Duke of Cleves. However, political expediency is not a secure aphrodisiac and Anne's scant charms failed to rouse the king to his marital duty. Annulment swiftly followed and Cromwell lost his head shortly afterwards.

If the Cleves incident was embarrassing, the next royal liaison was doubly so. Madly in love, Henry married the teenage Catherine Howard only days after the annulment of his union with Anne of Cleves. Already sexually experienced, the healthily active Catherine found the attentions of her 49-year-old husband endearing but not wholly satisfying. Unwise adultery brought the usual round of torture and executions. Her fall was also a grave blow to English Roman Catholicism as the Howards were among its foremost advocates.

Mortified, the following year Henry found consolation in the less demanding arms of the twice-widowed, Protestant-inclining Catherine Parr, to whom he remained contentedly married for the rest of his life. By now he was a sick man. Lack of exercise and an undiminished appetite caused his frame to fill out to an enormous size, and he was frequently laid low by bouts of fever and other ailments. He did not suffer from syphilis, as used to be thought, but from an ulcer in his left leg that was the result of an old jousting wound. The suppurating sore never healed properly and was a constant source of pain and inconvenience.

Nevertheless, the king remained mentally alert and very much in control of his government until almost the very end, and he was still capable of astonishing bursts of energy. As far as his soul was concerned, not once did he appear to consider a return to Rome. If anything, in his last years he leaned more strongly towards Protestantism as the preferred creed of the church he had seized.

Henry VIII's extraordinary 37-year reign ended when he suffered a series of strokes and died on 28 January 1547. Defender and breaker of the faith, soldier, lover, composer and scholar, he was in all ways a gigantic man. The imprint he stamped on the nation he helped create has yet to be erased.

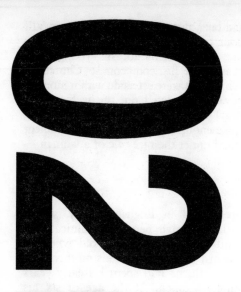

02

Edward VI, 1547–53

Parents: Henry VIII and
  Jane Seymour
Born: 12 October 1537,
  Hampton Court
Died: 6 July 1553, Greenwich
Did not marry; in infancy
betrothed for a while to Mary
Queen of Scots

Indomitable though he had been during his lifetime, Henry VIII could not rule his kingdom from beyond the grave. He tried, though, making elaborate arrangements for his young son's minority and the preservation of his compromise Church of England. All was in vain – his plans were set aside within months. In a broader sense, Henry's legacy lived on: the well-ordered realm with its respect (or fear) for authority, created by Henry and his ministers, proved durable enough to survive first a turbulent minority, then further turmoil under the rare rule of a woman.

The child king

The most urgently desired child in English history, whose creation had instigated such massive personal, political and religious upheaval, was still a tender nine-year-old when he ascended the throne as Edward VI. In place of his mother, who had died 12 days after his birth, he had spent his early years amid the company of kindly women. At the age of six his household was changed and he was transferred to the 'Prince's Side' at Hampton Court (given to Henry VIII by Cardinal Wolsey in 1525) where his entourage was largely male.

At the same time the future king's education began in earnest. It was ultimately supervised by John Cheke, one of the finest humanist scholars of his day and Protestant sympathizer. Indeed, the extent of Cheke's adherence to the new religion was probably not known to Henry VIII, and Edward grew up with a fervent belief in the reformed religion that his father had only half-heartedly embraced.

There was every sign that the young Edward would have matured into a man quite like his father. He inherited Henry's colouring, intellect and self-confident majesty. The idea that Edward was a weakling from birth, predestined to an early grave, has also been shown to be false: the boy appeared as energetic and keen on matters martial as most boys of his age.

Uncle Edward

Henry VIII had arranged for government to be in the hands of a balanced Regency Council of 16 members during his son's minority. Hardly had the old man's body cooled, however, before the Seymours, the family of the new king's mother, began pushing themselves to the fore.

At the head of the clan was Edward Seymour, Earl of Hertford, brother of the late Queen Jane and the young king's uncle. Also prominent was his younger brother, Thomas Seymour. Claiming to be acting on the wishes of the dying king, Hertford, a soldier of some repute and already the senior peer on the Council, awarded himself the title of Duke of Somerset. Within days he had become Lord Protector and Governor of the King's Person. His brother picked up a barony, the post of Lord Admiral, and the old king's widow, Queen Catherine. After she had died in childbirth, he made the kind of unwholesome approaches towards the teenage Princess Elizabeth (Anne Boleyn's daughter) that might nowadays have landed him in prison. He was executed for treason in 1549.

Somerset's premiership lasted two brief years. A self-seeking man of only moderate competence, his costly policies brought distress and hardship at a time of economic downturn. War with Scotland, a continuation of the 'Rough Wooing' that had been going on since Henry's day in an attempt to force the Scots to accept the betrothal of Edward VI to Mary Queen of Scots (see p.59), served only to drive Mary into the arms of the French dauphin. Renewed war with France added to the duke's difficulties.

Protestant reformation

Meanwhile, Somerset, with the backing of Archbishop Cranmer and the young king, had agreed strong steps towards making England a genuinely Protestant country. An English Prayer Book was introduced (1549), enabling a vernacular communion to replace the Latin mass. On government orders a whole range of Catholic practices and symbols was outlawed. Down came statues and other images, including much ancient stained glass; candles and elaborate crucifixes were removed; the use of such religious appurtenances as incense and holy water were banned.

Reformation continued under Somerset's successor, John Dudley, so that by the end of Edward's brief reign England was officially a Protestant country. However, it would take many years to change people's beliefs permanently and, where it had lay support, Roman Catholicism endured for generations. Nevertheless, the achievement of the administration of an under-age king in bringing about so momentous a change in so brief a time is little short of astonishing. It was to prove the outstanding legacy of Edward's truncated kingship.

Widespread revolt against Somerset and his policies provoked fellow councillors, led by John Dudley, Earl of Warwick, to remove the Lord Protector from office in his forty-ninth year. After a spell in the Tower, he was released and rehabilitated, only to fall again, this time permanently. In January 1552 he was executed on flimsy charges of treason.

John Dudley, Duke of Northumberland

As self-seeking as Somerset but rather more competent, John Dudley rejected the former's protectorship and dominated affairs between 1550 and 1553 as Lord President of the Council. He made a peace with Scotland and France, handing back Boulogne to the latter, and attempted to tidy up the financial and administrative mess left by his predecessor.

By now the king was beginning to exercise an influence in affairs of state. He was particularly enthusiastic in his support for the Reformation and took it upon himself, unsuccessfully, to convert his elder sister Mary away from the faith in which she had been raised. Just as his father might have done, the young prince took it as a personal affront that anyone should reject a church of which he was the head. The Lord President had the wisdom not to stand in Edward's way but tactfully allowed his young master an increasing voice in government policy.

Intolerance is a common feature of adolescence, so we have no way of knowing how Edward's beliefs would have settled down in maturity. There is a fair chance, however, that the rigid and fairly puritanical version of the Protestant creed he held at 16, visible in his journal, might well have stayed with him in adulthood. Had it done so, and had he lived another 20 years, how different the history of England (and perhaps also the US) might have been. In place of Elizabeth's broad and unusually tolerant Anglican communion, England would have had a Scottish-style, puritan church. All but the most righteous arts would have been frowned upon, limiting music, poetry and painting; theatre and dancing would have been banned, Sundays turned into periods of earnest reflection, and adultery become punishable by death. Such a land could hardly have inspired Shakespeare's dying John of Gaunt to speak of an 'other Eden, demi-paradise ... the envy of less happier lands.'[2]

Untimely end

Be that as it may, Edward did not survive. In April 1552 he fell seriously ill of some mysterious combination of diseases that permanently undermined his health and sapped his strength. Tuberculosis, previously thought to be his undoing, is now considered unlikely; a more probable diagnosis is complications arising from pneumonia. A royal progress in the summer of that year only made him weaker and by Christmas it was fairly clear that he did not have long to live.

For Northumberland this was a disastrous development. Should either of the king's two sisters succeed to the throne, the duke would be doomed. The Catholic Mary would lose no time in doing away with so enthusiastic a heretic, while Elizabeth was not the type to tolerate overmighty subjects, whatever their religion. Fortunately for Northumberland, the dying king shared his anxieties.

If Henry VIII's legislation was overridden and Mary and Elizabeth excluded from the succession, and the Stewarts (descended from the union of Henry VIII's sister Margaret with Scotland's James IV) also ruled out, then next in line to the English crown would be Lady Jane Grey. She was the oldest granddaughter of Henry VIII's youngest sister Mary, sometime Queen of France.

In May 1553, Northumberland arranged a marriage between Lady Jane and his own son, Guildford Dudley. It was a match to save English Protestantism and the Dudleys' skins. The king backed it by issuing dubious patent letters that purported to set aside the claims of his sisters on grounds of their illegitimacy and the possibility that they might marry foreigners 'to the utter subversion of the commonwealth'[3].

Edward died 16 days later. The news was kept secret for a while, then Lady Jane declared queen. Northumberland anxiously awaited the people's verdict.

03

Mary I, 1553–8

Parents: Henry VIII and
  Catherine of Aragon
Born: 18 February 1516,
  Greenwich
Died: 17 November 1558,
  St James's Palace, London
Marriage: Philip of Spain, 1554
No children

Of all the monarchs who have worn the crown from Tudor times onwards, none is more tragic than Queen Mary I. Although historians have scratched around to find things with which to credit her brief reign, the inescapable fact is that almost everything she set her heart upon failed. She was a non-political creature thrust into a role that demanded consummate political skill; furthermore, she lacked those most crucial of monarchical assets – luck and fecundity.

Claiming the throne

The Duke of Northumberland, having married his son to the Protestant claimant Lady Jane Grey earlier in the year, tried unsuccessfully to prevent the news of Edward VI's death from leaking out. He hoped, no doubt, to present Lady Jane's accession as a *fait accompli*. The intended coup was a dismal failure.

Summoned to London to be with her dying half-brother the king – and also to put herself within Northumberland's clutches – Mary had wisely taken off in the opposite direction and entered the loyal Catholic heartland of Norfolk. Here, when news of Edward's death emerged, she immediately had herself proclaimed queen. The opposition's proclamation of Lady Jane in London came a day later.

From the outset, the majority of English men and women, led by Catholics, turned instinctively to the daughter of Henry VIII whose right to succeed had been confirmed by statute three years before her father's death. Northumberland gathered his forces and rode boldly to confront the woman he had denounced as a bastard and a pretender. On the road, with his supporters melting away by the hour, he lost his nerve and ended up welcoming Mary as the rightful queen. It was a feeble gesture. He was executed for high treason shortly afterwards, although his son and Lady Jane were spared for the time being.

Teenage pawn

The first 11 or so years of Mary's life had been about as good as one could get in Tudor times. Her mother, Catherine of Aragon, had doted on her and ensured that she had an excellent education. Like most Tudors, Mary was a good linguist, a natural musician, and had a genuine liking for literature and learning. Unusually for the age, her proud royal father also took a close personal interest in her early-years development. The only clouds on an otherwise sunny horizon were abortive betrothals, for purely political ends, to the French dauphin and the Holy Roman Emperor.

Mary's world began to fall apart as she entered adolescence. Not only was she estranged from her father but, after his marriage to Anne Boleyn, she was forbidden even to meet with her mother. Although they conducted a clandestine correspondence, after 1531 the two never met again. Hated by Queen Anne, who obliged Mary to become a lady-in-waiting to the infant Princess Elizabeth, Mary's lot worsened when an act of parliament declared her a bastard. In 1536, pressured by the king and the Emperor (her mother's nephew), she finally acknowledged Henry as Head of the Church of England and the 'incestuous illegality' of his former marriage to Queen Catherine. For this, now that Queen Anne was out of the way, she was restored to much favour. It was a humiliating climb down that she regretted for the rest of her life.

We cannot be sure of the impact of these events on Mary's character. Certainly they affected her outlook, reinforcing her stubbornness. She had always been strong-willed, refusing all Anne Boleyn's attempts to force her into a convent, for instance. After the trauma of her mother's divorce and her own illegitimacy, she determined that if she ever had the power, whatever the cost, she would honour her mother's memory by returning England to the Roman Catholic fold.

Now Northumberland's clumsy coup had failed, the way was open for Mary to ascend the throne and turn her dream into reality. Widespread outbreaks of spontaneous rejoicing at the news of Dudley's demise led her to believe that the change was what her people wanted, too.

Restoring the faith

Massive transfers of land and wealth had accompanied the Henrician and Edwardian reformations. There was hardly a major family in the land that had not benefited from the change, so Mary and her council realized that popular support for a counter-reformation could be guaranteed only by acknowledging the material status quo: the Church would not get its riches back.

With that massive exception, parliament was persuaded to return the Church to a position close to the one it had enjoyed before Mary's father had experienced his fatal attraction for Anne Boleyn. To the surprise of some, even papal supremacy was restored. Mary and her friend the Cardinal Archbishop Reginald Pole did their best to see that the rebuilt Catholic Church was in better shape than its predecessor. They had some success, too, for although Roman Catholicism would shortly be outlawed again, they left it sufficiently robust to survive into more tolerant times.

Later, Mary's government engaged in a well-organized programme of persecutions that saw nearly 300 Protestants burned as heretics. Among their number were high-profile bishops, including the architect of the English reformation, Archbishop Thomas Cranmer of Canterbury. The aim of the most intense burst of religious persecution England has ever seen was to weed out Protestant malingerers and deter others from following them down the primrose path to perdition. It failed. Indeed, the flames seem to have had the opposite result, stiffening Protestant opposition to Mary rather than destroying it. The effect was magnified in later years when John Foxe's account of the Marian persecutions (*Foxe's Book of Martyrs*) became England's second most popular read after the Bible. For her key role in the campaign the queen was dubbed 'Bloody Mary', an epithet she retains to this day.

Choosing a partner

Mary was the first queen to rule England in her own right. This unprecedented exercise of her royal prerogative was considered by many to be unwise, even unnatural. Mary felt uncomfortable about it, too, so from the outset she expressed a wish to share her position with a husband. Despite her 37 years, she also hoped to produce an heir to maintain the restored Catholic Church.

In Tudor times, before colonial exploits had taught them about the rest of the world, the English were a notoriously xenophobic people. Although they had no objection to their kings taking foreign wives, as female consorts had little political power, for the queen to take a foreign husband was a wholly different matter. The male partner in a marriage was legally and traditionally dominant, so most believed union with a non-native would place England under foreign rule. That was considered at best distasteful, at worst totally unacceptable.

Unabashed, Mary rejected the thought of a home-grown husband and opted instead for union with Europe's leading Catholic principality, Spain. The man she set her heart on was her cousin Philip, the only son of Charles, Holy Roman Emperor and King of Spain (to whom she had been betrothed in her infancy). News of the marriage treaty helped spark a dangerous rebellion, led by Sir Thomas Wyatt (son of one of Henry VIII's court poets). The queen rose to the challenge with a demonstration of true Tudor grit and courage. London refused to rise and the Kentish rebels were seen off.

Philip, the queen's junior by 11 years, arrived in England five months after Wyatt's execution. His summer marriage to the delighted queen was conducted by the venerable bishop Stephen Gardiner in his cathedral at Winchester (1554). For Mary, now an earnest and rather plain spinster who was beginning to show her age, the dream of a lifetime had come true; for Philip, already a widower, the union was an awkward political duty. Although he would be married to Mary, whom he unflatteringly referred to as his 'aunt', for four years, he spent only 18 months in England. He was clearly not over-eager to be at her side, vertical or horizontal.

On at least two separate occasions Mary declared herself pregnant. She appears to have believed that she really was with child; others were more sceptical. When her time came and no child appeared, she became the butt of ribald remarks in her own kingdom and beyond. For a child of Henry VIII to be thus ridiculed was a painful letdown.

Calais in her heart

The marriage to Philip brought another humiliation. On his return visit to England in 1557 the Spanish king gained the queen's support for his war with France. To Mary's distress, the conflict also ranged England against the papacy. This was indeed a bitter blow for one whose policy had been built around reconciliation with Rome. Worse was to follow.

Anglo-Spanish forces enjoyed some initial successes. Then, in January 1558, these minor triumphs were completely overshadowed by the fall of Calais. The importance of the heavily-fortified Channel port was more symbolic than economic. As England's last toe-hold on continental Europe, Calais was the proud remnant of an empire that had once extended from Berwick to Bordeaux. Although English monarchs continued to style themselves 'King of France', the loss of Calais made the hollowness of the title ridiculously transparent. At the last, sick and depressed at her failures, Mary is supposed to have said that when her body was opened, 'Calais' would be found lying in her heart.

Mary died of stomach cancer in the winter of 1558. As the end approached she knew full well that her sister Elizabeth, Anne Boleyn's daughter, would swiftly undo most of what she had achieved. Many commentators, reflecting the queen's own desolation, have dismissed her reign as sterile. More recently, historians have attempted to paint a brighter picture, noting economic and administrative reforms carried out in her name. At the behest of Philip, now King of Spain, the Royal Navy and the realm's defences were improved, too.

Be that as it may, it is still difficult to reach any other conclusion than that Mary – the tragic Tudor – had failed in all that was dearest to her.

04 Elizabeth I, 1558–1603

Parents: Henry VIII and
Anne Boleyn
Born: 7 September 1533,
Greenwich
Died: 24 March 1603,
Richmond, Surrey
Did not marry

Elizabeth, the only surviving child of Henry VIII's passionate infatuation with Anne Boleyn, is probably more deeply embedded in the English 'heritage' industry than any other monarch. She is the first English ruler whose name is given to the age in which they lived. The buildings she visited and the beds she reportedly slept in draw tourists by the million. More quirkily, she is almost certainly the only king or queen recalled, albeit indirectly, in a type of tobacco (Virginia). While her father achieved monumental status at home, in terms of world-wide recognition, the daughter wins hands down.

Elizabeth's fame comes not from the length of her reign – both Henry III and Edward III occupied the throne for longer – although her longevity was an asset. Her martial exploits were notable, too, but pale beside those of Henry V. As a reforming monarch she hardly features in the top ten.

No, the 'golden' Elizabeth Age is, to a large extent, recalled with affection because the queen was blessed with that gift possessed of all successful political figures – luck. Had she died of smallpox in 1562, as she very nearly did, who now would talk of the Elizabethan Age? Twenty-six years later, favourable winds blew to help her sailors defeat the Spanish invasion fleet, and no PR organization, however skilful, could have arranged for her reign to coincide with the early working life of the greatest literary genius of all time.

Elizabeth's reputation is also enhanced by the fact that the era over which she presided contrasts so favourably with the troubles of the next century. Most important of all was the manner in which the queen, over many years, skilfully identified herself with all that was brightest and best in the burgeoning, proud little realm of which she was the mistress. Not for another two centuries would another monarch, also a woman, achieve such a fertile symbiosis.

Schooled in danger and disappointment

We do not know how either King Henry or Queen Anne reacted when told that their eagerly anticipated child was a girl, although anything other than disappointment is difficult to imagine. Elizabeth's lot did not improve. Before she reached her third birthday, her mother had been executed for adultery and the marriage with her father, the king, declared invalid (a logical inconsistency conveniently ignored). This made the little princess illegitimate in the eyes of both Catholics and Anglicans. Small wonder that visitors to the palace at Hatfield, where Elizabeth was brought up, found a child strangely serious for her age.

Elizabeth's life improved over the remaining years of her father's reign. She made public appearances on important occasions (such as Henry's last marriage) and, towards the end of the reign, was officially recognized as third in line to the throne. More important as far as her future was concerned, like her sister Mary, she received a first-class education that left her fluent in ancient Greek and Latin and several modern languages. She was also widely read in the literature recommended by humanist scholars of the day.

The reigns of her brother Edward and sister Mary were difficult for Elizabeth. During the former, now in her teens, she was molested by the unpleasant brother of Lord Protector Somerset; during the latter she was, consenting or otherwise, the focus of Protestant and nationalistic antipathy towards the restored Catholicism and the Spanish marriage. After Wyatt's rebellion (see p.30) she was arrested, detained in the Tower of London for a while, and subjected to close questioning about her links with the revolt. She was then held under virtual house arrest at Woodstock, near Oxford, before being restored to favour for the sad last months of Mary's life when it was clear that the crown would pass to the dying queen's younger sister. It is tempting but perhaps psychologically simplistic to assume that the difficult experiences of the first 25 years of Elizabeth's life shaped the virginal, secretive, cautious and pragmatic mould that marked her time as monarch.

Inherited headaches

Elizabeth was fortunate that her sister was so long a-dying – it gave her time to plan how she would conduct her own reign. It also gave the political nation time to decide that they wanted her and would not back an alternative, Catholic or otherwise. With the path to the throne carefully prepared, the young queen played her part with studied perfection. She made a gracefully flamboyant entry into her capital and was crowned amid widespread and genuine expressions of patriotic delight.

Elizabeth knew only too well that taking the crown had been the easy bit. Now she had the far more tricky task of keeping hold of it, governing her realm, and defending it and herself from all perils at home and overseas. Her immediate challenges were many.

The first difficulty, and something Elizabeth could do nothing about, was her gender. After the experiences of Mary's stunted and sterile reign there were still plenty of both sex who believed that a woman was not fit to rule. The best the new queen could hope to do was prove them wrong over time.

The queen's other problems were more practical. She had to choose a competent and loyal administration, and make the most of the crown's limited resources to avoid antagonizing tax payers. Equally pressing, she had to face the thorny religious question: during the course of her lifetime England had swung from Henry VIII's neo-Catholic Church of England to her brother's fully Protestant version of the same, then in her sister's reign back to full papal Roman Catholicism. Which, if any, of these options would Anne Boleyn's daughter adopt?

Religion was inseparable from foreign affairs. For example, England's long-standing friendship with Spain, begun with Catherine of Aragon's marriages to the sons of Henry VII and reinforced by the union of Mary and Philip II, meant partnership with the foremost opponent of the Protestant Reformation. As tricky was the potential problem of Elizabeth's young cousin, Mary Queen of Scots. As a Roman Catholic and granddaughter of Henry VIII's sister Margaret, Mary was considered by many in continental Europe to have a better claim to the English crown than the bastard Elizabeth. Moreover, Mary was now married to the heir to the French throne and styling herself 'Queen of England' – not a recipe for harmonious cross-Channel relations. (For the full story of Mary Queen of Scots, see pp.58–63.)

Mary's French union raises the question of Elizabeth's own position in the marriage stakes. As an attractive, healthy and presumably fertile young woman, it was universally assumed that she would marry. Her subjects wanted her to, the Tudor dynasty needed her to, and it is quite likely that Elizabeth herself believed she would choose a partner one day. But whom? For a woman who disliked making decisions of any kind, this was perhaps the toughest conundrum of all.

Loyal servants

Elizabeth's first act was not to select a single favoured individual but many. To make her lonely eminence a little less daunting she surrounded herself with family, friends, ministers and servants whom she could trust.

Henry VIII's principal secretary, Thomas Cromwell, had remodelled the medieval council, the traditional organ of central administration, into a smaller and more efficient privy council. This had swollen in size somewhat under Mary. Making it more manageable and at the same time purging Catholic and clerical members, Elizabeth cut it back to 19 (similar in number to the modern cabinet). Prominent were those already in her employ, Sir Thomas Parry and her secretary, William Cecil (later Lord Burghley), and her Boleyn cousins Sir Francis Knollys and Sir Richard Sackville. One of the new administration's first achievements, and one of which the queen was justly proud, was to restore the probity of the silver currency after years of debasement and confusion.

While the formal side of government was conducted in private by the queen and her privy council, the more public court and chamber were also important as vehicles for taking the temperature of the political nation and ensuring that influential families were kept on side. Governance and the maintenance of court and household were expensive, and on this score Elizabeth has received some criticism. Benefiting from reforms carried out under her sister, she managed to balance her books for most of her reign. But she and her councillors failed to exploit royal revenues efficiently and made ends meet (just) by keeping expenditure as low as possible. It is said that soldiers fighting in Scotland were instructed to save money by collecting used cannon balls for re-firing! (see p.60) This parsimony created tensions among those seeking royal bounty and increased the corruption of office-holders.

'Two-eyes'

As well as the Boleyns, Elizabeth restored to favour two other notable families, the Parrs, related to Henry VIII's last wife, and the Dudleys, relatives of Edward VI's erstwhile guardian and mentor, the Duke of Northumberland. The young queen quite lost her heart to the good-looking and talented Robert Dudley, one of Northumberland's younger sons. At the start of her reign she appointed the dashing 'Two-eyes', as she affectionately called him, master of the horse. The position meant she could guarantee his close attendance at all times. Tongues began to wag. In the dark corners of London taverns it was even whispered that the queen was carrying her lover's child.

Under normal circumstances the union of two such young, able, attractive and noble-born young people in their mid-twenties would have been an ideal match. The golden circle of the crown, however, was far larger and more potent than the wedding ring. Elizabeth's marriage could never be simply a personal or even a family matter: it was a political issue of supreme national and international importance. For Elizabeth to select one of her own subjects would invariably raise jealousies and lessen her own power and influence. As for taking a partner from abroad, the sad experience of Mary's reign had shown how fraught with dangers that could be.

Nevertheless, over the summer of 1560 romance blossomed between the queen and man the court equivocally nicknamed 'the gypsy' for his dark good-looks. All things seemed possible. Then, as the autumn began to close in, the relationship received a blow from which it could never recover.

While still a teenager, Dudley had married the heiress Amy Robsart. The marriage, it seems, had gone well to begin with, but by the time of Elizabeth's accession its initial ardour had cooled and Amy was complaining of a 'malady in the breast'. Modern speculation has suggested cancer. Whatever her illness, it did not prove fatal. Instead, perhaps weakened by sickness, on 8 September 1560 the unfortunate young woman was found dead at the foot of the stairs in Cumnor Place, Berkshire. Her neck had been broken, presumably as a result of a fall.

How convenient! muttered Dudley's many enemies, alienated by his apparent arrogance. Suspicion of foul play could not be uttered out loud, but it hung in the air of court and city like a pestilence. Elizabeth, with her sure nose for political trouble, immediately picked it up and took the only sensible course of action open to her. Any lingering thoughts she might have had about a marriage with Dudley were locked in the back of her heart and the key cast away. Earlier she had told Dudley that she would marry no one but him: she remained true to her word.

The Church of England

Unlike her sister, Elizabeth was not an overtly religious person. Rather, as with so many aspects of her personality, she kept her innermost thoughts and beliefs to herself. As she once famously declared that she had no wish to open 'windows into men's souls', so she wanted no one to peer into her own. Conforming to Catholicism during her sister's reign might have been distasteful, but it was better than the alternative. She had no thirst for martyrdom.

Nevertheless, the queen clearly was no papist. How could she be? Her mother had been the very occasion of England's split with Rome, and Elizabeth had been educated by Protestant tutors. One of her first acts as queen had been ostentatiously to reject the use of candles in church other than for purposes of illumination. Furthermore, Elizabeth was astute enough to see that it was far more advantageous for the monarch to control the English Church directly as its Supreme Governor (not Supreme Head as her father had been because, as a woman, she could not be attached to the metaphorical body of the Church) than as a loyal subject of an alien master, the Pope. Finally, the Church, with its paid network of ministers and pupils, was the Tudor equivalent of a state broadcasting service. To privatize it, as Mary had done, would not have been Elizabeth's style at all.

Guided and goaded by Elizabeth and her council, the first parliament of the reign undid Mary's religious legislation and, through Acts of Uniformity and Supremacy, re-established the Church of England. Its new form was similar to that existing at the end of the reign of Edward VI. In the slightly revised edition of 1662, the Elizabethan Prayer Book – with its famous compromise wording over what happens to the bread and wine at mass/communion – is essentially that still used by traditional Anglicans (Episcopalians) to this day.

The Church presided over by Elizabeth and her first archbishop of Canterbury, Matthew Parker, was a strange, hybrid creature. It was essentially Protestant in theology and practice (for instance, using the vernacular, frowning on idols and other aids to worship, and allowing priests to marry), but retaining distinct and conspicuous features of the old religion, such as a hierarchy of bishops and archbishops. The Supreme Governor presided over what was clearly a compromise church. This middle-of-the-road position made it a soft target for attack by both Roman Catholics and more earnest Protestants.

The Catholic fightback

There is no way of knowing the faith of the majority of Elizabeth's subjects when she came to the throne. It is likely that most still hankered after some moderate form of the old religion, albeit moderated by a Henry VIII-style independence from foreign interference and with all pre-reformation wealth remaining securely in secular hands. Consequently, they did not find the new ecclesiastical arrangement too antagonistic. Office-holders were required to swear an oath accepting the royal supremacy and those who failed to attend church were, in theory, fined. However, since the unpaid local officials charged with collecting such fines might themselves be sympathetic to the old cause, there was often plenty of leeway.

This was just as Elizabeth wanted: a well-administered church demanding outward uniformity only. Excessive persecution, as she had seen in Mary's reign, merely provoked reaction. Although by the end of her reign Elizabeth had executed about as many Catholics as Mary had Protestants, there was a subtle difference between the two persecutions. While the latter died for their faith, Elizabeth's victims were executed as traitors who had sworn allegiance to an enemy power – the Pope.

A relatively happy-go-lucky attitude towards Catholic dissent lasted about ten years. After 1568, when Mary Queen of Scots turned up unheralded in northern England and asked for political asylum, the atmosphere turned sour. A major Catholic revolt broke out the year after Mary's arrival. Later, giving up hope of Elizabeth's conversion, the Pope belatedly excommunicated her. This inspired a series of dangerous plots to replace Elizabeth with Mary. Finally, from 1574 onwards, a stream of secular and Jesuit priests, trained on the continent, arrived in England to guide its people back to Rome.

Elizabeth's government, backed by popular xenophobia, tightened anti-Catholic legislation and hunted down the missionaries with unpleasant fervour. A turning point was reached in 1588, when the Spanish Armada threatened to convey an army of Spanish Catholics over to England. Forced to choose between loyalty to their queen or to their pope, England's remaining Catholics took the nationalist option. Thereafter, Elizabeth recognized that the danger from domestic Catholicism was more imaginary than real.

Purification

Protestantism lacked the monolithic uniformity of Catholicism. It took its inspiration for church organization largely from descriptions of the earliest Christian communities. As they regarded the Bible as the revealed word of God and therefore their sole source of authority, the keener, more literal-minded Protestants rejected anything not found within its pages. Hence their rejection of the traditional Catholic hierarchy, monasteries, altars, and anything that smacked of idolatry. To such a way of thinking Elizabeth's new church was clearly far from perfect – it needed to be 'purified' of remaining elements of Roman Catholicism. Enter the puritans.

Puritan opposition was a constant source of annoyance to the queen because it threatened to undermine her ability to govern her own church. She saw, for example, that the puritan desire to do away with bishops also struck at the heart of royal power. Order and central authority held the state together just as it did the Church. The Protestant alternative to the Church of England – a presbyterian church of congregations whose representatives periodically gathered together in synods – meant a powerful state-wide organization existing outside royal control. That was something Elizabeth would not even contemplate.

With this as her touchstone, Elizabeth demanded that her servants, lay as well as ecclesiastical, rooted out puritan opposition as ruthlessly as they did Catholic. Priests were to wear official-looking vestments, not just a sober form of mufti. When Archbishop Grindal, Parker's successor, refused to clamp down on unauthorized extemporary prayer meetings (who knew what dangerous sentiments might be uttered by someone claiming inspiration from the Holy Spirit?), the queen suspended him from office for the remaining six years of his life. Incidentally, he had hardly helped his cause by tartly reminding Elizabeth, 'And although ye are a mighty prince, yet remember that He which dwelleth in Heaven is mightier.'[4]

Fortunately for Elizabeth, Grindal died in time for her to appoint an archbishop of her own mindset to tackle the crisis of the 1580s. With the Queen's full backing, Archbishop John Whitgift used the rigours of the Court of Ecclesiastical High Commission to conduct a vigorous and successful campaign against the intelligent and well-connected puritans attempting to establish an underground presbyterian church parallel to the Church of England. The government was even more ruthless in its approach towards separatists – the forerunners of the Pilgrim Fathers who eschewed all church hierarchy in favour of wholly independent congregations.

Thus Elizabeth and her officers sustained beyond babyhood the Church whose birth they had presided over. By the end of her reign, having survived a number of perils, the child was in good health and had a relatively secure place in the affections of her subjects. By then most had known no other monarch or church.

A new enemy

With a population of around four million by the early seventeenth century, Elizabethan England was a small and comparatively weak country in comparison with the major continental powers of France, Spain and Austria. Elizabeth had to tread warily in her relations with such superpowers, especially because of religious differences. She was helped by the protracted domestic upheavals in France, known to historians as 'Wars of Religion'. These nullified the traditional cross-Channel threat. She also benefited from the replacement of Scotland's Catholic Queen Mary by her Protestant infant son James. Thus, once she had concluded the French war inherited from her sister and made a brief foray north to support Scottish anti-Catholic rebels, Elizabeth remained largely free from the traditional danger of a north-and-east pincer.

The removal of one set of hazards did not leave Elizabeth free to sail in untroubled waters. The new danger was Spain or, strictly speaking, the Spanish Habsburgs. Philip II's rich and puissant empire embraced the Iberian Peninsular, the Netherlands (modern-day Holland and Belgium) and vast swathes of the New World from whose mines poured a seemingly endless river of treasure. As an enemy of France, Spain had long been seen as England's friend. After the first decade of her reign, however, Elizabeth was caught up in a diplomatic revolution that left her head-to-head with the major power of the western hemisphere.

Elizabeth's former brother-in-law was a pious man who believed it his God-given duty to spearhead the Catholic Church's counter-attack on Protestantism. After Philip had waited ten vain years for Elizabeth to abandon her heresy (even suggesting marriage with her), Anglo-Spanish relations deteriorated rapidly. Many factors were to blame, not all of them within Elizabeth's control.

The queen might have done more to rein in semi-piratical raiders such as Hawkins and Drake (knighting the latter after a Spanish-tormenting circumnavigation was little short of deliberate provocation); she might also have limited semi-official support for the Protestants rebelling against Spanish rule in Holland; and she certainly did not have to pocket the cash en route to pay Spanish soldiers in the Netherlands. On the other hand, there was little she could have done about the troublesome presence in England of the Catholic pretender Mary of Scots, surrounded by a sinister cloud of treasonous plot; nor could she have done much to calm the rising tide of anti-Catholic feeling fed by stories of cruel inquisition and the ghastly massacre of thousands of French Protestants in Paris on St Bartholomew's Day, 1572.

Armada

However complex and convoluted the reasons, by the summer of 1585 England and Spain were officially at war. A force led by the beloved Dudley, now Earl of Leicester, was sent to assist the Dutch, and English sailors were given a free hand in disrupting Spanish plans for a seaborne invasion. Now the die was cast, Mary Queen of Scots' life was no longer so precious: she was tried for treasonous plotting against her cousin, found guilty and executed. Elizabeth, unwilling publicly to endorse regicide, pretended that the signing of her cousin's death warrant had been a ghastly mistake.

Philip's plan was to use a vast armada of Spanish ships to convey the Duke of Parma's large and professional army, based in the Netherlands, across the Channel. The grand design was a miserable failure. Spain did not command a suitable deep-water port on the eastern side of the Channel in which Parma's forces could be taken on board. Furthermore, the seamanship, tactics and gunnery of the English fleet was far superior to that of the Spaniards. Finally, the great armada was scattered by storms that left its remnants limping back to Spain as best they could.

In August 1588, when a Spanish invasion was still on the cards, Elizabeth, truncheon in hand, rode among the troops assembled at Tilbury and addressed them thus:

> 'I know that I have the weak and feeble body of a woman, but I have the heart and stomach of a king, and of a king of England too, and think foul scorn that Parma or Spain or any prince of Europe should dare to invade the borders of my realm.'[5]

Surely, it was her finest hour.

The Virgin Queen

Elizabeth was born regal. She was naturally elegant and in her youth her pale face beneath a halo of red hair was thought genuinely lovely. Later, masked in thick white make-up, her appearance was more noble than beautiful. She dressed the part, too, always most elegantly clad and dripping with jewels. Unsurprisingly, her successor inherited an empty treasury but a wardrobe stuffed with hundreds of dresses. Appearance and demeanour, however, were but an indication of her power. To them she added the mystery and mastery of a great actress. She never revealed the true Elizabeth; just when courtiers felt they were beginning to get to know her, she pulled away, flummoxing them with a seemingly out-of-character gesture or display of withering hauteur.

In a very real sense the Virgin Queen (a deliberate attempt to replace the illegal cult of the Virgin Mary) wooed her people, declaring herself to be their bride. She controlled her parliaments, which on occasion showed signs of angry frustration at her religious policies and failure to marry, with a similar mix of charm and command. When the situation demanded, as during a bout of MPs' criticism in 1601, she could be almost pathetic:

> 'And though you have had and may have many princes more mighty and wise sitting in this seat, yet you never had nor shall have any that will be more careful and loving.'[6]

There was literally not a dry eye in the House.

In the same vein, Elizabeth used her single status to political advantage. On separate occasions she hinted that she might marry the kings of Spain and Sweden, the Archduke of Austria and two royal French princes. In truth, though, she had no intention of putting herself in thrall to any of them. She was at best a supreme manipulator, at worst a tease.

For all her successes, Elizabeth was by no means faultless. She made misjudgements, as when she opted to give military aid to the French Huguenots (Protestants) in the 1560s, and she was forever procrastinating. For instance, her refusal formally to recognize a successor, even on her deathbed, drove her councillors to distraction. Moreover, as she neared the end of her life, the edifice she had so carefully erected began to show distinct signs of wear. When she finally passed away on 24 March 1603, the ending of so majestic a reign was marked not with great sadness but with an almost audible sigh of relief.

Decline and death

During Elizabeth's last years a series of bad harvests (1593–6) fed a major economic downturn. The price of bread rose steeply, bringing many to the edge of starvation. At the same time, the government's financial demands made life difficult for the better-off. Acting on the queen's request, the House of Commons grudgingly voted a series of subsidies. These were the traditional tranches of land and property tax raised only in exceptional circumstances.

The exceptional circumstance was war. Most costly were a series of expeditions to quell a massive Catholic revolt in Ireland, the part of the Tudor realm over which the crown's sway was at best tenuous. Large sums were also spent assisting the Dutch, the Huguenot Henry IV of France, and on further (largely unsuccessful) naval expeditions against Spain. The mood was further darkened as, one by one, the queen's old favourites passed away – 'Two-eyes' Dudley (1588), Drake (1596), Burghley (1598), the Countess of Nottingham (a cousin and bosom friend, 1603) – leaving the antique queen virtually the sole representative of her generation still in a position of power.

There were also signs that Elizabeth's judgement was not what it had been. With the foolishness of a fond old maid she lavished attention and favours on her handsome 30-year-old cousin Robert Devereux, Earl of Essex. The young man, Dudley's step-son, was brave and gallant – an ideal courtier – but lacked the wisdom and judgement for high office. Sent to Ireland with a large and costly force in 1599, he botched his commission and returned home in disgrace. At this point he lost his reason. Having made a futile attempt to purge the court by force, he was tried and beheaded as a traitor in February 1601. Essex's demise was the queen's greatest failure.

The end came two years later. A few weeks before her death Elizabeth become melancholic and ate only fitfully. Sensing the inevitable, she refused physic. At the last she called for the ministration of Archbishop Whitgift. Then, cradled in a bed of silken cushions, she slipped away in the early hours of 24 March, 'as the most resplendent sun setteth … in a western cloud'[7].

part two

The House of Stewart, 1489–1714

Introduction

The royal Stewarts ('Stuarts' is merely a sixteenth-century Frenchification of the original name), Scotland's premier ruling dynasty, had their origins in Brittany. As their name suggests, they first made a name for themselves as stewards of noble and royal households. They moved to England with Henry I, the ruthless third son of William the Conqueror (1066–87), and were given land on the border with Wales. In 1136, Walter FitzAlan (as the family was then known) trekked north to serve as steward to the up-and-coming King David I of Scotland. Other Anglo-Breton families, including the Bruces, made a similar move.

The dynasty of hereditary stewards flourished, expanding the scope of their responsibilities and acquiring widespread estates in the south and west of Scotland in return for unfailing loyalty to the monarch. In the late thirteenth century two events occurred that enabled them to scramble even further up Scotland's socio-political ladder. First, King Alexander III fell from his horse one stormy night and was killed; second, his granddaughter and heir, the romantic-sounding Margaret, Maid of Norway, died en route for her kingdom.

England's Edward I promptly declared himself Scotland's overlord. This instigated a series of campaigns and battles known as the Wars of Independence, in which English designs on Scotland were eventually thwarted. The heroes of the Scottish resistance were William Wallace (meaning 'of Wales', from where the family had originally been brought by the Stewarts) and Robert Bruce, who was eventually crowned Robert I. Bruce's son David inherited his father's crown while his daughter Marjory married the dashing Walter the Steward. She gave birth to a son (another Robert), then slipped from the saddle and died. Road deaths were all too common in Scotland even before the age of the motor car.

Royal Stewarts

David proved a competent monarch in all areas except one – he failed to produce an heir. Consequently, upon his death in 1371, the throne passed to his sister Marjory's son, the laid-back 55-year-old Robert the Steward, or simply 'Robert Stewart'. Crowned Robert II, the new king was everything the Bruces had not been: while pretty ineffectual as a leader and administrator, he did at least father nigh-on two dozen (legitimate and illegitimate) children. The eldest of these, John, changed his name and succeeded his father as Robert III (1390–1406).

The second Stewart monarch, who said he wished to be buried in a midden (dunghill), was stricken with chronic depression that rendered him incapable of conducting the business of government effectively. His hereditary ailment brought to the Scottish and, eventually, English monarchies a level of incompetence that almost proved their undoing. In the end, though, the same ineptitude may ironically have contributed to their preservation (see p.3).

When his profoundly melancholic father died, James I (1406–37) was both a child and a prisoner in England. Although his scheming uncle declined to ransom him until 1424, once back in Scotland James ruled with centralizing vigour. His ruthless enthusiasm made him several enemies, a band of whom broke into his residence, cornered him in a drain and stabbed him to death.

Like his father, the fourth Stewart king was a mere child when the burden of Scotland's crown came upon him. After an unsettled minority, the distinctly-birthmarked James II (1437–60) set about the customary task of all early Stewart monarchs: reducing the power of overmighty subjects who made the task of governing Scotland so trying. Focusing on the Livingstones and Douglases, the energetic king met with such success that, in 1460, he felt strong enough to challenge his more powerful neighbour to the south. The attack on England got no further than Roxburgh Castle. Obsessed with guns, 'James of the Fiery Face' was killed by an exploding cannon.

As James III (1460–88) was only nine at the time his father was blown up, the endless cycle of early death and troubled minority was perpetuated into the next reign. James's success in reasserting royal authority is open to question. Smitten with debilitating bouts of depression, he never commanded sufficient loyalty to enable him to dominate his kingdom. At one stage conspirators held him prisoner in Edinburgh Castle, and he was eventually murdered after a battle in which the rebel forces were led by his own 15-year-old son.

Such was the extraordinary history of the early Stewarts. It was this dynasty, manic and depressive by turns, that continued to rule Scotland while the Tudors were in power in England, and which took over the crowns of both countries upon the death of Elizabeth I. Whatever else the Stewarts might bring to the British monarchy, it was certainly not going to be dullness.

05

James IV, 1489–1513

Parents: James III and
   Margaret of Denmark
Born: 17 March 1473,
   place unknown
Died: 9 September 1513,
   Flodden battlefield,
   Northumberland
Marriage: Margaret Tudor, 150⬛
Children: (i) James, Duke of
           Rothesay, b.150⬛
      (ii) Arthur, Duke of
           Rothesay, b.150⬛
    (iii) James V, b.151⬛
    (iv) Alexander, Duke
           of Ross, b.1514⬛

The Scottish monarchy boasts few heroes. Robert I (the Bruce), the victor of Bannockburn and saviour of Scottish independence, stands pre-eminent, the national all-time gold medal winner. The bronze is usually contested between the early-medieval Malcolm Canmore (Big Head or Chief) and two Alexanders (the second and third kings of that name) of the doughty House of Dunkeld.

The silver medal, for sheer strength of personality and the force with which he dragged his tiny state towards the European mainstream, hangs undisputed around the neck of James IV. Like so many Scottish idols, however, James's glory is not untarnished. In the end he proved no more than a gallant loser, squandering all he had achieved in one vain, foolish and fatal last throw.

James of the Iron Belt

Little is known of James's early life. He seems to have spent much of it within the secure granite walls of Stirling Castle in the company of his Danish mother. For a thorough academic education he was indebted to the humanist scholar Archibald Whitelaw. His mother may have had a questionable hand in his political instruction, sowing the seeds of disaffection for her ineffectual husband.

At the age of 15 James was persuaded to join rebellious lords seeking to purge the court and administration of 'deceitful and perverse council'. The plan went horribly wrong when, fleeing after defeat in the battle of Sauchieburn, the king was mysteriously murdered. His son, now prematurely launched onto the throne, was genuinely distraught and for the rest of his life wore an iron belt next to the skin as a mark of penance.

Peace, balance and order

The rebellion that had brought James to the throne was shortly followed by another serious uprising. Three years later the king was fighting the wily Archibald, Earl of Douglas (also known colourfully as the 'Red Douglas' and 'Archibald Bell-the-Cat'), and the year after that he faced disloyalty among the 'savages' of the Western Isles.

The king adopted an instinctively astute policy to end this endemic disorder. He was continually on the move, personally intervening wherever the rule of law was flouted. At the same time, he studiously avoided siding with any noble faction, making sure that powerful groups and families were represented and recognized at court. All this he achieved without noticeably raising the burden of taxation. Although always short of money, he managed to make ends meet by making better use of the royal lands and prerogatives.

Scotland never had a more restless monarch. James discovered that by alternating hanging with hunting, and fining with fornication, he could dispense justice, make money and enjoy himself all at the same time. He mixed pilgrimages in with his travels, too. Like many monarchs, he saw nothing wrong with exploiting the Church when it suited him, making his illegitimate 11-year-old son Archbishop of St Andrews, while simultaneously supporting the ultra-strict Observant Friars. His obsessive womanizing was hardly in keeping with church teaching, although it did not stop Pope Julius II from honouring him with a golden sword and the title 'Protector and Defender of the Christian Faith'.

'Lord of the world'

Despite his country's fringe status on almost all counts – geographically, economically, militarily and diplomatically – James of the Iron Belt was determined to cut a dash on the European scene. He built great ships and halls, employed poets, musicians, tumblers and craftsmen from countries far and wide, and when possible acted the part of the noble Renaissance prince and patron. It was the duty of all well-to-do Scottish parents, he decreed, to see that their children were properly educated.

Nor was this all show. The king himself was genuinely learned, speaking many languages (including Gaelic, 'the tongue of the savages who live in some parts'), and fascinated by new ideas. He tested the strength of his flagship, the *Great Michael*, by firing a cannon at it, and he backed the crackpot schemes of Doctor Damian who attempted to fly from the ramparts of Stirling Castle on home-made wings. More seriously, he supported Edinburgh's new College of Surgeons and his country's first printing press.

Sadly, a very big fish in a very small pond, James's head was turned by his achievements and the flattery of those around him. He did not like being criticized and was probably driven by an inner core of self-doubt. So when described as 'lord of the world', he allowed his heart to overrule his head and half believed it – if he set his mind to it, surely there was nothing he could not achieve? After almost quarter of a century on the throne, he told himself that all he needed to crown his many and glorious achievements was a Bannockburn-style victory over the old enemy. Simple, surely?

The Tudor union

James's initial forays into the diplomatic field were fortunate, even moderately skilful. Realizing that conflict with England invariably brought costly disaster, he made a truce with Henry VII in 1491. A few years later he gave temporary backing to Perkin Warbeck, the pretender to the English throne who masqueraded as the younger of the two murdered Princes in the Tower. This persuaded Henry VII to make a further truce that eventually matured into a full-blown peace treaty.

Peace was cemented by James's marriage to Margaret Tudor, the awkward sister of the future Henry VIII. The union was not a success. Margaret found her husband quickly unfaithful and prone to vaunting displays of unwarranted self-glorification; he found her self-willed and arrogant. Nevertheless, the marriage achieved its primary purposes, ending some two centuries of sporadic but intensely bitter conflict and producing a healthy heir. Indeed, had James been prepared to leave things there, he might well have died in his bed and been remembered as one of the foremost monarchs of his generation.

Flodden

It was not to be. James annoyed his southern neighbours by emphasizing that his wife was next in line to the English throne (this remained true until the birth of Henry VIII's daughter Mary), thereby raising the hateful possibility of Scottish rule at Westminster. Salt was rubbed into the wound when the very English name of Henry VIII's dead brother, Arthur, was usurped by James and Margaret for their third child. Worse was to come.

As Henry VIII prepared for his French campaign in 1512 (see p.13), Louis XII tempted James into an alliance with promises of great quantities of arms, men and money. It was too good to be true. The moment his brother-in-law shipped his army across the Channel, all James had to do was slip over the undefended border and loot and harry to his heart's content. The French deal was concluded.

At first all went according to plan. As Henry left for France, James led 20,000 men, the largest Scottish army ever assembled, into England. Four hundred oxen were needed to haul its massive siege cannon. After making some easy gains, James had fulfilled his bargain with Louis XII and was free to return home with his substantial booty. Tragically for Scotland, he wanted more.

The English force sent to head off James's incursion was led by the Earl of Surrey, a 70-year-old veteran of the Wars of the Roses. Cautious, wily, uncharismatic, he was everything the Scottish king was not. He managed to goad his opponent, who had no experience of command during large-scale encounters, to commit to battle on a grassy site known as Flodden Field, near the River Til. Here the man of the iron belt made a series of elementary errors. He failed to position his guns effectively, missed the opportunity to attack as the enemy were deploying, and ordered his inexperienced pikemen to break ranks and charge the well-trained and orderly English infantry.

James led the Scottish assault in person. Fighting like a man possessed, he hacked his way to within a few spear lengths of Surrey before, smitten by multiple wounds, he fell dead to the ground. By the time the battle ended, the hapless monarch had been joined by virtually the entire Scottish ruling class. As well as thousands of ordinary soldiers, an archbishop, a bishop, two abbots, nine earls, 14 lords and numerous lesser chiefs and lairds were slain in the worst military disaster in Scottish history.

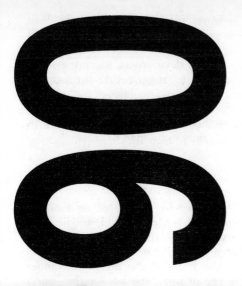

06 James V, 1513–42

Parents: James IV and
  Margaret Tudor
Born: Linlithgow, 1512
Died: Falkland Castle, 1542
Marriages and children:
1 Madeleine Valois, 1537
  No children
2 Mary of Guise, 1538
  Children: (i) James, Duke of
                  Rothesay, b.1540
             (ii) Arthur, Duke of
                  Albany, b.1541
             (iii) Mary Queen of
                  Scots, b.1542

The most attractive of Stewarts was succeeded by the least attractive. Today James V is primarily remembered as the father of a semi-legendary superstar, Mary Queen of Scots. In his own day he was known largely for his deviousness, viciousness and sexual profligacy. It is tempting to suggest that through his parents he inherited the least sympathetic qualities of the Stewarts and Tudors, although his nastiness is probably more accurately explained by his appalling childhood. Whatever the reason for his twisted personality, he was certainly not a man to cross.

A mere pawn

James V was 19 months old when his father fell on Flodden Field. His mother, pregnant with another child, might have considered it her duty to devote herself to the upbringing of her deceased husband's children – but that was not Margaret Tudor's way. Shortly after the birth of the infant Alexander (who survived only to the age of one), she fell for the hearty charms of Archibald Douglas, Earl of Angus (Bell-the-Cat's grandson and the latest Red Douglas). She promptly married him. The marriage was based upon lust, not love, and swiftly fell apart. Margaret was soon in the arms of another and found precious little time to devote to the young king.

As well as Margaret and Archibald, champions of the English cause in Scotland, two other relatives played a prominent part in James's tortuous minority. These were the Earl of Arran and his French-speaking cousin, the Duke of Albany, supporter of a French alliance. A pawn in the hands of these power brokers, the young king was buffeted by periods of neglect and flattery, threat and even virtual house arrest under Earl Angus. His education was fragmented, leaving him with broken French and little Latin or Italian. Although quick-witted, he was an ignorant buffoon in comparison with such Renaissance luminaries as Henry VIII and Francis I of France. This did little for his already fragile self-esteem.

In 1528, James fled Angus's detention in disguise and was reunited with his mother and her latest paramour. Shortly afterwards he entered Edinburgh at the head of a great host. The Red Douglas fled, barricaded himself in his castle for a while, then escaped to England. Finally in personal control of his kingdom, by this time the 17-year-old king was as calculating, mistrustful and insecure an individual as one might imagine.

Power and money

James's minority had taught him to trust no one, least of all the nobility. It is said that he preferred the common people to the mighty and mixed with the latter disguised as the 'Gudeman of Ballangeich' in order to ascertain the mood of the nation (and seduce unsuspecting country maidens). He relied upon the advice of lawyers and others of the middling sort rather than the traditional ruling class, whom he further alienated by exorbitant financial demands.

The king imposed a centralized royal authority, symbolized in the new, lay-staffed central court (the College of Justice), more effectively than any of his predecessors. His campaign to 'staunch all theft and rieving within this realm' began in the Borders, where he used rugged Highlanders to round up known villains.[8] He then overawed the Highlands and Islands themselves with 'letters of fire and the sword' and a threatening circumnavigation of the region in a fleet of 12 heavily-gunned vessels. Local chiefs, awe-struck by such a display of power, were powerless to prevent their sons being shipped down south for a little Renaissance education.

James was swift to exploit the prevailing religious uncertainty. The Pope, his authority crumbling in much of northern Europe, was eager to keep Scotland on-side. James sized up the position with Machiavellian astuteness and, turning a deaf ear to Uncle Henry's pleas for British and family solidarity, opted to remain a loyal Roman Catholic. In return for condemning Protestantism and burning a few heretics, the pope granted James a perpetual £10,000 a year from ecclesiastical revenues, a further temporary tax of one tenth of the same, and the right to nominate appointments to Scottish episcopacy. The deal was a real bargain: as well as filling his coffers, the king was able to furnish his illegitimate sons with comfy positions in the Church.

Madeleine and Mary

For the first few years of his reign James avoided aligning himself firmly with any foreign power. His bachelor status gave him leverage and at one time or another he was offered Habsburg, English (Mary Tudor) and French brides in return for alliance. In the end, he rejected his mother's efforts to keep him in the English camp and chose to renew the Auld Alliance with

France. The move brought short-term gain at the expense of long-term disaster.

The first French bride on offer proved, upon closer inspection, to be a hunchback; the king was something of an expert on female charms and turned her down flat. In her place he chose a skinny 16-year-old consumptive, Princess Madeleine. That the poor girl was not expected to live long did not worry James one jot. In fact, it was just what he wanted. His only concern was that she survived long enough for her dowry of 100,000 gold crowns to be handed over. It was. Seven weeks after landing in Scotland, Madeleine was dead (1538).

Nothing daunted, James looked to France for a replacement. He found one in the form of the recently widowed Mary of Guise. The shapely, golden-haired and blue-eyed noblewoman, already the mother of two, was an altogether different proposition from the feeble Madeleine. Tough, intelligent, accomplished, she was a real asset to the Scottish monarchy. So too was a second six-figure dowry.

Solway Moss

By his late twenties James was not a well man. He had suffered a heavy fall from his horse and was smitten with periodic bouts of debilitating depression. In 1541 a series of unfortunate happenings exacerbated his melancholic disposition. His mother and two sons by Mary of Guise died. France and Henry VIII reconciled their differences, and relations with England worsened when James failed to keep an appointment with Henry VIII at York.

By 1542 there was sporadic fighting along the southern border. Upping the stakes, Henry VIII renewed his crown's ancient claim to Scottish overlordship. James struggled to raise forces sufficient to defend his realm – memories of Flodden were still sharp and the king had done little to endear himself to his people, least of all those who had traditionally provided military leadership. When two sizeable armies did eventually meet, at Solway Moss, the Scots' simply disintegrated.

For James this was the last straw. Deeply unsettled, he rode around the country until he reached Falkland Palace. Here he took to his bed, turned his face to the wall and died. His supposed last words – 'It came with a lass; it will pass with a lass' – are as mysterious as they are well-known.

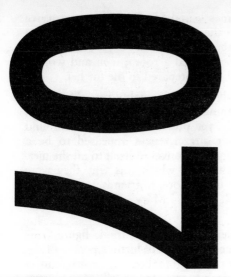

07 Mary Queen of Scots, 1542–67

Parents: James V and
  Mary of Guise
Born: Linlithgow, 1542
Died: Fotheringhay Castle,
  Northamptonshire, 1587
Marriages and children:
1 Prince Francis, briefly King
  Francis II of France, 1558
2 Henry Stewart, Lord Darnley,
  1565
  Child: James VI and I, b.1566
3 James Hepburn, Earl of
  Bothwell, 1567

Mary, the only child of James V and Mary of Guise to survive into adulthood, was one of the few British monarchs possessed of that indefinable quality that makes a star. People remembered her; heads turned when she entered a room; men and women became devoted to her and were prepared to die for her.

It is difficult to say precisely what this quality was. Mary was good-looking but not stunning, quick-witted without being in any way intellectual, lively yet prone to bouts of profound depression. The key to her attractiveness appeared to be a radiating warmth and energy that conveyed itself to all she met. To her enemies it was frightening, which was why they were quick to brand her a witch or a whore; to friends and admirers it was almost magical. With Mary there were no in-betweens.

The Queen of Scots is widely regarded as a tragic figure. This may well be so, but her tragedy was one of birth: a person of her qualities should never have been called upon to lead a government. Her misfortunes were almost all of her own making. She was simply the wrong person in the wrong place at the wrong time. If one needs confirmation, one might simply ask how her cousin Elizabeth would have coped in the same situation. Not with such crass and tactless ineptitude, surely?

A Rough Wooing

Mary was six days old when she became queen. She was crowned in a specially adapted ceremony at the age of nine months. It goes without saying, therefore, that she had only ever known herself as a queen – not the ideal upbringing for an impressionable child.

As was by now customary in Scotland, the minority of the new monarch triggered a round of feuding for control of the administration. On this occasion it was given added bitterness by religious differences: despite the efforts of James V and Cardinal Archbishop David Beaton, Protestantism was making considerable headway in southern Scotland. To some sections of the population, therefore, the traditional Auld Alliance with Roman Catholic France was losing its appeal.

The wavering heir presumptive, James Hamilton, Earl of Arran (great-grandson of James II), opened his innings by arranging the betrothal of the infant Mary to England's Prince Edward.

When Hamilton and the Scottish parliament changed their minds, Henry VIII responded with the 'Rough Wooing' – a series of devastating cross-border incursions (1544–5). When Lord Protector Somerset continued the campaign (see p.23) and secured an overwhelming victory at the Battle of Pinkie, the desperate Scots signed the Treaty of Haddington with Henry II of France.

The key clause of the treaty stated that Queen Mary was to move directly to France, where she would be betrothed to Dauphin Francis. The six-year-old Mary bade farewell to her mother, who remained in Scotland to safeguard her family's interests, and sailed for France in August 1548. She remained abroad for 13 years. When she finally returned to Scotland, it was as a complete stranger.

The French princess

The French fell in love with Queen Mary. At court the little queen, whom Henry II dubbed his 'most perfect child', was a sort of exotic exhibit – a lovely waif whom the French believed they had rescued from northern barbarity. Her childish speech delighted, her looks were praised, her simple gestures envied. Rarely had a child been more fawned over.

In between the flattery, Mary received a sound education. As well as music and dancing, she learned several languages and was even given some instruction in government and diplomacy. The latter, however, was largely theoretical and only marginally related to the narrow feuding and cruel power struggles that marked the politics of her native land. In other words, Mary was raised to be the ideal consort to the King of France, not to govern a troubled state single-handed.

At the age of 16, already a tall, elegant and lively young woman of undoubted sexual appeal, Mary was married to the dauphin. Her husband Francis, the heir to the French throne, was her chronological junior by two years; in terms of physical and emotional development the gap was more like five – or even 15. He was a little boy, reportedly physically incapable of sexual activity, who doted on his bride as if she were his older sister. The couple had been friends for many years and marriage appears not to have altered their innocent friendship.

Mary's other kingdom

Affairs in Mary's other kingdom, Scotland, had settled down after her departure. Mary of Guise had replaced the Earl of Arran as regent (1554) and striven on her daughter's behalf resolutely to maintain the French and Catholic cause. For a time she was helped by the presence of a Catholic on the English throne (see p.27). The extent of Mary Stewart's participation in Scottish government was sending her mother blank sheets of paper signed 'Marie'.

France's domination of Scotland fed a nationalistic backlash that made common cause with religious reform. The inspirational Protestant leader John Knox returned to Scotland from Switzerland, Elizabeth I committed English forces to the rebel cause (see p.36), and, following the regent's untimely death, in the summer of 1560 a treaty was signed that obliged French and English troops to leave Scotland. A Reformation Parliament then severed links with the papacy and abolished the mass. Across the Channel, Queen Mary rejected both moves. It made no difference. Willy-nilly, in her absence her Scottish kingdom was swinging rapidly towards Protestantism.

Queen of Scotland

In July 1559 Dauphin Francis succeeded to the throne of France. Now queen of two nations, Mary's star was at its highest. Its long, slow decline began less than 12 months later. In June 1560 her 45-year-old mother died. Then, shortly before Christmas, her feeble husband also passed away. Power passed into the hands of Francis's mother, Catherine de Medici, who was opposed to the Guise faction and therefore no friend of Mary Queen of Scots. The young widow had no option but to return home.

Mary's position was not an enviable one. Rejected by France, as a Catholic she was regarded with suspicion by the prevailing Protestant faction in Scotland and by her cousin Elizabeth in England. She was also expected to govern an unstable realm about which she knew little and whose political and social fabric had been torn by a protracted minority and religious upheaval. That she failed dismally comes as no surprise: the fault lay not with her but with the system of hereditary monarchy that selects rulers for their genes not genius.

Mary's reign lasted six years. To begin with things went quite well: she took wise advice, principally from her half-brother, the Earl of Moray, and avoided open religious confrontation. Beneath the surface, though, tensions were building. There was an unsettling contradiction in having an ostentatiously Roman Catholic queen in a country where attending mass was forbidden.

Nor did Mary endear herself to her people by tactlessly harking on about how, as the true queen of England, she was determined to oust her cousin Elizabeth. This tactlessness gave the distasteful impression that she saw Scotland as a third-rate state she could not wait to leave. Moreover, Scottish Protestants looked upon Elizabeth as an ally, not a usurper. They broke into a cold sweat at the thought of a military campaign against England – ending no doubt in yet another crushing defeat – simply to satisfy the ambition of their Catholic queen.

The English issue was just one example of Mary's lack of political skill. Her volatility, her bouts of depression, her craving for attention and praise – were all indications of a personality fundamentally unsuited to the subtle task of government. Her scandal-tinged, French-influenced court of poets and songsters, dancers and revellers annoyed her more puritan-minded subjects. To cap it all, she fell madly in love and made a disastrous marriage.

The object of Mary's affections was her cousin, Henry Stewart, Lord Darnley: 'the lustiest and best proportioned long man that she had seen.'[9] Her junior by three years, Darnley certainly had good looks and a superficial charm – but nothing else. He was immature, capricious, scheming, unreliable and cruel. Marrying in July 1565, within a year the queen was arousing her husband's jealous fury by showing affection for her Italian secretary, David Rizzio. Darnley and a band of cronies dragged the unfortunate man from the presence of the terrified queen, now six months pregnant, and stabbed him to death.

Prince James, Mary's first and only child, was born in June 1566. By this time she and her husband were irreconcilably estranged. The queen, after two unsuccessful marriages with younger men, now fell for the rugged masculinity of James Hepburn, Earl of Bothwell. Older but no wiser than her, he arranged for Darnley to be murdered in bizarre circumstances. When declared not guilty in a dubious trial, he had his first marriage annulled, seized Mary (perhaps raping her), and promptly married her at Holyrood House, Edinburgh.

This was more than the Scots could take. Their queen was now the scandal of Europe. She was arrested, deprived of her crown and imprisoned in Loch Leven Castle. Her infant son was taken from her and crowned as James VI. Bothwell fled abroad and died insane in a Danish prison. Mary may have lost her crown, but she still had her magnetic charm: beguiling her captors into helping her, she escaped and raised an army. This force was defeated at Langside. Four days later Mary crossed the border into England and begged her royal cousin for asylum and assistance. Elizabeth was not amused (see p.39).

The prisoner

On board the fishing boat carrying Mary across the Solway Firth to England, the fugitive queen had a sudden change of heart: she did not want to go to England after all, she told the captain, but France. It was an impossible request. The vessel was far too small to sail around Britain, and Mary was delivered to her original destination.

Mary's misgivings were fully justified. Did she really expect Elizabeth to show generous assistance to the woman who wished to replace her on the throne? At the same time, the English queen was unsure what to do with her unwelcome guest. To release her would be to court disaster; to execute her would be to make her a Catholic martyr. As so often when faced with an awkward dilemma, Elizabeth did nothing.

Mary was placed under house arrest, a condition she remained in for the rest of her life. To increase security, she never spent more than two years in one place, finally ending up in Fotheringhay Castle, Northamptonshire. The public explanation for her detention was the result of an enquiry into Darnley's death, held shortly after her arrival in England, which concluded that she was implicated in her second husband's murder.

The longer Mary remained alive, the more of a liability to Elizabeth she became. For a short time it was thought she might be safely married off, even to Elizabeth's own Dudley. By 1570, though, she was clearly the focus of Catholic plots, some of which she almost certainly participated in. The full extent of her treasonous guilt towards Elizabeth is difficult to judge because English agents under the control of Secretary Francis Walsingham, eager for a kill, were prepared to use any methods to trap the Catholic queen.

Birth of a legend

The end came after the discovery in 1586 of a Catholic plot to assassinate Elizabeth and replace her with Mary. Its instigator was most cruelly executed. Presented with clear evidence of her royal cousin's guilt, Elizabeth still prevaricated: taking the life of an anointed queen, whatever the circumstances, was not something she wished to be associated with. When she finally signed Mary's death warrant, it was rushed to Fotheringhay before Elizabeth could change her mind.

After long years of detention, much of Mary's attractiveness had long since faded. Nevertheless, she made a good end. Dressed in blood red, the Church's colour of martyrdom, she faced the axe with noble serenity. Perhaps, kneeling at the block, she knew instinctively that a good final performance would blot out all previous bungling and even mark the birth of a legend. It was just as her motto had predicted: 'In my end is my beginning.'

08

James I & VI, 1567/1603–25

Parents: Mary Queen of Scots and Henry Stewart, Lord Darnley

Born: 19 June 1566, Edinburgh Castle

Died: 27 March 1625, Theobalds, Hertfordshire

Marriage: Anne of Denmark, 1589

Children:
(i) Henry, Prince of Wales, b.1594
(ii) Elizabeth, b.1596
(iii) Margaret, b.1598
(iv) Charles I, b.1600
(v) Robert, b.1602
(vi) Mary, b.1605
(vii) Sophia, b.1606

In terms of the British monarchy the reign of James VI of Scotland and I of England is of major importance – for the first time the crowns of the two nations were formally and voluntarily united. This paved the way for the full political union between the two countries a little over a century later, although if James had had his way it would have come much sooner.

James Stewart (or 'Stuart' using his mother's French spelling) is also a fascinating character in his own right. Perhaps the only genuine intellectual to wear the British crown, he had the double misfortune of being personally somewhat unsavoury and reigning between his much lauded cousin Elizabeth and his disastrous son Charles. This has led to accusations, unwise and inaccurate, that he laid the road that led to civil war in both kingdoms and republicanism in England. To assume that great events have great and deep-seated causes is to read history backwards. James, in many ways a remarkable king, deserves better than that.

Hard schooling

The heartless upbringing of Mary Queen of Scots' son bears testimony to the startling resilience of the human psyche. He had no memories of his mother, whom he knew only as the 'bawd' and 'whore' of endless puritanical moralizing. The toys she sent him from England were never delivered. Later, he believed his childhood lessons confirmed when the captive Mary still refused to recognize him as king, referring to him simply as 'Prince of Scotland'. He displayed formal grief and anger at her eventual execution in 1587, severing diplomatic relations with England for a while. In his heart, though, he was relieved. With Mary out of the way he was now Elizabeth's undisputed heir.

Confined for much of the time within the granite fastness of Stirling Castle, James's childhood was grim. His governess, the Countess of Mar, was not renowned for warmth or sympathy. His principal teacher, George Buchanan, was as rigid in discipline as he was in thought, although he did instil his pupil with a sharp sense of humour. The young king's other teacher, Peter Young, was only marginally less fierce.

In their unyielding hands James acquired a genuine love of learning. He absorbed much history and theology and became fluent in several ancient and modern languages, including his native Scots. When he grew up he joined his great-great uncle Henry VIII as one of the few British monarchs to write a book. In fact, he wrote several on a range of subjects. *The Trew Law of Free Monarchies* and *Basilikon Doron* dealt with political ideas. *Demonology* was a treatise on one of the king's favourite subjects, witchcraft, while the *Counterblaste to Tobacco* was a health warning almost 400 years before its time.

An old young man

Although crowned when 13 months old, James did not begin to participate actively and regularly in government until the early 1580s. His long minority witnessed the usual vicious jostling for position among the ruling class. Power rested, with varying degrees of security, in the hands of a string of regents. The first of these was James Stewart, Earl of Moray (Macbeth's old stamping ground), one of the many bastard sons of James V. An enthusiastic presbyterian, he was linked to the murders of both Rizzio and Darnley (see p.61). After three years in office he received a fatal dose of his own medicine: assassination by a fervent Roman Catholic.

Other regents fared little better. One of the more able was James Douglas, Earl of Morton, another of the Rizzio murder gang. His period of power saw an improvement in relations with England and greater church stability. When James, eager to exercise power himself, obliged him to stand aside in 1578, parliament swiftly restored him. The king took revenge a few years later when Morton was found guilty of participating in the Darnley murder. He was unusually executed by a guillotine machine – charmingly named the 'Maiden' – that he had helped introduce.

Finally, there was the Esmé Stuart incident. In the middle of the Morton debacle James invited his 37-year-old French cousin, Esmé Stuart, Seigneur d'Aubigny to Scotland. So sophisticated and charming a man the boy had never met before and he was completely bowled over. The rugged Scottish nobility were less impressed, particularly when their king began to address the scented papist in highly emotional terms and shower him with honours and gifts. The liaison ended in tears when a group of lords seized James in the Ruthven Raid and gave the Seigneur no option but to return to France. Small wonder that around this time a foreign visitor described Scotland's emotionally scarred king as 'an old young man.'

King of Scots

Against all the odds, James turned out to be a very good king of Scotland. Some say he was the best the country ever had. Given his childhood experiences and 40-odd years of what he disparagingly dismissed as rule by 'women, little children and traitorous and avaricious regents', this was a quite remarkable achievement.[10]

The young king's tasks were much the same as those that had confronted his predecessors – because each reign invariably began with a minority during which the work of the previous monarch was unravelled, there is a depressing similarity to the pattern of Stewart rule in Scotland. The only difference for James was that the usual struggle to restore central authority was spiced with religious controversy.

Unlike the more macho Stewarts, the intellectually-inclined monarch was not one to blast or bombard his subjects into submission. Where possible he preferred more subtle methods: compromise, balance, conciliation or, perhaps as a last resort, trickery.

Subterfuge may have been behind the famous Gowrie Conspiracy of 1600, when, visiting the household of the powerful Ruthven family, James became involved in some sort of affray. His cries for help attracted courtiers who slew the head of the Ruthven family and his brother. Their pierced bodies were taken to Edinburgh where they were incongruously convicted of treason. The Ruthven family possessions were forfeit and use of their name proscribed. Opinion is divided over whether James had been in serious danger or had engineered the incident to remove the Ruthvens. He owed them money and bore a grudge against them for the part they had played in the Rizzio murder and Ruthven Raid.

In ecclesiastical matters James built upon the progress made during his minority gradually to enhance the powers of bishops and maintain royal power over church as well as secular business. This was confirmed in the Black Acts of 1584. Obstreperous nobles, such as the Catholic 'Northern Earls' (Huntly, Crawford, Errol) and the overpowering Francis Stuart, Earl of Bothwell, were out-faced rather than confronted directly. Where possible, James relied upon 'new men', those who owed their status entirely to him, rather than traditional families. The best example was the able Sir John Maitland, the first chancellor for over a century who was neither a prelate nor a noble.

The king's pacific instincts were prominent in his foreign policy, too. History taught him the folly of war with England, in which the Scots were invariably walloped in nine out of every ten campaigns. Moreover, the last thing he wanted was to alienate the promised land in the south to which he aspired. A treaty signed at Berwick cemented Anglo-Scottish friendship and gave James a much-needed £4,000-a-year. (This may seem a paltry sum but for a monarch with an annual income of only £15,000 it was a godsend.) The new spirit of amity and co-operation enabled James to bring more law and order to the border region than it had probably ever seen. Only in the Highlands and Islands did his softly-softly style of government make little impression.

Solomon goes south

Elizabeth never formally accepted James as her heir. Perhaps she did not wish to be reminded of her mortality? Certainly, while she was still around, she had no intention of creating the circumstances in which a pro-successor faction might develop. That said, Elizabeth never denied that her Scottish cousin would succeed her. James prepared the way carefully, too, developing links with key figures at the English court and administration. He corresponded with Robert Devereux for a while, then with Robert Cecil, Lord Burghley's immensely capable son who replaced his father as Elizabeth's chief minister at the end of her reign.

It was Cecil who sent news of Elizabeth's death to Scotland and arranged for James to be proclaimed in London. The change-over went remarkably smoothly. Elizabeth's war-ridden final years had been less than glorious and the English warmly welcomed a change. Although, after centuries of feuding, there was little love lost between the English and the Scots, rumour had presented the 'Northern Solomon' favourably to his new subjects. James was thrilled to find the route south to London lined with cheering crowds.

The vulgar intellectual

Whatever they had been expecting from their new monarch, James took England by surprise. He was so un-Tudor. Physically he did not impress. A wispy beard and moustache partly hid a small mouth. His nose was large and in later life his eyes bulged. The ungainly manner in which he carried himself lacked dignity and has led to the suggestion that he suffered from a mild form of cerebral palsy.

James's style was even further removed from what had gone before. Where the Tudors had been stern and regal, he was witty and informal. Where they had been frugal, he was profligate. Where they had dictated, he discussed. The English did not necessarily find their new monarch any easier to manage, however. He was so contradictory: an academic-minded man who wrote books and delighted in philosophical discussion, yet at the same time could be most unroyally vulgar and coarse. When pressed by English courtiers he once protested angrily, 'God's wounds! I will pull down my breeches and they shall also see my arse!'[11] One can hardly imagine Elizabeth, her sister or her father indulging in such ribaldry.

Two other aspects of James's personality the English found hard to stomach were his Scottishness and his penchant for attractive young men. The English hated his insistent use of the hard-to-follow Scots tongue (similar to that used later by the poet Robbie Burns), and the swarm of fellow countrymen who flocked south with him in search of rich pickings. The English had long been prejudiced against 'northern adjectives'. Marriage to one of them was compared to being tied to a rotting carcass and thrown into a ditch. The most vitriolic racial abuse was reserved for royal favourites like Robert Carr, whom James made Earl of Somerset. The king was himself not above cruel racial discrimination, either. To entertain his brother-in-law, the King of Denmark, for aesthetic reasons he arranged for a troupe of black Africans to dance naked in the snow. He knew full well that the traumatic experience would probably kill them – which it duly did.

James had a weakness for hunting and attractive young men. The former, which he took to excess, was socially acceptable. The latter was not. Considering James's childhood, his homosexual predilections are not surprising; nor are they shocking to modern sensibilities. His contemporaries, steeped in fundamental Christian teaching, were less tolerant. We do not know the intimate details of James's relations with his young men, but it was enough for him to fondle and pinch them in full view of the court for people to believe the worst.

Rex Pacificus

James was by conviction and instinct a man of peace. His detractors said that he was a physical coward. True or not, one of his first acts on ascending the English throne was to end the war with Spain that had been dragging on for so long. The move was universally popular and set the tone for the whole reign.

Styling himself 'Rex Pacificus' – the king of peace – James saw himself as the arbiter of Europe, the wise and tolerant mediator between Catholic and Protestant. Since his wife, Anne of Denmark, had (somewhat embarrassingly) converted to Catholicism while he remained a staunch Protestant, he offered his own household as an example of peaceful cohabitation. He planned to take the matter further through the marriages of his children.

James had married his 15-year-old Danish princess by proxy in 1589. Then, with an unaccustomed dash of heterosexual gallantry, he had crossed the seas to fetch her. The marriage was not close and there were rumours that the king was not the true father of some of the couple's later children. Before that, though, James performed his marital duty effectively enough to father several children. This suggests that his sexuality was more what we would term AC/DC than straightforward gay.

The peace plan was to marry Henry, the able Prince of Wales, into a leading Roman Catholic dynasty (Spanish Habsburg or French Bourbon) and Elizabeth, James's lively daughter, with a leading European Protestant. The idea fell apart for a number of reasons but primarily because England, although vastly more powerful than Scotland, was not sufficiently influential to play the role of arbiter of Europe.

The Protestant side of the scheme went well enough. Princess Elizabeth, the original 'Queen of Hearts', married Frederick, the Elector Palatine, a key figure in German Protestantism. No Catholic bride had been found for Henry, however, before he died in 1612. His place was taken by his immeasurably less able younger brother Charles. To ensure that England did not join the major European conflict that flared in 1618, the Spanish artfully played along with the marriage idea. It finally collapsed shortly before James's death. Although the king's masterplan had failed and war was inevitable by 1625, he had maintained the peace for over 20 years.

'No bishop, no king'

The Church of England had not been influenced by the Presbyterian ideal as strongly as had the Church of Scotland, and James was determined to keep it thus. His famous maxim 'no bishop, no king' indicates how well he understood the link between monarchical authority and a church hierarchy under royal control.

As in the previous reign, pressure on the Church came from puritans as well as Catholics. Shortly after James's accession a meeting was held at Hampton Court to discuss puritan ideas for church reform ('purifying' it of remaining traces of Catholicism). The bishops, backed by James, made no concessions and the only notable outcome of the gathering was a decision to produce a new, authorized version of the Bible. The King James Bible, published in 1611, remains to this day one of the finest books ever written in the English language and an enduring monument to the king who patronized its production.

The religious history of James's reign has been studied in great detail because of the Puritan Revolution that followed (see p.84). One looks in vain for signs of impending turmoil during his lifetime. Ever the moderate, James knew when to pull back to avoid confrontation. In 1618, for example, he issued a *Book of Sports* that listed suitable sports, such as archery, for Sunday practice. Puritans, equating Sunday with the Sabbath and determined to uphold the fourth commandment, objected. The king withdrew his order that the book be read aloud in church.

Similarly, James refused to back the ambitious high-church Bishop of St David's, William Laud, although the objectionable prelate was a favourite of the king's last and dearly beloved favourite, George Villiers, Marquess of Buckingham. Laud, James wisely observed, 'hath a restless spirit, and cannot see when matters are well.'[12] The bishop was a confrontational man, the king was not. The latter maintained a balanced and relatively peaceful church; the former, backed to the hilt by the inept Charles I, would lead both England and Scotland into civil war (see p.81).

James was initially inclined gradually to extend the hand of toleration towards Roman Catholics. His mind was changed by the foolish Gunpowder Plot of 1605. A band of young Catholic zealots had grown disillusioned with the new king for not doing more for their cause. They rented a cellar beneath the Palace of Westminster and hired Guy Fawkes, a fanatical ex-soldier, to stuff the room with gunpowder. The daft idea was to blow up the older members of the royal family (and hundreds of others) at the opening of parliament and somehow put either Prince Charles or Princess Elizabeth on the throne. One of the conspirators warned a friend who might have been in danger. The secret leaked. In the nick of time Guy Fawkes was apprehended amid his explosives. The terrorist plot put paid to any hope the Catholics might have had of better treatment, and the day of Protestant salvation (5 November) has been celebrated ever since.

God's agent

Always eager to lecture those willing (or even unwilling) to listen, James was a keen supporter of the idea of the 'divine right of kings'. This held kingship to be a divinely ordained institution and monarchs to be answerable, ultimately, only to God. They were, therefore, God's lieutenants upon earth.

This was the theory – a sure recipe for tyranny. Ever the pragmatist, James tempered this extreme view by stating that kings should be as fathers to their people, ever mindful of their needs and wishes. What father, he argued, would ever knowingly harm his children? It was beholden upon kings, therefore, to have their subjects' best interests always at heart. Moreover, if they put themselves first or acted foolishly or harshly, God would surely punish them severely in the life to come.

James's study of history and practical experience in government had also taught him that there was always a wide divide between theory and practice. He knew only too well that politics was the art of the possible, not of trying to guide events down pre-ordained channels. No one would sacrifice him on the altar of principle.

Canker of want

James's biggest failing – setting aside his sexual proclivities – was money. His 'canker of want', as he put it, arose quite simply because he always spent more than he had. His difficulties arose partly because of his experience in Scotland, where he had been embarrassingly impecunious. Arrival in England was like Christmas, and he engaged in a wild spending spree before he realized that even in a time of peace England's coffers were by no means bottomless.

The problem was intractable. As in Tudor times, the king was expected to 'live of his own' – meet all personal (including court) and governmental expenses from his regular revenue. This came from crown lands, customs duties and various traditional feudal rights, such as wardship (the right of the crown to control the estates of important minors until they came of age). Anything extra had to be voted by parliament – specifically, the House of Commons – in the form of subsidies (see p.44).

Various factors, including inflation and the depletion of crown assets, had led to a fall in royal income to the point where it was extremely difficult to make ends meet. James's roaring expenditure – £3,300 on a single 1600-dish Twelfth Night banquet, for instance – certainly did not make things any easier. There were three possible ways out: cut expenditure, squeeze more from the crown's assets, or persuade parliament to vote the crown a regular supply.

The first proved impossible. Lord Treasurer Lionel Cranfield's brave attempt, 1621–4, made as many enemies as cuts. The second was tried but proved a political hot potato. As Elizabeth had done, for example, James granted monopolies (the sole right to trade in or manufacture a particular commodity) as rewards and favours for courtiers. The procedure aroused a storm of protest in the House of Commons. The third solution, a regular parliamentary grant, was negotiated by Robert Cecil, Earl of Salisbury, but eventually collapsed amid bitter in-fighting in 1610. As a consequence, under James's lax accountancy, the royal debt rose from some £400,000 to close on £1 million – a formidable sum.

'So mild and gentle a prince'

Monopolies were not the only subject disputed in parliament. James neither understood nor managed the English version of the institution too well and often bemoaned its existence. From time to time there were rows over religion, foreign policy and various other issues, largely as a result of the king's failure to manage the Commons as well as Elizabeth had done. The assembly sat for only three of his 22-year reign, however, and at no time was there a serious crown v parliament stand-off. That would be left to his son's reign.

In the spring of 1625 James was afflicted with convulsions. These led to a stroke and, wallowing in the consequences of uncontrollable dysentery, he died in great misery on 27 March. He was little mourned in England. The Scots, whom he had latterly governed with his pen for over 20 years, were more sorry to lose their 'Blessed James'. The antiquarian Sir Simonds d'Ewes was surprised that 'so mild and gentle a prince' should not have been more esteemed by his southern contemporaries. Perhaps, he mused further, 'the ensuing times might yet render ... his memory more dear.'[13]

The words proved uncannily prophetic.

09 Charles I, 1625–49

Parents: James VI & I and Anne of Denmark
Born: 19 November 1600, Dunfermline
Died: 30 January 1649, Whitehall, London
Marriage: Henrietta Maria, 1625
Children: (i) Charles, b.1629
(ii) Charles II, b.1630.
(iii) Mary, b.1631
(iv) James II, b.1633
(v) Elizabeth, b.1635
(vi) Anne, b.1637
(vii) Katherine, b.1639
(viii) Henry, b.1640
(ix) Henrietta, b.1644

Legend and popular history have been much kinder to Charles I than he deserves. Of course he did not choose to be king – indeed, had his elder brother lived a few more years he would probably not have been – but once in that position he displayed such staggering ineptitude that his decapitation in 1649 comes as more of a relief than a tragedy. So why is he remembered so fondly in some circles – Charles the Martyr, the heroic victim of tyranny?

Charles's popularity is partly a cultural matter. He made enemies of a type – earnest, rigid, puritanical folk – who are nowadays distinctly out of fashion. The confused reasoning, mixing modern-day issues with history, runs like this: as Charles was executed by killjoys who, Taliban-like, closed theatres and outlawed Christmas, he must have been a good bloke. In fact, he was no more tolerant than those who opposed him: it was his inflexibility, prejudice and narrowness of vision that stirred up conflict in the first place.

Charles also found himself, posthumously, on the winning side. Republicanism did not take root in England and, 11 years after Charles's death, the crown, House of Lords and Church of England were all restored. The winners inevitably maintained that they should never have been done away with. Since all three still remain more or less intact, the folk memory of Charles the Martyr rests secure.

To those seeking a reason to value Charles's reign, a more balanced estimation might be that he inadvertently saved the British crown. Paradoxically, he did so by bringing it down. This allowed his subjects to try their hand at republicanism. When this too failed, they compromised by restoring a watered-down version of the old monarchy. Dilution of royal power continued over the next half century to the point where the crown became part symbol, part active political force. Consequently, when old-style monarchies were being jettisoned all over Europe in the nineteenth and twentieth centuries, the British were happy to hold on to their tamed variety. Enthusiastic monarchists, therefore, might want to welcome the execution of Charles I rather than bemoan it, for in the long run it helped preserve a popular British institution.

The forgotten son

When King James made his triumphant progress into England he left his two-year-old son Charles behind in Scotland. The boy child was not that important and it was feared that the journey might damage his already frail health. There were also rumours, surely apocryphal, that the boy was ill-fated.

One story tells how King James was woken at night by the crying of Charles's nurse. When asked what the matter was, she declared that she had seen a dark figure enter and throw a cloak over her charge's cradle. James, a self-professed expert on such matters, declared that the devil had cast his cloak over Charles and, if the child were ever to reign, no good would come of it.

It seems that the young Duke of Albany, as Charles was titled, suffered from rickets. He was slow to walk and grew to only about 1.55 metres (just over five foot) in height – very short for a Stewart. As king he wore specially made high-heeled shoes to help him appear taller. Prominent eyes, fleshy lips and the notable Stewart nose were all inherited from his father. His scornful expression, however, was all his own. So too was a speech impediment that made him stammer on all but one public occasion.

As a young boy Charles was overshadowed by his exuberant elder brother and sister. Where they shone, he glowed dimly. By the age of 12, when he became heir apparent on Henry's death, he already had something of an inferiority complex. His intellect was plodding, his personality reserved, his thinking narrow. Worst of all, he lacked judgement in all areas but art. Painfully aware of his flaws, he defended himself by adopting an aloof persona and an infuriating stubbornness.

Buckingham

Charles's reputation, never high, suffered a blow even before he became king. The cause was the proposed marriage deal with Spain, by which Charles should marry Maria, the Spanish Infanta (king's daughter). With the Spanish prevaricating over the deal, in 1623 Charles and Buckingham decided to sneak down to Spain incognito to take a peek at the lady.

Travelling as the Smith brothers and feebly disguised in beards and wigs, they were immediately recognized in Madrid. Charles fell madly in love with the Infanta (although he scarcely saw her) and came close to agreeing a marriage treaty that would have removed virtually all penalties against English Roman Catholics. In the end the prince and the duke (Villiers had recently been made Duke of Buckingham) gave up and returned home to agitate for war against the power that had been instrumental in their humiliation.

The first five years of Charles's reign were a disaster. He got his war with Spain then made things doubly bad in 1627 by going to war with France as well. The land and sea operations, particularly a Buckingham-led attempt to assist the Huguenots of La Rochelle, were expensive and humiliating failures.

The young king and Buckingham made the situation worse by simultaneously giving open support to the new high-church movement known as Arminianism. This denied the Church of England's gloomy Calvinist doctrine of predestination. (God, being almighty and all-seeing, knows everything that will happen; as a consequence, however they live their lives, the good are earmarked at birth for heaven and the wicked for hell.)

Ordinary citizens were less concerned with the theology of Arminianism than with its outward manifestations. These included a greater emphasis on ritual and the sacredness of places of worship. To many Englishmen there was a distinctly popish feel to the Arminians' penchant for moving the communion table to the chancel and railing it off as an altar. And popery, as everyone knew only too well, meant burning people alive, Spanish armadas and Gunpowder Plots. In short, it spelt danger. In the popular imagination Catholicism and tyranny were inseparable.

Rights and wrongs

The traditional place for airing grievances was parliament, more specifically the House of Commons. MPs were elected on a variety of different franchises in unevenly distributed constituencies. Although the system was in no way democratic, research has suggested that the early seventeenth-century Commons was much more representative of the nation's adult males than had previously been thought. The lesson is clear: if MPs spoke with a degree of unanimity on an issue, it behoved a monarch to listen. Charles did not.

Charles's first parliament reluctantly voted him a meagre war chest and registered its dissatisfaction at the way things were going by voting him tunnage (duty on wine imports) and poundage (duty on all imports and exports) for a year only instead of the customary lifetime. Charles ignored the warning and continued to collect the taxes as if they had been agreed. He also demanded a loan from all his better-off subjects.

The parliaments of 1626, 1628 and 1629 were unprecedentedly tumultuous. While voting further inadequate subsidies, MPs tried to impeach (put on trial, with Parliament acting as the court) Buckingham, passed a Petition of Right to limit arbitrary action by the monarch, and held the speaker in his chair while the minority present agreed Three Resolutions against Arminianism and non-parliamentary taxation. Outside Westminster events were equally fraught. When the courts backed the king's right to imprison those who refused to pay the forced loan, the refusniks were hailed as national heroes. Buckingham, by now an almost universal hate figure, was assassinated in Portsmouth while preparing another military venture (1628). Small wonder that when Charles dissolved parliament in 1629 he determined never to call another.

Personal rule

After the collapse of the proposed Spanish match, Charles had promptly married Henrietta Maria, the youngest daughter of Henry IV of France. At first the bubbly teenager found her husband a bit of a bore, but once Buckingham was out of the game their relationship deepened into genuine love.

Henrietta Maria was a mixed blessing for the king. Her Catholicism and belief in the divine right of kings (see p.72) reinforced opposition fears that Charles was trying to erect a continental-style Catholic tyranny in Britain. On the other hand, she had vigour and marginally more political sense than him. The latter led her to oppose the direction of policy during the 1630s and urge Charles to compromise after 1645.

Charles was a fastidious man of impeccable taste. An extravagant patron of Inigo Jones and Van Dyck, his art collection was the toast of Europe. Unfortunately, his attempt to create in government the same order and neatness that he found in art proved disastrous. Working closely with William Laud, now Archbishop of Canterbury, and Thomas Wentworth, Earl Strafford (President of the Council of the North then, 1632, Lord Deputy in Ireland), he pursued a policy of 'Thorough'. This was a sincere but tactless attempt to tidy up local administration, restore royal authority in Ireland, put the royal finances on a sound footing, and reform religion along Arminian lines.

In all these spheres royal policy came up against established rights or practices. One of the most contentious issues was raising Ship Money – a traditional tax on maritime counties for the maintenance of the navy – from inland counties. This made it potentially a source of considerable revenue collectable without parliamentary approval – a real threat to the standing of the House of Commons. Opposition was so widespread that by the later 1630s England was gripped by a virtual strike of all taxpayers.

However, it was the religious aspect of 'Thorough' that really annoyed people. Churches were tidied up, rearranged and decorated in the Arminian fashion, and those who opposed the popish-looking policy in print were punished with exemplary harshness. For a work that was supposed to have libelled Henrietta Maria, the puritan lawyer William Prynne was sentenced to have his books burned, his ears cropped, expulsion from Oxford University and the Inns of Court, a £5,000 fine and, to cap it all, life imprisonment. The last was not enforced and three years later he was in court again, on this occasion for being rude about the Archbishop of Canterbury. He was given another £5,000 fine, a time in the pillory, a bit more taken off his ears, and the letters 'S' and 'L' (seditious libeller) branded on his cheeks. He said the brand stood for 'Stigmata Laudis', the stigma of Laud.

Archbishop Laud had other things on his mind. He and the king had been particularly distressed at the puritan inclination of the Scottish Church (the Kirk). To rectify the situation, the busy archbishop got a group of bishops sympathetic to his cause to produce a new Scottish prayer book. With Charles's blessing the new missal was issued in 1637. Neither the Scottish parliament nor the General Assembly of the Kirk, the country's principal representative bodies, had been consulted. Not surprisingly, the popish-sounding book was about as welcome as the Spanish Inquisition, and its use immediately provoked angry riots. Before long these grew into a full-scale national revolt.

Kingdoms in turmoil

Although he retained a hint of a Scottish accent, Charles had visited the country of his birth only once during the first part of his reign – for his belated coronation in 1633. He showed little understanding of his northern realm. For their part, the Scots resented his aloofness and were suspicious of his high-church worship. The prayer book revolt led to many Scots signing a

Covenant (a sort of religious pledge) to purify the Kirk. The National Assembly went on to abolish episcopacy, which had become a symbol of an alienated king's insensitive interference.

The situation was more serious than any monarch had faced for almost a century: one kingdom was in armed revolt, the other was seething with discontent. A marginal court decision upholding the legality of Charles's collection of Ship Money had been greeted with widespread disbelief and alarm. Diffusing the situation would require political skills of the highest order, qualities neither the king nor his ministers possessed.

To bring the Scots to heel, Charles could afford to raise only a token force led by unwilling nobles serving at their own expense. In response the rebels gathered a large army under the command of Alexander Leslie, an experienced veteran of European wars. Unwilling to risk battle, the English made peace at Berwick and disbanded. Although there were signs of opposition to the Covenanters within Scotland, Charles could not take advantage of the situation without further funds. That meant summoning the English parliament.

The so-called Short Parliament met in April 1640. A barrage of pent-up anger burst upon the ears of the king and his advisors (although protocol meant that it was only the latter who were criticized directly) and the assembly was dissolved the following month. No supply (money) had been voted. Nevertheless, urged Strafford, the traitorous Scots had to be brought to heel. So, begging and borrowing where he could, Charles raised another paltry force. The second 'Bishops War' lasted scarcely longer than the first: after a brief skirmish at Newburn, the Scots, who were in contact with the opposition leaders in England, made peace on their own terms. By the Treaty of Ripon Charles had to pay £850 a day to keep them at bay. There was only one body that could raise so large a sum: the English parliament.

The road to war

What would become known as the 'Long Parliament' met at the end of 1640. For a few months Charles agreed concession after concession. These included the imprisonment of Laud, the execution of Strafford, legislation to curb the royal prerogative (requiring parliamentary approval for the collection of tunnage and poundage and Ship Money, for example), and a law giving parliament a veto over its own dissolution. The comprehensive opposition programme was masterminded by the skilful Somerset MP John Pym.

MPs became divided over two issues: command of the forces sought to quash the Irish rebellion that had broken out after Wentworth's return to England, and, even more contentious, religion. Pym had steered clear of the religious issues for as long as possible. When they eventually came up, for the first time two sides began to emerge. Few liked what Laud had been doing, but moderates feared that the Anglican baby might be jettisoned along with the Arminian bathwater.

In both England and Scotland Charles botched or rejected attempts at compromise. He refused to recognize the realities of the situation and was convinced, deep down, that because it was traitorous the opposition would eventually collapse. Everyone, even his own family, ministers and supporters, found him unreliable and difficult to work with. Rash acts, such as a failed counter-coup in Scotland and an attempt to arrest leading MPs in England, only increased suspicion and mistrust.

Eventually, at the beginning of 1642, Charles and his court left London. The capital, which had never taken to him, was glad to see him go. The Long Parliament continued to legislate by 'ordinance', laws not signed by the monarch. An early example placed the militia under parliament's control. When Charles raised his standard at Nottingham (ominously, it blew down in a gale that night) and called on loyal subjects to support him, the country was at war.

Civil wars

Charles was a better soldier than politician. He was a good horseman, had a sound grasp of tactics, and was completely fearless. At Naseby (the last battle on English soil in which a reigning monarch participated, 1645) he was forcibly restrained to prevent him from charging to certain death. (Those solicitous of his welfare undoubtedly did him a disservice: death at this point would have gone a long way to salvaging his reputation.) Bravery, though, was not enough. Parliament had the money and, in the end, the better troops and commanders.

The king's best hope was a swift victory. He went on the offensive in the autumn of 1642, fighting an inconclusive engagement with parliamentary forces at Edgehill (Warwick-shire) then advancing on London. Outnumbered at Turnham

Green to the west of the capital, he was forced to retire for the winter. The royalists, based in Oxford, had some success the following year in the north and west. Territorial gains, though, were undone by a tactical loss: parliament signed the Solemn League and Covenant with the Scots, bringing Leslie and his formidable Covenanter army into play against the king.

The Scots played a key role in the battle that proved the turning point of the war, the royalist defeat at Marston Moor (Yorkshire) in July 1644. Victories in the south west could not compensate for the loss of the entire north of England. As at other times during the war, attempts were made to reach a negotiated settlement. No agreement was forthcoming. Parliamentarians feared for their safety once the armies had been disbanded, while the king could not bring himself to take talks with rebels seriously. The issue had to be decided on the battlefield.

So it proved the next year, when parliament had created the professional and well-trained New Model Army. Led by Sir Thomas Fairfax and Oliver Cromwell, it destroyed the king's army at Naseby before wiping out the remaining royalist army at Langport (Somerset). For Charles, hit by periodic bouts of the age-old Stewart melancholia, the outlook was grim. 'I must say', he wrote, 'there is no probability but of my ruin.'[14] He was right, of course, although it need not have been so if he had played the cards remaining in his hand with any degree of skill.

The block

As the parliamentary forces closed in on the King's headquarters at Oxford, the king cut his splendid long hair (his finest physical attribute) and fled in disguise. Eight days later he appeared at the camp of the Scottish army near Newark and gave himself up. Protracted negotiations followed during which the king professed himself willing to surrender episcopalian government in the Scottish Church. The gesture was neither convincing nor sufficient. In the end the Scots stopped trying to negotiate with Charles and handed him over to their English allies.

The king was now held at Holdenby House in Northampton-shire, under parliamentary wardship. All was not well in the parliamentary camp, though, as MPs found that in the army they had raised a monster they could no longer control. As in so many coups, however well-intentioned initially, power ultimately ended up in the hands of the military. When ordered to disband without the backlog of pay owed to it, the New Model Army refused. In June 1647 it went a step further by seizing the king.

During the next few months Charles had a golden opportunity to get himself back into the political frame. Relations between the Scots, parliament and the New Model Army were strained. Within the army, ordinary soldiers were urging further social and political reform of a most radical nature. Presbyterians at Westminster clashed with Independents (those who wanted autonomy for each congregation) in the army and elsewhere. Many, tiring of the whole business, were eager for a settlement. It was there for Charles's taking.

Henrietta Maria, writing from exile in France, urged moderation and compromise. Sometimes her husband seemed to take her advice, offering concessions such as a willingness to accept Presbyterianism in England. (He later admitted saying this simply to obtain his release – he had no intention of holding to it.) On other occasions he proved as openly intractable as ever, insisting, 'You cannot do without me. You will fall to ruin if I do not sustain you.'[15] That is what he really believed. God had ordained that he should be king; to question his authority, therefore, was to question the wisdom of the Almighty. His opponents, many as set in their beliefs as he was in his, claimed divine support for their cause. Impasse.

In November 1647 Charles escaped and fled to Carisbrooke Castle on the Isle of Wight. The governor was less welcoming than the king had anticipated and he was detained. From his island captivity Charles negotiated an agreement with the Covenanters, sparking a Second Civil War in which his new allies were thrashed by Oliver Cromwell. The net was now tightening around a king whom nobody trusted. Fresh talks were opened with the army commanders. By the end of 1648 they too had given up – it was impossible to negotiate with someone who did not mean what he said or say what he meant.

By the beginning of 1649, Oliver Cromwell, the most able and forceful of the army commanders, had decided that no solution to England's problems was possible while the king was still around. A court was assembled and Charles put on trial for his life. His defence was simple: since the crown was the source of all law, the court was illegal and therefore had no jurisdiction over him. Technically speaking, he was correct. Legal theory, however, was overwhelmed by political necessity. Charles was found guilty and condemned to death. He spoke well at his trial, even losing his stammer. He rather spoilt things, though, by crying out at the last, 'I have a plan … for a lasting peace!'[16] No one believed him.

On 30 January 1649 Charles was led from a first floor window of his father's magnificent banqueting hall in Whitehall onto a specially constructed platform. A huge crowd gathered and hundreds of soldiers put on duty to keep order. With great dignity, the king knelt and placed his neck on the low wooden block.

Charles's head was severed with one blow. The crowd uttered a great groan, then, eager for souvenirs, surged forward to dip their handkerchiefs in the royal blood. Mounted soldiers moved swiftly to clear the street. Thus ended the most momentous act in the history of the modern British monarchy.

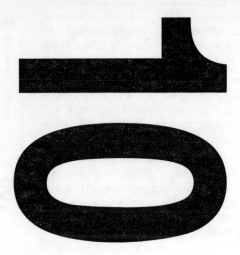

10

Charles II, 1649/1660–85

Parents: Charles I and
  Henrietta Maria
Born: 29 May 1630,
  St James's Palace, London
Died: 6 February 1685,
  Whitehall, London
Marriage: Catherine of
  Braganza, 1661
No children

The keynote of much of Charles II's reign was uncertainty. When did his reign begin, for instance? The Scots always maintained it was from the moment his father's severed head plonked onto the scaffold in Whitehall. The English rejected this timing until 1660; then, out of politeness, backdated their chronology to equate with the Scots. The missing years, though, could not simply be forgotten.

Once he was firmly on the throne, what powers did Charles have? The settlement known as the Restoration ensured he could not do what his father had done, but it did not make it clear what he could do. The new boundaries of royal authority had to be worked out over time – a messy business.

We can now see that having rejected republicanism, after 1660 Britain was at a divide in the road. One path, the more familiar one, led towards royal absolutism of the variety emerging on continental Europe. The other, unknown and untrodden, led towards parliamentary and eventually constitutional monarchy. During Charles's reign steps were taken and retraced in both directions, leaving the future as uncertain as ever when he died.

The prince

As the oldest surviving child of Charles I and his French wife Henrietta Maria, the future Charles II was thrust early into the political arena. At the age of one he was sent into the House of Lords to beg their lordships to spare the life of his father's favourite, Thomas Wentworth (see p.79). Three years later he was made nominal commander of the royalist forces in the south-west.

By the end of the civil war the royal family were scattered far and wide. While the king, Charles I, was surrendering himself to the Scottish army, his wife and one daughter (Henrietta Anne – 'Minette' – Charles II's favourite sister) were in exile near Paris. Mary, the eldest daughter, was in the United Provinces (Holland) with her Dutch husband, Prince William of Orange. Three other children – James Duke of York, Henry Duke of Gloucester and Princess Elizabeth – were prisoners of the English parliament. The heir to the throne might have been with them had he not escaped down a secret passage in the nick of time and boarded a ship for the Scilly Isles. From here he made his way to Jersey, then on to St Germain, France, to be with his mother. He was joined later by his lively but slow-witted younger brother, the Duke of York, who had managed to give his captors the slip and flee London in disguise.

The formal life at St Germain irked Charles and two years later he was relieved to move to the household of his married sister in the United Provinces. Eager to play a part in the drama that was unfolding on the other side of the Channel, Charles relieved his brother of the post of Lord High Admiral and commanded a flotilla of royalist ships on a fruitless patrol along the south coast. Back on shore he overcame a bout of smallpox and fell madly in love with Lucy Walter, the first of his many mistresses.

The news of Charles I's execution reached his son's meagre court in a newspaper report. This was read first by one of the prince's chaplains. Not the most tactful of men, he broke the tragic news by approaching his young master respectfully and addressing him as 'Your Majesty'. Charles burst into tears. It was one of the last occasions when he made a public display of his inner emotions.

Exile

Scotland's Covenanters (see p.81) had made common cause with the Westminster parliament during the civil war in the hope that England would adopt a Presbyterian church system similar to their own. The shift of power from parliament to army, symbolized by Colonel Pride's forcible ejection of Presbyterians from the House of Commons in December 1648, destroyed the Covenanters' plans. Consequently, on hearing the news of Charles I's execution, they swiftly proclaimed Charles II king of Scotland.

Charles was wary. He was easy-going and tolerant by nature, a young man who took pleasure in earthly delights. Neither Scotland's puritanism nor its rugged simplicity appealed to him. Furthermore, the Covenanters were the very people whose prayer book rebellion had begun his father's downfall. Even so, Charles was in no position to bargain. He accepted his hosts' strict terms and stepped onto Scottish soil in June 1650. Subjected to endless petty humiliations and kept as a sort of captive figure-head, within a few days he was wishing he had never come. His dour masters were not impressed either, finding him nothing but 'vanity and lightness.'[17]

Paradoxically, it was Oliver Cromwell who inadvertently came to the king's rescue. Returning from Ireland, where he had brutally overwhelmed Catholic rebels with fire and the sword, the brilliant general swept north and crushed the Covenanters at Dunbar. Keeping well out of the way of the New Model Army now occupying much of southern Scotland, Charles was crowned at Scone on 1 January 1651. That summer, just as his great-nephew Bonnie Prince Charlie would do almost a century later, he risked all on a daring dash into England.

Charles's army got further than the Bonnie Prince's would do, but to no avail. The English did not flock to his banner in their thousands. Cromwell caught up with him at Worcester, where the royalist army was annihilated. Charles fled for his life. A price of £1,000 was put on his head and bills posted asking for information on the whereabouts of 'the pretender, Charles Stuart, a dark man more than two yards high.'[18] The penalty for harbouring him was death. For six weeks Charles sneaked around the countryside, heavily disguised and hiding in priest holes and, most famously, in an oak tree. Finally, passing as a coal merchant, he crossed from Shoreham, Sussex, to the safety of Fécamp in northern France.

Restoration

The eight years that followed were Charles's most miserable. He was poor, powerless and often treated with disrespect. The experience left him determined, after his eventual return to England, that he would never, under any circumstances, go on his travels again. Until the death of Cromwell, who had become Britain's Lord Protector and even contemplated taking the crown, there was no way Charles could have recovered his crown. Foreign powers – and even the American colonies – had recognized Cromwell's government. None was prepared to risk money and men on trying to overthrow it for the sake of a peripatetic and impecunious adventurer flitting (and flirting) about the Netherlands.

The passing of Cromwell changed everything. His son Richard was neither interested nor capable of filling his father's gigantic shoes, and before long the republican regime was crumbling. Order was restored by General Monck, who marched down from Scotland with a large and disciplined force, restored the Long Parliament of 1640, and opened negotiations with Charles.

The 29-year-old king, now back in the United Provinces, was too intelligent to let the opportunity pass. From Breda he issued a masterly manifesto setting out the terms on which he was prepared to return home. Everyone saw in the brief document what they wished to see, and it was immediately accepted. When Charles came ashore at Dover on 25 May 1660 he was greeted with scenes of unprecedented jubilation. It is said that one old Cavalier, still in exile, laughed himself to death when he heard the news.

The Merry Monarch

England's new king was an odd fellow. Exaggerated versions of the Stewart features – the long nose, fleshy mouth, heavy brows – meant he was far from handsome. He was tall, though, as Mary Queen of Scots had been, and carried himself well. Obsessed with keeping fit, he took long walks, rode and sailed. His patronage of horse racing was generous and his court was an excellent place for gaming. Theatres, closed during the Interregnum, reopened and the king introduced women actors onto their boards. Clearly, this was a man who relished life's cheerier, lighter moments – hence the epithet by which he is widely known: the 'Merry Monarch'.

Like all his family (and unlike most of the Tudors), Charles was sexually vigorous and fathered numerous children. Unfortunately, not one of them was legitimate. Apart from Lucy Walter, his longer-standing mistresses included Barbara Villiers (Duchess of Cleveland), Louise de Kéroualle (Duchess of Portsmouth), and the captivating, full-figured actress Nell Gwynn. The unfortunate Catherine of Braganza, whom he married in 1662 as part of a political deal with Portugal, was physically incapable of childbearing. Distressed at first, she learned to tolerate her husband's philandering and on his deathbed he is supposed to have apologized to her for all the wrong he had done. Whether he meant it or not is another matter. He might have done, or it might have been one last example of his unfailing good manners. The inner Charles was impenetrable.

From his grandfather, the king inherited a sharp brain and a quick wit. Although not especially interested in administration, particularly not in details, by the age of 18 he possessed more political sense than his father had acquired in a lifetime. His approach to matters of state was invariably pragmatic, his style laid-back. Difficulties, he generally found, had a habit of resolving themselves if one did not stare at them too hard. As far as underlying principles went, a quiet determination to uphold the power of the monarchy was the most obvious. A life-long

Anglican, Charles was accepted into the Roman Catholic church as he lay dying – a final twist in the tale of a charming enigma.

Liberty?

The open-ended Declaration of Breda offered a general amnesty and a free pardon to all except those who had signed Charles I's death warrant. (The bodies of dead regicides, including that of Oliver Cromwell, were dug up and mutilated.) It also promised a free parliament and 'liberty to tender consciences' – some form of religious toleration. The details were to be sorted out by parliament.

The Declaration got Charles his throne back but settled little else. The monarchy was restored, shorn of some of its feudal powers, but in no better financial state than it had been previously. The funds allocated to it by parliament proved woefully inadequate for most of the reign, and the quest for further income drove Charles to some pretty underhand diplomacy. Meanwhile, a decision not to restore land sold to assist Charles I caused much bitterness among royalist gentry, one of whom was a Dorset gentleman named Sir Winston Churchill.

Tender Protestant consciences were left with precious little liberty after parliament had passed a series of laws (inaccurately known as the 'Clarendon Code' after the chief minister, Earl of Clarendon) that made life tough for all non-Anglicans. Twice, Charles attempted to use his remaining prerogative to mitigate the lot of Catholic and Protestant non-conformists, but his efforts were largely ignored. The old Cavalier squirearchy, back in the saddle with a vengeance, was in no moody for mercy.

Instability returns

While the restoration settlement was being worked out Charles relied heavily on Edward Hyde, Earl of Clarendon, who had been a constant friend and support during his exile. He was ditched in 1667 after reverses during a war fought with the Dutch for largely commercial reasons.

For the next five years there was no leading minister. Charles relied instead on a disparate group known as the Cabal, from the initial letters of their names. During this period the king made the first of several secret agreements with Louis XIV of

France, now the leading power in Europe. In return for funds, Charles promised (perhaps even using French troops) to bring his country back into the Roman Catholic fold. He almost certainly had his fingers crossed when he gave such a dangerous undertaking.

By the time Sir Thomas Osborne, Earl of Danby, took over the reins of government in 1673 and led the country into another costly war with the Dutch, the political temperature was rising high. Why, asked increasingly frustrated MPs, was England allied with the arch Catholic Louis XIV against the Protestant Dutch? What secret agreements had the king made with France? Who would succeed Charles? Surely not his brother James, a Catholic convert and married to a Catholic wife of childbearing age? Alternatively, would the king divorce and marry again in an attempt to father a Protestant heir? Might he even legitimize James Scott, Duke of Monmouth, his favoured son by Lucy Walter?

Amid growing anxiety that England was being pulled into the orbit of France, parliament passed an act that made it illegal for Roman Catholics to hold office. The Duke of York was promptly obliged to resign his reinstated post of Lord High Admiral. The development infuriated James and left Charles unusually worried.

Crisis and conclusion

It is difficult to comprehend the near-hysteria generated by fear of Catholicism in seventeenth-century Britain. The closest modern parallel would be Western paranoia about communism during the Cold War. Generation after generation had poured over *Foxe's Book of Martyrs* (see p.29), fed on stories of Drake and the Spanish Inquisition, and cheered, danced and burned the Pope in effigy every 5 November. In the popular imagination (and to some extent in reality) Catholicism had been equated with cruelty and lack of freedom since mid-Tudor times.

Louis XIV, the 'Sun King', had taken over the mantle of popish demon once worn by Spain's Philip II. France, it was pointed out, had no parliament; its king could imprison and tax at will; even now he was starting to persecute his Protestant subjects, forcing them to convert or flee into exile. If England had a Catholic king, as James would be, what tyranny might he impose in league with France? It did not bear thinking about!

This was the febrile atmosphere into which the fraudster Titus Oates launched his story of a 'Popish Plot' to kill the king. Fortuitous circumstances gave the story credence and the country went wild. Plots and plotters were suspected everywhere. There were denunciations, trials, executions. Seizing the moment, anti-Catholic politicians, led by the diminutive Anthony Ashley Cooper, Earl of Shaftsbury ('Little Sincerity'), proposed that the Duke of York be excluded from the succession on account of his religion. The Duke of Monmouth, it was suggested, would make a suitable Protestant alternative. The illegitimate son of Lucy Walter conveniently claimed to have his parents' marriage certificate hidden in a little black box.

The country divided. York's supporters were damned with the name 'Tory' – Irish bandits; pro-Monmouth exclusionists were branded 'Whiggamores' (soon just 'Whigs') – Scottish Covenanters. The world had it first parliamentary political parties.

Elections were held, parliaments met and dissolved, supply halted, Exclusion Bills presented and voted upon. Charles stood firm behind his brother's right to succeed. Giving way to Whig demands, he realized, would weaken the monarchy immeasurably. If parliament could choose who would wear the crown, then it, not the monarch, would be the ultimate source of all authority.

In the end Charles called the Whigs' bluff. He summoned parliament to meet in Oxford, his father's headquarters during the civil war, and then dissolved it before an Exclusion Bill could be passed. All legitimate means of getting their way having been blocked, the Whigs' only alternative was force. The memories of the previous reign were too fresh for that, and they returned home defeated.

There followed a 'Tory Reaction' in which, where possible, James's supporters were promoted to positions of influence. With money arriving from France and increasing trade, the treasury was fuller than it had been for ages. The discovery of a genuine plot to assassinate the king and his brother further boosted the Tory cause, and Monmouth was obliged to go into exile. So when Charles finally passed away – muttering at the last, 'Let not poor Nelly starve' – he left his brother a secure succession to a relatively stable and prosperous realm.

It was up to James to make the best of it.

James II & VII, 1685-8

Parents: Charles I and
  Henrietta Maria
Born: 14 October 1633,
  St James's Palace, London
Died: 16 September 1701,
  St Germain, France
Marriages and children:
1 Anne Hyde, 1660
  Children: (i) Charles, b.1660
    (ii) Mary, b.1662
    (iii) James, b.1663
    (iv) Anne, b.1665
    (v) Charles, b.1666
    (vi) Edgar, b.1667
    (vii) Henrietta,
      b.1669
    (viii) Katherine,
      b.1671
2 Mary of Modena, 1673
  Children: (i) Katherine,
      b.1675
    (ii) Isabel, b.1676
    (iii) Charles, b.1677
    (iv) Elizabeth,
      b.1678
    (v) Charlotte,
      b.1682
    (vi) James the Old
      Pretender,
      b.1688
    (vii) Louise, b.1692

The reign of James II of England and VII of Scotland, as brief as it was important, confirmed the worst fears of those who had opposed his accession during the Exclusion Crisis: the Catholic king sought to increase royal power at the expense of parliament in order to promote his faith as an alternative to Anglicanism. The reaction to these policies produced one of the most significant upheavals in British history. Its impact went on to be felt worldwide and persists even to this day.

During much of the reign of Charles II it was unclear whether Britain would move towards an absolutist-style monarchy, or devise a compromise that balanced the crown and parliament. By 1685, with the crown as secure as it had been all century, the former seemed possible. However, by trying to push his religious policies too far too fast, and failing to take the political nation with him, in three years James undid all his brother's work, lost his throne, and ensured the survival of parliamentary government in Britain.

Limited vision

In appearance James was similar to his brother Charles, although his features were more sympathetically arranged and proportioned. Even at 51, the age at which he ascended the throne, he was strong, upright and fit. James liked it so – indeed, he liked everything neat and well ordered. Compromise and muddle were an anathema to him. He was understandably happier dealing with military matters than politics. In this he took after his father.

A liking for tidiness, however, did not make James a straightforward personality. Beneath the deceptively plain surface contradictory passions surged, passions that caused him much personal misery. Here was a man who believed the divinely appointed king should have his subjects' interests at heart, but who, like Charles I, did not believe it necessary to consult widely with them about what those interests might be. Here was a devout, almost puritanical Roman Catholic who despised 'private ease', yet who was also a sexual gourmand. Besides his 20 legitimate children, there were numerous illegitimate offspring by a collection of mistresses (one of whom was Arabella Churchill, daughter of the Sir Winston of Charles II's court). For this sexual incontinence James felt a deep guilt that led him to harsh episodes of self-punishment. His brother

Charles had taken a very different view of the matter, remarking laconically that because James's mistresses were so ugly they were a penance in themselves.

James inherited his father's political tunnel vision. A number of his contemporaries believed him to be similarly dim. Charles described him as 'sotise' (stupid), while the witty Duke of Buckingham summed up the difference between the two brothers with a neat aphorism: 'The King could see things if he would, and the Duke [of York] would see things if he could.'[19]

Exile

After his daring escape from London during a game of hide-and-seek in 1648, James Duke of York spent the next 12 years in impecunious exile. As Lord High Admiral he was entitled to a share of all booty seized by the royalist navy based on the continent. He also shared small pensions from the French and Spanish governments. Shopkeepers and tradesmen gave credit and friends and supporters made gifts and loans. All in all, though, James and his brother felt embarrassed and constrained by lack of funds. This was a major reason why Charles determined in 1660 never to travel again, whatever the circumstances. Not so James.

The Duke divided his time in exile between serving in the Catholic armies of Europe and leading a fairly riotous social life. He hunted furiously and when in Paris rarely got to bed before four in the morning – and then seldom alone. In the later 1650s he met Anne Hyde, daughter of his brother's advisor who would become chief minister in the restored administration. At the time Anne was with the household of James's sister Mary, married to William of Orange.

The couple became deeply attached. James promised to marry his beloved commoner and in 1660 she became pregnant. They were married in secret later that year. Charles had objected to the match but eventually accepted it. Anne's father was less tolerant: hearing of his daughter's behaviour he asked the king to cast her into the Tower of London and cut off her head. Charles thought this a little excessive and politely declined the request.

Conversion

It was not James's marriage that caused the biggest storm but his conversion to Roman Catholicism. He had been raised an Anglican, although of the Laudian, high-church variety with its emphasis on the mystery of the communion and the need for order and seemliness in church buildings and practices. There was no getting away from the fact that the Church of England, however 'high', was a middle-of-the road institution, born out of compromise. James, as has been noted, was not the compromising type. His vision was black and white, so when he began to think about religion in the 1660s he came to the conclusion that there could be no logical middle ground between Roman Catholicism, the faith of his mother, and extreme Calvinist or even Separatist Protestantism.

There were other factors in James's conversion. To get French money, Charles had secretly declared himself willing to convert to the Catholic Church, and Anne, Duchess of York, became a Catholic in 1669. Finally, there was the question of authority. The Roman Catholic Church was an hierarchical institution under a father-figure pope – just the kind of pattern James believed should be followed in the secular world. Again, he saw no middle road between authority and anarchy.

James stopped taking the Anglican communion in 1671 and was received into the Catholic Church the following year. The Test Act of 1673, obliging office holders to profess their Anglicanism publicly, forced James to make his conversion public and resign his post as Lord High Admiral. Following the death of his first wife, he confirmed his new position by marriage to Mary of Modena. In accepting James, the devout young Catholic sacrificed her ambition of entering a convent.

New York and Exclusion

Samuel Pepys noted that James, although sometimes distracted by his pursuit of women (which the famous diarist tactfully referred to as his 'pleasures'), was generally attentive to his duties as Lord High Admiral. During the two Dutch wars (see pp.91–2) he managed his forces with competence. The duke also showed some interest in commercial and colonial matters. He put money into Brazilian and African trading ventures and was nominal governor of the Hudson's Bay Company.

During Charles's first war with the Dutch the crown laid claim to a vast swath of territory stretching inland from the eastern seaboard of North America. The region had already been partly settled by colonists from the Netherlands. When it came into English hands, the king presented it to his brother. In honour of its royal owner, the Duke of York, the name of the principal settlement was changed from New Amsterdam to New York. The Duke took some interest in his acquisition, granting religious toleration but refusing requests for an assembly.

Suspicion of James's Catholicism and awareness of his somewhat blunt, inflexible approach to matters of state prompted the Exclusion Crisis of 1679–81. At the height of the troubles Charles sent his brother abroad to get him out of the limelight. He came back for a spell as Lord High Commissioner for Scotland, where he displayed his dislike of religious dissenters, before resuming his post as Admiral the year before his brother's death.

Rebellion

James's age at the time of his accession may help to explain the extraordinary – and ultimately disastrous – haste with which he set about implementing his Catholic policies. First, though, he had to overcome two linked rebellions.

One was led by Charles II's illegitimate son, the Duke of Monmouth. Returning from exile in Holland, the Duke landed in Dorset and attracted a following of some 4,000 men. Many were Protestant dissenters. The royal army, ably led by its second-in-command John Churchill (Arabella's brother), scattered the rebels at Sedgemoor (5 July 1685), killing perhaps as many as one third of them.

Monmouth was captured, taken to London and beheaded. He met his end well and execution made him something of a Protestant martyr. The Sedgemoor massacre was followed by Judge Jeffreys' 'Bloody Assize' in which 300 supposed rebels and their supporters were condemned to death. Such harshness did James's cause little good in the long run, especially as immediately afterwards he appointed Jeffreys lord chancellor.

Before Monmouth's ill-fated exploits in the south-west, Archibald Campbell, Earl of Argyll, had raised the standard of revolt in the Highlands of Scotland. The Earl, a staunch Protestant, had fallen foul of James during the latter's spell in Scotland and had fled abroad under sentence of death. Linking up with Monmouth in Holland, after James's accession he returned home. The swift defeat of his small force led to the equally swift execution of its leader.

Suspending and dispensing

Not since Henry VIII dissolved the monasteries had the crown been as comfortably off as James found himself after the first year of his reign. Customs revenues were rising and his English and Scottish parliaments had both voted him a substantial income. With the Monmouth and Argyll rebellions safely crushed, the king's prospects looked rosy indeed.

Part of the royal prerogative left intact at the Restoration was the medieval power to suspend the operation of a law (the suspending power) and dispense with a law, thus legalizing an illegal action (the dispensing power). Charles II had attempted to use the former to suspend the operation of the Clarendon Code. Although the legality of these much-disliked royal powers was questionable, James proceeded to use them to set aside anti-Catholic legislation. This enabled fellow religionists to take up civil and military posts. In a blatant effort to win the support of Protestant dissenters, a Declaration of Indulgence (1687) lifted restrictions on all Christian religious minorities. When the dispensing power was challenged in the courts, James dismissed six judges who might have found against him and won a favourable judgement by a 12–11 majority.

A shudder of horror ran through the political nation. It deepened as the king began to interfere with the ancient charters that set out how MPs were to be elected. He sought a subservient parliament which would repeal the Test Act and probably make him financially secure for life. His opponents feared that, backed by armed force, the crown would be able to overturn the traditional balance of power between court and country. No longer would a monarch need to take into account the wishes of its leading subjects. In short, both Whig and Tory started to believe that James was attempting to establish a new and tyrannous government along the lines of Louis XIV's France.

The warming pan baby

The end came swiftly. The Archbishop of Canterbury and six other bishops were imprisoned in the Tower and put on trial for refusing to order that a second Declaration of Indulgence be read out in church. Before the verdict was given, in June 1688 the 30-year-old Queen Mary, all of whose previous children had died young, gave birth to a healthy boy. Protestants did not believe that the baby was hers and spread the story that he had been smuggled into her bed in a warming pan.

Interloper or not, the child raised the prospect of a dynasty of Catholic kings. The nation might have put up with James, now 55, knowing that on his death the crown would pass to Mary or Anne, Protestant daughters by his marriage to Anne Hyde. With the birth of a Roman Catholic son, however, the prospect of a Protestant succession receded alarmingly. A desperate situation called for desperate remedies.

Twenty days after the birth of Prince James Francis Edward, the seven bishops were found not guilty. Their acquittal was greeted with uproarious celebrations – even James's soldiers, camped on Hounslow Heath to overawe the capital, seemed delighted. James got the message and began to back-pedal by abolishing his unpopular church court and reinstating remodelled town charters. It was all too late.

Seven of the nation's leading political figures, Whig and Tory, wrote to his sister Mary's husband, William of Orange, inviting him to come to England to ensure a free parliament. This was just what the clever and ambitious William had been waiting for. A 'Protestant wind' carried the Dutch fleet to Torbay where the prince and his army came ashore on 5 November – an auspicious date for the would-be saviour of Protestantism.

James's nerve now failed him. As deserters by the hundred (including Princess Anne and the up-and-coming John Churchill) went over to the invader, the king dithered. His plight was worsened by depression and debilitating nose bleeds. Giving up hope of resistance, he packed his wife and son off for France. Two days later he threw the Great Seal into the Thames, disguised himself and, as William and his supporters had hoped, set off down the Thames Estuary in a small boat. Unfortunately, diligent fisherman on the look out for Catholic priests recognized the royal fugitive and brought him back. James wept uncontrollably. Two weeks later the king whom no one wanted was allowed to flee a second time. He reached France on the morning of Christmas Day, 1688.

Exile once more

Setting himself up at St Germain, as his mother had done, James received enough support from Louis XIV (the arch enemy of William of Orange) to believe he might be able to get his throne back by force of arms. The first attempt came in Scotland, although James was not there in person. A Highland rising by John Graham – 'Bonnie' Viscount Dundee – triumphed over pro-William forces in the pass of Killiecrankie, but Dundee's death left the rebellion without a leader and it soon fizzled out.

Meanwhile, James went in person to Ireland where he summoned a parliament and attracted thousands of eager Catholics to his ranks. William, an able and experienced soldier commanding over 30,000 professional troops, confronted James on the banks of the River Boyne (30 June 1690). The old king was no match for the new, and the Catholic army, despite its core of French soldiers, was routed. Once again James fled, still plagued by nose bleeds and melancholia. He was back in St Germain by the end of July.

James was to all intents and purposes a broken man, although he did manage to summon up enough energy to father just one more child. Even Louis XIV deserted him in 1697 when he recognized William of Orange as King William III. By this time James was slipping into senility. As he did so his religious obsession increased. He spent hours on his knees confessing his past failings, attended mass at least twice a day, and took to wearing spiked garters round his thighs as a masochistic form of penance. A stroke in March 1701 left him partly paralysed and he died six months later. His wife Mary lived on for another 17 years, doing her best to keep alive the cause that her late yet scarcely lamented husband had so singularly bungled.

12

William III (& II) and Mary II, 1688–1702

Mary
Parents: James Duke of York (James II) and Anne Hyde
Born: 30 April 1662, St James's Palace, London
Died: 28 December 1694, Kensington Palace, London
Marriage: William of Orange (William III), 1677
No children

William
Parents: William II, Prince of Orange, and Princess Mary Stuart
Born: 14 November 1650, The Hague, Netherlands
Died: 8 March 1702, Kensington Palace, London
Marriage: Princess Mary (Mary II), 1677
No children

The reigns of William and Mary are remarkable. They were the first and only time that Britain had a joint monarchy. The fact that the two were there at all was deeply significant. In what became known as the Glorious and Bloodless Revolution, an unpopular and unwanted monarch, James II, had been forced off the throne and replaced by his daughter and a man whose claim to the crown was distant. William, the prime mover in the partnership, was a largely political choice. The Divine Right of Kings was dead and buried.

William's position as king *de facto* rather than *de jure* (in reality rather than by right) was established when he retained the crown after his wife's death in 1694. The same principle applied to the 1701 Act of Settlement that stipulated where the crown was to go upon William's demise. From this time forwards no monarch could forget that they were there to perform a duty, and if they failed or exceeded their brief there was a chance they might be removed from the throne as James II had been.

Nevertheless, the scales were not yet obviously weighted in parliament's favour. The Glorious Revolution confirmed what the Restoration had shown, that the political nation needed a monarch as much as a monarch needed the support of the political nation. When James II had proved to be such a danger, no one had seriously suggested trying a republic again. As a consequence, although the post-revolutionary parliament was now an equal partner in the constitution with the monarchy, William and Mary retained considerable powers. To be successful, the settlement required a new working partnership; this in turn introduced a whole new era of politics.

Mary the heir

We are told by Samuel Pepys that the birth of Mary, the second child of Anne Hyde and James Duke of York, provoked little reaction at court or among the public at large. If that were so, then the unfortunate child began her life as it would continue – relatively anonymously.

James was fond of his daughter and was seen playing with her on occasion. When he converted to Catholicism, however, Charles II insisted that Mary and her sister Anne be moved to a separate household lest they become similarly infected with popery. The precaution was necessary because Mary's elder brother had died young, leaving her heir apparent. Her other brothers were similarly short-lived. For 17 years, between the death of the three-year-old Edgar Duke of Cambridge in 1671 and the birth of her half-brother James (the warming pan baby) in 1688, Mary was due one day to succeed to the thrones of England and Scotland.

Mary grew into a tall, comely young lady of limited talent. She danced well in her youth and liked playing cards. Politics never interested her, which was just as well for she inherited her father's slowness of wit. He also passed on to her a fervent interest in matters religious, although unlike him she never veered from the high Anglican creed into which she had been brought up. When queen, the only branch of state she participated in – the only one her husband permitted her to participate in – was church appointments.

Mary and William

Mary married her Dutch cousin William III, Prince of Orange, on 4 November 1677. It was a Protestant political union engineered by the Earl of Danby to counterbalance the growing Catholic influence. It infuriated Louis XIV so much that he cut his clandestine funding of Charles II. William was the posthumous son of William II, Prince of Orange, who had married Charles I's daughter Mary. (It was she who had sheltered the exiled Charles and James for a while – see p.87). On the announcement of her engagement, the future Queen Mary II wept for at least 24 hours.

The tears were an omen. The marriage of William and Mary radiated little warmth, although the depression he fell into at her death suggested a depth of sentiment not shown while she was alive. Mary became pregnant three times but produced no living child. Her husband took a mistress not long after their marriage and abandoned his wife for long spells when called away on military or political duties. When resident in the same building, the couple did not dine together.

Mary found life in England even worse than in Holland. Prompted by her husband, who had no time for the superficial household of Princess Anne and her husband George, Mary even fell out with her sister. The pair did not speak after 1692. Doing her best to fill her lonely days with a mix of gossip and prayer, the puppet queen lamented how she was 'very much neglected, little respected, censured of all, commended by none.'[20] Although her English subjects did begin to warm to her as time went by, the impression left by her death from smallpox was not markedly greater than that made by her birth 32 years earlier.

The Stadtholder

Most of his English contemporaries had a hearty dislike of William III. Modern academic historians, on the other hand, have scarcely a bad word to say about him. The stark contrast tells us much: William the man was not appealing in any way; William the king and politician was brilliant. Although not necessarily a great accolade, he was the last genuinely intelligent monarch to occupy the British throne. The way he towered over the rest of the royal family was neatly summed up in the cryptic remark, 'King William thinks all, Queen Mary talks all, Prince George drinks all, And Princess Ann[e] eats all.'[21]

Raised by his mother after his father's early death (also from smallpox), William III grew up in turbulent times for the Dutch Netherlands. Wars with England put a considerable strain on the small state's resources and, when in the third war the old enemy sided with France, the odds were seriously alarming. It was under these difficult conditions that William showed his skill as a leader, saving his country from conquest by France (1672–9). He was rewarded with his family's former position of 'Stadtholder'. The title was supposedly military but in fact made William the practical head of state.

In this position William devoted himself to the preservation of his precious republic by forming coalitions to prevent the France of Louis XIV from dominating the whole of western Europe. The Stadtholder's ability to see the 'big picture' – the future of the continent rather than just a single state – marks him down as a statesman of rare vision. This is the context of his marriage to Mary and later willingness to accept the thrones of England and Scotland.

The crown of England

By marrying Mary when she was heir apparent to the twin British crowns (1677), William had a reasonable hope that those precious jewels would come into his hands one day. Britain's wealth and naval power would be invaluable assets in his struggle with Louis XIV. At the time the obvious stumbling block had been the pro-French attitude of James Duke of York, who had recently (1673) married a Catholic wife young enough to bear him children.

William played his cards carefully during the Exclusion Crisis – it was clearly not in his interest that the cause of the Duke of Monmouth should flourish too vigorously. When it was over, though, he visited his wife's native land and met with several Whig leaders. When James became king, William befriended Monmouth but did not approve of his armed rebellion – indeed, he sent troops to England to make sure that it failed! Once the tide had turned against James, William's ambassadors had meetings with leaders of the opposition to see how the land lay. It was obvious what William's reply would be, therefore, when he was asked to come to England with sufficient troops to ensure the holding of a free parliament.

Once James had fled, William made it clear, as did his wife, that he would not be prepared to serve as either his wife's consort or as a regent for James: only an equal share of the royal prerogative would do. The new arrangement was set out in a Bill of Rights, which inaccurately declared that as James had abdicated, William and Mary were now king and queen. Many clergy, including the Archbishop of Canterbury, would not go along with this lie: having sworn an oath of loyalty to James II, they could not bring themselves to do the same for the new king and queen. These 'non-jurors' were deprived of their livings.

The Bill of Rights also said that no monarch was to be or marry a Catholic, and declared illegal a string of powers and practices employed by James II and his predecessors. These included the suspending and dispensing powers (see p.99), maintaining a standing army in peace time without the consent of parliament, and non-parliamentary taxation.

Curbed though his powers might be, William was still indisputably the dominant figure in British politics. Moreover, in return for his helping them out of their nasty predicament, the English political nation kept their side of the bargain by giving massive support – largely financial – to their king's European enterprise.

King of England

The new king was as unattractive as he was clever. His nose was large and hooked, his body thin and bent, his eyes sunken and dull. He wheezed and coughed so badly that he had to move from the smoky Palace of Whitehall to less polluted surroundings. He had few social graces, which he frowned upon anyway as mere vanities, and certainly had no time for fools like his sister-in-law's simple husband George.

Those Englishmen and women who met William were unimpressed by his appearance and lack of civility. They disliked, too, his foreign accent and mannerisms. The Dutch favourites upon whom he lavished rewards and gifts were detested. Yet, despite all his failings, William was vastly preferable to the departed James. His political and diplomatic skills won grudging admiration, as did his faultless memory and fluency in many languages. Most important of all, not once did he attempt to break the rules he had accepted at his accession. Unlike his predecessors, he worked through and with parliament rather than trying to get round it.

New king, new system

Slowly and painfully a new political system was being born. The Bill of Rights was followed by acts extending limited religious toleration, requiring triennial parliaments, and defining royal power over the armed forces. In the financial sphere a distinction emerged between the Civil List – monies for the crown's personal needs and some official expenses – and extraordinary expenditure which came wholly under parliament's control. Passive obedience to the crown was a thing of the past.

All government was still conducted in the monarch's name. William decided on policy, appointed and dismissed ministers, and had the power of veto over legislation (which he used frequently). At the same time, in order to get the funds necessary for the conduct of government and especially the vastly expensive war with Louis XIV (1689–97), William had to ensure that a majority of MPs was on his side. This developed the embryonic party system that had first emerged in Charles II's reign.

William was inclined to the Tories as the natural supporters of monarchy, but they were not keen on the unprecedentedly high levels of taxation required for the war. This obliged the king to work with a 'junto' (group or faction) of Whigs for a while. Outside both parties were a group of independent MPs who went by the name of the 'country' group. They adhered to certain principles (essentially putting the interests of the country as a whole above those of the court or a particular interest group), but no party.

William achieved his main aim, curbing the expansionist aims of Louis XIV, at the Treaty of Ryswick (1697). It had not been easy. Parliament had been a hotbed of wrangling and bitterness over cost and strategy, appointment and policy. Behind it all there was also the possibility that the exiled James II and his supporters (the Jacobites) might re-appear on the scene. Peace did not make things much easier. New tensions arose over Irish and Scottish policy, what to do with the army raised to fight the French, and the king's Dutch favourites.

Never a strong man physically and always suffering from respiratory problems, by the turn of the century William seemed old before his time. His condition had not been helped by the way he had driven himself, working tirelessly into the night, day after day. As a consequence even the smallest injury might lead to serious complications.

This is precisely what happened. On 21 February 1701 the king's horse stumbled over a molehill in the grounds of Hampton Court. The rider was thrown to the ground, breaking his collarbone. Pneumonia set in and on 8 March William III died. At the time few mourned the passing of so cold a character, although many since have had cause to thank him.

13

Anne, 1702–14

Parents: James II and
  Anne Hyde
Born: 6 February 1665,
  St James's Palace
Died: 1 August, 1714,
  Kensington Palace
Marriage: George of Denmark,
  1683
Children: (i) Mary, b.1685
        (ii) Anne, b.1686
        (iii) William, Duke of
             Gloucester,
             b.1689
        (iv) Mary, b.1690

The reign of Queen Anne was momentous. By its close Britain was in the midst of a commercial revolution that would make it the West's leading economic power and enable the Industrial Revolution that followed. The profits of expanding trade allowed parliament to raise unprecedented sums in taxation. This money, which had funded William III's war against France, was now used to continue the struggle during the War of Spanish Succession (1702–13).

The English fleet had always been useful. Now, for the first time since the Middle Ages, the English army also became a force to be reckoned with. Brilliantly commanded by John Churchill (Duke of Marlborough, 1702), it won a series of striking victories that eventually brought Louis XIV to his knees. The Treaty of Utrecht (1713) confirmed Britain's status as an arbiter of Europe.

It was not just finance that made possible these martial triumphs. The defusing of ancient Anglo-Scots' animosity was hastened by an Act of Union (1707) that joined the two nations' parliaments and some of their administration. The political system created during the reign of William III was also bedding in, albeit with much rancour. This provided the platform on which Marlborough was able to operate and ensured that on Anne's death the crown would pass with relative ease to a virtual stranger.

The queen played only a fitful role in all of this. She was a statuesque figurehead, a symbol rather than a prime mover. With the creation of the Bank of England and the launching of the National Debt in the previous reign, the political nation's loyalty was increasingly focused on the system in which it had a vested financial interest rather than on the individual who presided over it. In short, Britain was entering an era of parliamentary monarchy.

Loneliness and love

Anne was not raised to be queen. As the second daughter of James Duke of York, she was far back in the line of succession. Consequently she was not afforded the level of education needed to cope in a world of aggressive males well versed in sophisticated ancient culture and sharp modern practices. Other than English, she spoke only halting French and made copious errors even when writing her own language. The death of her mother when she was six and removal from her father's household because of his Catholicism left her emotionally dependent upon her elder sister. When Mary was shipped off to Holland at the age of 16 to marry Prince William, the 12-year-old Anne was left very much alone.

Solace came from an unexpected quarter. Six years later policy required that Anne marry Prince George of Denmark. Unusually for such planned liaisons, the marriage blossomed into a relationship of genuine love and affection. Anne's endless stream of pregnancies – virtually one a year for the first 17 years of her married life – was testimony to George doing more than just his contractual duties. The couple had much in common. Neither was very bright – Charles II declared of the roly-poly Dane, 'I have tried him drunk and I have tried him sober and there is nothing in him.'[22] That was no handicap as far as Anne was concerned, and the pair happily shared the same pleasures in bed, at the table and on the racecourse. They had no time for music or the theatre.

George had not married a beauty. Although Anne was once said to have had pretty hands and an attractive speaking voice, these were her best features. Always large, she grew ever more so with age and childbearing. After the devastating grief of her husband's death in 1708, she consoled herself with gorging. This made her bigger than ever, so that at the end of her life she could hardly walk. Childhood smallpox had ravaged a frowning, bland face that in middle-age was further marred by red blotches. The frown, caused by a chronic short-sightedness that defied the doctors, gave the impression of perpetual disapproval. In truth, it was normally just indifference or boredom.

Ambition

Anne's lack of intellectual prowess did not mean she was without opinions or ambition. She was deeply patriotic, taking much pride in being crowned on St George's Day. Raised as her sister had been in the Anglican faith, she remained all her life a stout supporter of the Church and its doctrine. She abhorred Catholicism, the creed that had seduced away her father and united him with a bride nearer her age than his. (Mary of Modena had been 15 at the time of her marriage to Anne's father, the 40-year-old James Duke of York.)

Anne made a point of not being present when the 'warming pan baby' was born (see p.100), and she helped spread the myth of the child's non-royal parentage. This came more easily because, her sister Mary being childless, by now Anne was beginning to realize that the crown might one day pass to her or her children. To this end she had no compunction about abandoning her father in 1688 and accepting the joint rule of her sister and brother-in-law. After the death of the former, with whom Anne had fallen out, the heir apparent tactfully made up with King William. There was no way she wanted to give hope to her exiled father, half-brother and their Jacobite cronies across the Channel.

'Sometimes counsel'

Anne inherited the same powers as William but did not have the skill to employ them as he had done. As a consequence, political power was absorbed further into the grasp of parliament, especially the financially omnipotent House of Commons. This inevitably raised the party stakes, increasing the temperature of debate and the sharpness of policy disagreement. Anne's parliaments were marked by ferocious party and factional rivalry. Although stopping short of the kind of witch-hunt that had culminated in the execution of Strafford (see p.81), they led, nevertheless, to out-of-favour political notables being sent to the Tower (Robert Walpole) or driven into exile (the Duke of Marlborough).

Through all of this Anne claimed to steer a non-partisan course: 'party' was still a dirty word, having overtones of plot and subterfuge. Favoured ladies of the royal household were believed to have influenced her decisions, although contemporaries probably over-estimated their power. The most prominent of these confidante women of the bedchamber were Sarah Churchill, wife of the Whig Duke of Marlborough, and her cousin the Tory-inclined Abigail Masham.

Whether guided by her girlfriends or not, the queen appointed and dismissed ministers. However, since a ministry had to be able to command the support of the Commons in order to obtain funding for its policies, her choice was perforce limited. She also sat through some cabinet meetings and dropped in on the House of Lords from time to time. It took a poet, Alexander Pope, to sum up most succinctly the queen's butterfly interest in affairs of state:

There stands a Structure of Majestic Fame,
Which from the neighb'ring Hampton takes its Name.
Here Britain's statesmen oft the fall foredoom
Of foreign tyrants, and of nymphs at home;
Here thou, great Anna! whom three realms obey,
Do sometimes counsel take – and sometimes tea.[23]

Anne favoured the Tories at first, swung towards the Whigs,
then moved back to the Tories as the nation tired of the long
war with France and its attendant high taxation. In a muscular
display of her remaining prerogative she created 12 new Tory
peers to get the Utrecht peace terms through parliament.

During her final illness, Anne was persuaded to make one last,
vitally important political move. The more extreme Tories,
worried about a post-Stuart future, were making overtures
towards the Jacobites. Their nominal leaders, the highly
experienced Earl of Oxford and the younger and more vigorous
Viscount Bolingbroke, were finding it difficult to control them.
The pair even showed Jacobite sympathies themselves, though
perhaps for strategic reasons.

Although dying, Anne refused to put her beloved Anglican
Church and the Glorious Revolution in jeopardy and appointed
the worthy Duke of Shrewsbury her Lord Treasurer. He had
been a key mover in the events of the Glorious Revolution and
was as capable as anyone of ensuring a smooth transition to the
Hanoverian monarchy. Thus, the unfortunate, ill-favoured
queen, who had for years been gently mocked and often
ignored, at the last performed a deed of truly national
significance.

The Jacobites

As Queen Anne lay dying, across the Channel in St Germain hopes were rising. This was the moment James, the warming pan baby of James II and Mary of Modena, had been waiting for – a chance to regain the throne which by the traditional right of succession should be his.

The situation was relatively straightforward. Anne's last surviving child, William Duke of Gloucester, had died in 1700 aged ten. Since the marriage of William III and Mary II had remained childless, next in line was the half-brother of Anne and Mary: the boy whose birth in 1688 had sparked the Glorious and Bloodless Revolution. However, the Succession Act barred Roman Catholics and those married to Catholics from the throne (a situation that pertains to this day). James had only to change his religion, therefore, and the British crown would be his. One hundred years earlier Henry IV of France had made a similar move (Protestant to Catholic) to win his crown, observing somewhat cynically that 'Paris was worth a mass.'

However, London was not worth a communion to the would-be James III and VIII. A change of faith might have been acceptable to a consummate politician such as Henry IV, but to James it was unthinkable. His father (James II and VII) had sacrificed everything for this new-found faith and it was not for his son to abandon it, whatever the earthly inducement. The Catholic faith was a defining badge that the exiled Stuarts wore with pride and dogged, unshakeable conviction.

The supporters of James II and his successors were known as 'Jacobites', from *Jacobus*, the Latin word for James. Opponents also referred to the self-styled James III as the 'Old Pretender' – the man who pretended to the throne – and to his son as the 'Young Pretender'. In Britain, Jacobites showed their allegiance to 'the king over the water' by proposing a loyal toast ('the King!') while simultaneously passing their drinks over a bowl of water. Another favoured Jacobite toast (still drunk in obscure circles) was to 'the little gentleman in the velvet waistcoat' – the mole that had raised the little hill on which William III's horse had tripped, fatally throwing his master. Romance was always the Jacobites' strongest suit.

Hanover

With the Old Pretender ruled out on account of his Catholicism, and all other descendants of Charles I being dead, where were the Protestants of the Glorious and Bloodless Revolution to find a successor to Queen Anne? The only answer was to consult the Stuart genealogical tree. There, perched on a branch reaching back to the beginning of the previous century, they found what they were looking for.

The answer was surprising. To bring it home, the searchers crossed the Channel, skirted north of the Jacobite haunts in France and Lorraine, and entered northern Germany. Here, in the small state of Hanover, they met with their salvation: George Guelph, the great-grandson of James VI and I. Middle aged, squat, not too bright and unable to speak much English, a less prepossessing king would be harder to imagine. And this, howled the Jacobites, was the buffoon who kept the rightful king from his crown. If ever they had a favourable moment to strike, surely this was it.

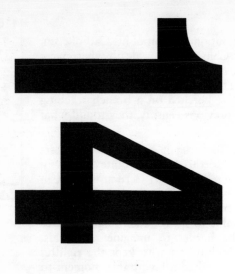

14

James Stuart, the Old Pretender (James III & VIII), 1688–1766

Parents: James II and
  Mary of Modena
Born: 10 June 1688,
  St James's Palace, London
Died: 1 January 1766, Rome
Marriage: Mary Sobieski, 1719
Children: (i) Charles, the
              Young Pretender,
              b.1720
          (ii) Henry, the
              Cardinal, b.1725

While the Old Pretender's upbringing would have been unfortunate for any child, for one who needed to woo an entire nation it was a calamity. By the standards of the time his mother was middle-aged (30) when she bore him, while his father was a positively geriatric 55. The couple's court in St Germain was a gloomy place, overlain with guilt, bitterness and oppressive religious fervour. The young James met few children of his own age – play was regarded as frivolous – and grew old before his time. More important as far as his future was concerned, his narrow education gave him little insight into the raucous, confident little country to which he was assured God would one day return him as king.

The Catholic crusader

After his unsuccessful foray into Ireland, James II returned to St Germain plagued by guilt (see p.101). He became more and more convinced that his exile was divine punishment for the sins of his youth, particularly the sexual ones. 'Nothing is more fatal to man,' he agonized, '… than to be given over to the unlawful love of woman'.[24] As he had sowed, so he was now reaping. This he urged upon his earnest, impressionable son, demanding that at all times he lead a virtuous life, remember his exalted position, and give praise to his Maker.

When James II eventually died in 1701, Louis XIV infuriated William III and the majority of his English and Scottish subjects by instantly recognizing the 13-year-old James as the rightful heir to his father's kingdoms. Louis also took over his protégé's education, trying to provide him with a few more kingly qualities than the boy's father had done. James's languages were brushed up and his ability at riding, shooting, dancing and fencing made him a useful adornment at the court of the ageing Sun King.

An adornment, yes, but not much more. James's virtues were real enough: honesty, loyalty, determination, tact and clean-living. He was tall and well-formed, too. None of these, however, was enough to make up for his shortcomings, for he lacked all those qualities, definable and otherwise, that combine to give a man charisma. To put no finer point on it, he was boring. His brain was slow, his sense of humour non-existent, his expression dull and, in time, he developed his family's hereditary depression. His singular lack of personality might have suited the role of constitutional monarch, but to a self-appointed Catholic crusader it was an insuperable handicap.

False start

James had his first opportunity to make an impact on the European scene in 1708. Britain's triumphs in the War of Spanish Succession had not been welcomed throughout the kingdom. The Scots were especially wary, having been obliged by their economic difficulties to accept a full political union with England the previous year. The arranged marriage had fanned Scottish nationalism and enthusiasm for the Stuarts, whose dynastic roots ran deep north of the border.

James's ancestry might have been Scottish but his current backing was all French. Pretty useless it turned out to be, too. Louis XIV gave his blessing to a plan to land 5,000 men in Edinburgh, seize the castle and then launch an invasion of England to restore the Stuarts. English spies had got wind of the threat from the outset and the Royal Navy was on the alert. Reaching the Scottish coast too late to meet up with Jacobites waiting there, the French ships were hammered by Admiral Byng then scattered by a storm. James, smitten with a nasty combination of sea-sickness and measles, did not even set foot on Scottish soil. He spent the rest of the war fighting with some distinction in the French army as the 'Chevalier de Saint George': he liked military life and was unafraid of battle. He also welcomed the opportunity to get away from weighty problems and decisions.

'The Fifteen'

The year 1712 was a bad one for James – his beloved younger sister Louise died of smallpox. The following year, 1713, was worse. By the terms of the peace he made with Britain at Utrecht, Louis XIV agreed to abandon the Jacobite cause and stop sheltering its leader. Unemployed and homeless, 'Jamie the Rover' (James was better at accumulating nicknames than kingdoms) drifted to Lorraine where the duke kindly gave him the use of Bar Castle. This was James's base when events finally caught up with him: Queen Anne died, leaving the crown of Britain up for grabs. Although speed was of the essence, James was not built for speed. George I arrived in England from Hanover seven weeks after Anne's death; the Old Pretender turned up in Scotland almost 15 months later.

The moment had passed. The British government had rounded up known Jacobites and raised the price on James's head to

£100,000. The delay had not all been James's fault – he had no significant European backer and his British supporters were an odd concoction of opposition politicians (of both parties and none), Scottish nationalists, Catholics, non-jurors (see p.106), rabid xenophobes and a riff-raff assortment of highwaymen, frauds and crooked opportunists. It would have taken a leader of outstanding talent to weld such a motley crew into an effective force. The one man who might have done it – James's illegitimate brother the Duke of Berwick (son of James II and Arabella Churchill) – was prevented from helping by his French citizenship and James's tactless insistence that he was 'a disobedient servant and a bastard too.'[25]

The Jacobite revolt in Scotland, intended to coincide with the Rover's arrival broke out in August 1715. Led by 'Bobbing John' Earl of Mar, it had some success before running out of steam by the end of November. James's arrival in December with three attendants did nothing to re-invigorate the movement. The weather and the prince were cold and wet. 'Old Mister Melancholy', as he soon became known, had neither a plan nor a liking for the unpolished enthusiasts who came to him for leadership and inspiration. So dourly taciturn was he, some of them even wondered whether he was able to speak.

Struck down by an ague brought on by depression and the climate, James took to his bed. Finally, as Hanoverian troops closed in, he summoned up sufficient energy to move north to Aberdeen and thence by sea to Flanders. The Scots were neither surprised nor upset that he never returned.

Dust to dust

Fiasco though it had been – or his part in it, at least – the 'Fifteen' rebellion was the high point of the Old Pretender's career. Back on the European continent, he fell out with his most able supporters, continued to shun the Duke of Berwick, and lost his base in Lorraine. A Spanish-backed venture to the Western Isles of Scotland turned out to be yet another Jacobite damp squib. After further wandering, James finally settled in his spiritual home, Rome. The Pope backed his claim to the British crown, gave him a generous pension and palace to live in. Having achieved a degree of stability and respectability, Old Mister Melancholy sought a wife. Eventually, through the mediation of a go-between who wildly exaggerated his master's attractive qualities, he married the 17-year-old Polish princess

Maria Clementina Sobieski. Like all his other ventures, this too was a disaster. The lively girl tolerated her lugubrious husband just long enough to produce two sons, Charles and Henry, then fell out with him in spectacular fashion. Her early death in 1735 was yet another example of everything that James touched turning to dust.

Worse followed when the sad, shambling king fell out with his eldest son, the dashing Bonnie Prince Charlie. As early as 1740 the British traveller Thomas Grey had found James an unprepossessing figure. He laughed rarely and prayed continually, Grey remarked, and had the alarming appearance of an idiot. Clinging to empty ritual and hollow honours, the stooped and gape-mouthed dreamer shambled around his shadow court in the Palazzo Muti for another 18 years. Had he been crowned when his father died, his reign would have been the longest of any British monarch.

To the very end James insisted that he was King of Great Britain by the divine will of the Almighty. When he first made that claim, those who agreed numbered many thousands. At his death they might possibly have been counted on the fingers of both hands. Such was the miserable achievement of an equally miserable man.

15

Charles Stuart, the Young Pretender (Charles III), 1720–88

Parents: James the Old Pretender and Maria Clementina Sobieski
Born: 31 January 1720, Rome
Died: 31 January 1788, Rome
Marriage: Louise of Stolberg-Gedern, 1772
No children

In recent times the British monarchy has been short on stardom. Queen Victoria is afforded some pale, nostalgic glow but we have to go further back to find the last truly brilliant figures. Henry VIII's light, though bright, is perhaps too bloody for modern tastes. About his remarkable daughter Elizabeth there can be no dispute. Her cousin Mary Queen of Scots has her advocates, too, earning the pity of generations of romantics for her enthralling incompetence. And then there is Bonnie Prince Charlie.

Like a glorious comet, the Bonnie Prince illuminated the European firmament for 14 brief months. He attempted the well-nigh impossible, and came closer than anyone expected to achieving it. For that and for his heart-throbbing adventures on the way, he is remembered with indiscriminate affection while the drunken ignominy of his later years is forgotten. In the face that launched a thousand whisky bottles and shortbread tins, the last, largely mythical star of British monarchical history lives on.

Charisma

Few if any of the monarchs in our story enjoyed what we would regard as a healthy, affectionate family life. Prince Charles was no exception. At this distance no one can say what effect the violent rift between his parents had on the young child. It might have prepared the soil for seeds of hereditary depression and augmented the prince's dislike of his pedantic, hectoring father, whom he grew to hate. Charles also came to despise his effete younger brother Henry, the pretty but dim childhood favourite of both parents. In fact, the prince proved unable to establish an enduring relationship with anyone: not one of his adult affairs developed into a secure, long-term friendship. In this, as in other aspects of his personality, there was something of the Hollywood about him.

Charles was quick-witted but disliked study, once threatening to kill an over-zealous tutor. Nominally Catholic, he lacked the passionate religious commitment of his father – a major source of tension between them. In his youth, convinced that he would soon be called upon to perform some great task, he was obsessed with keeping fit. He showed considerable skill as a horse rider and marksman outdoors and danced with elegant grace within. Tall and brown-eyed, he was considered good-looking but not wildly so. That did not in any way lessen his attraction, which emanated from him like a captivating scent, drawing both men and women into feeling that here was a young man they would lay down their lives for. Such powerful charisma can have terrible consequences.

To Scotland

By 1740 Britain and France were at war again, nominally over the succession to the throne of Austria. Three years later the government of Louis XV prepared an ambitious scheme for the invasion of southern England and Charles, eager to be part of the action, fled from Rome against his father's wishes and presented himself at Versailles, Louis' court. He never set eyes on his father again.

The French knew that by this time, after more than 25 years of Hanoverian monarchy, the Jacobites were at best a very long shot. Indeed, the Old Pretender was such a farcical figure that he had made his cause more of a liability to France than an asset. Consequently, Louis' policy was to promise the Stuarts support if and when they had proved their popularity in Britain by raising a serious revolt there. The most French strategists hoped for was to fracture the 1707 Act of Union through the formation of an independent Scotland under Stuart rule. This made sound strategic sense. Charles, however, did not see it that way and railed against Louis' refusal to back him after the collapse of the 1743 invasion plan.

If the king of France would not support him, Charles declared, he would go it alone – by canoe if necessary. His target was Scotland, where reports of unrest in the Highlands had been coming in for many years. Of the country itself he knew next to nothing. Before going there, like most educated Europeans of his day he regarded the place as a geographical and cultural backwater that at its extremities verged on the barbaric.

In command of just two ships, Charles set sail in June 1745. En route for the Western Isles his small squadron was badly mauled by a British warship so that when the prince reached the island of Barra he had at his disposal just one ship and 11 men. 'Go home!' urged one of the first men he met, echoing the sentiments of both Rome and Paris. But this was Charles's great moment – the time he had been preparing for all his life – and he had his famous reply ready: 'I am come home.'

The Prince drew clansmen to his standard as filings to a magnet. London grew alarmed and took to singing 'God save great George our King' – a new patriotic song that would later become the national anthem. Soldiers were put at the ready and a price of £30,000 put on Charles's head. He responded by offering only £30 for King George's – all it was worth, he quipped. With his army swelling by the day, the invader marched south and met up with the experienced soldier Lord George Murray. In Perth, Charles had the Old Pretender proclaimed King James VIII and III before sweeping down through Stirling to Edinburgh. The rebellion reached its apogee when the Jacobite army routed a force of Hanoverians at the Battle of Prestonpans. Charles, with almost no military experience, was horrified at the slaughter.

Derby to Culloden

After Prestonpans, Murray wished to consolidate the rebels' position and await the reinforcements promised by France. Charles feared that this would mean surrendering the initiative. Speed and surprise were his sharpest weapons, he argued, and the only target worth aiming for was London. His point of view narrowly prevailed and the Jacobite army, around 5,000-strong, headed south. The Scots met neither resistance nor support. After trudging through the pouring rain and a series of indifferent towns, they reached Derby in early December. Here, on 'Black Friday' (6 December 1745), they made the momentous decision to reject their leader's advice and retire whence they had come. Down in London, only 120 miles away, it was said that George II had ordered his bags to be packed.

As Charles had known by instinct, the decision was the wrong one. His army had little chance of taking the capital – but at least it had a chance. On the retreat it was doomed. Stirling and Edinburgh Castles were held against them and now the Hanoverian administration had time to gather a force sufficient to subdue the rest of Scotland. The Bonnie Prince – the title was popular currency by this time – was never the same again. The old charm returned from time to time, but the spell had been broken. He had bouts of sullen depression, drank too much, fell ill and had an affair with the young lady, Clementina Walkinshaw, who nursed him back to health.

The Jacobite forces, reinforced with some Irish regulars from France, scored minor successes before retreating into the Highlands. Here they were followed by a large, well-armed force commanded by the Duke of Cumberland. In April, advancing like a skilful stalker, 'Butcher' Cumberland closed in on his prey. Cornered, Charles chose to give battle on Culloden Moor. It was the wrong place and the wrong time, and the Prince's brave but weary and dispirited army was annihilated by Hanoverian shot and steel. Charles escaped, dragged from the field by his friends, but there was no escape for the clanspeople who had supported him. Over the ensuing weeks Cumberland subjected the Highlanders to a brutal campaign of rape, murder and destruction that broke for ever the clan culture on which Charles had been able to base his rebellion. When on the run after Culloden, overcome with guilt, the stricken Prince was heard to cry out in his sleep, 'Oh God! Poor Scotland! Poor Scotland!'[26]

Hero and beyond

Charles did not manage to get back to France until September, five months after Culloden. In the intervening period the myth of the Bonnie Prince was honed by a series of hair-raising and romantic adventures. Cared for by highland men and women at the risk of their lives, the royal fugitive was pursued by red-coated Hanoverian soldiers around the Highlands and Islands. Sleeping in caves and boats, ill and lice-ridden, seasick, disguised and starved, he was not once heard to complain, nor did anyone ever consider betraying him. Yet while Flora MacDonald was winning immortality for bravely disguising Charles as her female servant, her charge was confirming his taste for Scotch whisky – and any other alcoholic beverage he could lay his hands on. Thus in his triumph were the seeds of his destruction sown.

Stepping ashore from a French warship in Brittany, Charles was immediately the wonder of Europe. Stories of his adventures had made him the most famous man on the continent, and he made the most of it in a series of official and unofficial engagements. It could not last. Louis XV was unwilling to back another Jacobite debacle and Charles, frustrated and depressed, diverted his energies to an embarrassing orgy of debauchery. His father tut-tutted in impotent disgust, while his brother Henry became 'Cardinal of York' and prepared to join the Catholic priesthood. Charles saw the move as an admission that the Jacobite cause was lost and swore never to meet Henry again. The next year France and Britain made peace and Louis XV ordered Charles from his kingdom. When he refused, he was carried off by force to the papal territory of Avignon.

Sadly for Charles the end did not come quickly. The adamantine constitution that had enabled him to withstand the hardships of the Highlands kept him alive for another 40, sodden, self-reproachful years. He had affairs, even calling Clementine Walkinshaw from Scotland for a while and having a daughter (Charlotte) by her. At the age of 52, swollen, gouty and red in the face, he married the 18-year-old Louise of Stolberg. His pretty, blue-eyed bride tolerated her revolting husband's unseemly demands for a while before falling in love with a poet and then running away to a nunnery to get away from both of them. Even more depressed, Charles upped his consumption to six bottles of fortified wine a day.

Charles travelled widely, even sneaking secretly over to London on one occasion and converting to the Anglican Church to make himself eligible for the throne. It was a pathetic gesture. On his father's death the prodigal son went to live in Rome, where he tried to get the Pope to recognize him as 'Charles III'. The request was refused, so he had to make do with the self-concocted title 'Baron Renfrew'. Although Britain and France went to war on two further occasions during the Baron's lifetime, not once was he asked to come out of retirement and weave his old magic again.

In 1784 Charles's daughter Charlotte, sometime mistress of the Archbishop of Cambrai, sought out her father and came to Rome to look after him. She also persuaded Cardinal Henry to become reconciled to his debauched brother before it was too late, although the devout churchman might not have been so willing to fall in with Charlotte's plan had he known of her former occupation. Finally, far from young and certainly no longer Bonnie, Charles died in the arms of his loving daughter. The Jacobite cause had long since predeceased him.

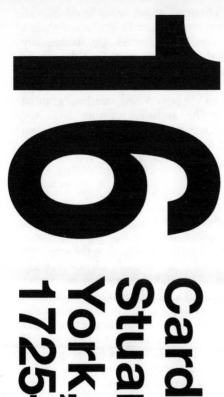

16

Cardinal Henry Stuart (Cardinal York, Henry IX), 1725–1807

Parents: James the Old
  Pretender and Maria
  Clementina Sobieski
Born: 21 March 1725, Rome
Died: 13 July 1807,
  Frascati, Italy
Did not marry

Cardinal Henry Benedict Thomas Stuart, who liked to call himself 'Henry IX' during his latter years, is little more than a footnote in the history of the British monarchy. Technically speaking he was the last of the Stuart pretenders, although he did little pretending. Indeed, by the end of his life the cause he professed periodically to espouse was so moribund that George III, taking pity on his distant, impoverished relation, granted him a handsome pension. The gesture, together with the cardinal's heartfelt celibacy, confirmed what many had known for years – Jacobitism was finished.

Duke of York

As a young child, Henry 'Duke of York' (the title given Henry by his father was also conferred by George III on his second son, Frederick) was by all accounts more attractive and more popular than his elder brother Charles. Sadly, once the winsome curls and babblings of babyhood had passed, Henry was left totally devoid of all charm. This did not prevent his father finding more in common with his short, hazel-eyed second son than he had with the first: Henry's mind was methodically academic, like the Old Pretender's, and his personality similarly earnest. Both qualities are epitomized in the mind-blowingly tedious diary he kept. Perhaps recognizing in Charles qualities that he secretly yearned for, as a teenager Henry doted on his brother and made pitiful efforts to emulate him.

Once out of his teens Henry became more his own man. He joined his father in finding serious fault with Charles's rash and irreligious ways, but displayed a certain sinfulness himself. It is said that his bent was homosexual – a practice utterly condemned by the Roman Catholic Church – and he developed a certain cunning and self-righteousness that would also have merited mention in the confessional. Not surprisingly, Henry did not marry nor have we any record of his taking a mistress. He was terrified of women and the celibate priesthood offered welcome refuge from their intimate company and the dreaded duties that would have followed an arranged marriage. Thereafter, the apparent blamelessness of his lifestyle won the respect of several notable clerics of his day.

From Jacobite to archbishop

Henry was never much of a Jacobite. The very thought of what his brother did – risking life and limb in battles by sea and land

– filled him with horror. That said, he did his bit in 1745 by travelling to France on hearing of Charles's successful landing in Scotland. The worldly-wise king of France was little impressed with the tactless pleading of a pious prig and Henry had to be content with nominal command of the invasion force being prepared to cross the Channel after the Bonnie Prince had seized London. Henry remained in Dunkirk – talking a great campaign but doing nothing – until news came through of the Culloden disaster.

Sneaking back to Rome after a few unhappy weeks' service in the French army, Henry met with the Pope and emerged as 'Cardinal of York'. Although the title did not require ordination, Henry immediately began his training for the priesthood. Charles said the decision had put a dagger through his heart, while in England the Hanoverians delighted in the spectacular Jacobite own-goal: as the chances of either England or Scotland accepting a cardinal as their king were zero, the entire Jacobite cause now rested on the beating of the overburdened and still unmarried heart of the self-destructing Young Pretender.

The Church gave the Cardinal of York a good life. He enjoyed the fruits of benefices in Italy, France and Spain, and collected a number of profitable perquisites. As Archbishop of Corinth, Bishop of Tusculum (Frascati) and Vice-Chancellor of the Vatican he enjoyed a selection of magnificent residences, art collections, libraries and the use of 60 coaches. He also earned a reputation as a generous entertainer and benefactor of those less fortunate than himself. As far as the Romans were concerned, he was not the pretender to a throne but the admired 'Protector of the Poor'. Pope Benedict XIV expressed a more widely held view of Henry when he remarked that if all the Stuarts were as boring as him it was small wonder the English had thrown them out.

Once a churchman, Henry did nothing to further the Jacobite cause. Surprisingly, therefore, after Charles's death he sported the title 'Henry IX' and insisted that his servants call him 'Your Majesty'. It was largely vanity. His true position was expressed on a medal he had struck in 1788. One side hailed him as king, while the other explained that this was *Non Desideriis Hominum, Sed Voluntate Dei* ('Not In The Eyes Of Man, But of God') – a neat compromise acceptable to most parties.

Henry's final years were rendered miserable by the turmoil of the French Revolution and its attendant wars. He lost much of his fortune and only just managed to escape when French soldiers ravaged his Frascati diocese. After long years of painful wandering when he was believed dead, he turned up in Venice. Here his case was taken up by an English MP and *The Times* newspaper. Unwilling to see a fellow member of the royal family reduced to poverty, George III granted Henry a pension of £4,000 a year.

Twelve years after the snowy haired Cardinal's death at the age of 83, the Prince Regent caught his father's spirit of reconciliation and commissioned a Stuart monument for the Chapel of the Virgin in St Peter's, Rome. Beneath marble busts of the Old Pretender and his two sons the Latin inscription reads, 'The last of the Royal House of Stewart.' Although a branch of the Stuart line might still be traced through the descendants of Charles II's sister, Minette, as far as the British monarchy was concerned the Prince Regent's words were exactly right.

part three

The Hanoverians, 1714–1840

As part of an ambitious plan to become arbiter of a European peace, James VI and I had married his lively daughter Elizabeth to Frederick, Elector Palatine (see p.70). The elector was one of a group of elite German princes who from medieval times had exercised the right and privilege of electing the Holy Roman Emperor. The fact that there had been no disputed election for years (the job always went to the head of the Austrian Habsburgs) was immaterial, for the valuable position of elector was much sought after. In prestige it was second only to the emperor himself and it opened the door to highly remunerative positions within the imperial network.

Unfortunately, Frederick was a dead loss at just about everything except fathering children. In 1618 the Bohemians (Czechs) rebelled against their Austrian masters and invited him, as a leading Protestant prince, to become their king. Against the best advice, Frederick accepted, ruling for one winter only before Habsburg troops ejected him from both his new throne and the Palatinate. While exiled in the Hague, Elizabeth the Winter Queen (also known as the 'Queen of Hearts', a title borrowed much later by Princess Diana) gave birth to her twelfth child, a daughter named Sophia. From her mother the child inherited a long face and a sharp mind.

Sophia of Hanover

After an upbringing in exile with a mother whom she said (unfairly) cared more for her dogs and pet monkeys than her children, Sophia's principal quest was for a quiet and settled life. Her husband having died, on the cessation of European hostilities in 1648 she returned to the Palatinate with her brother Charles, the new Elector Palatine. Some years later she became engaged to George William, a German duke from the house of Brunswick-Lüneburg. George then went off on holiday in Italy, changed his mind about Sophia, and persuaded his brother Ernst August to take her off his hands. The bride-to-be was somewhat taken aback but eventually accepted the deal: at 28, in those days she was perilously close to being left on the shelf. George William died in 1705, having made good his missed opportunity for family advancement by marrying his illegitimate daughter to Sophia's son.

Once Sophia had reconciled herself to the fact that Ernst Augustus was idle, intellectually her inferior and unashamedly unfaithful, she found him a reasonable husband. He was amusing, always cared for her and, in 1692, came into the prestigious post of Elector of Hanover. Moreover, he gave Sophia the freedom to get on with the things she cared for. One of these was her Anglo-Scottish heritage.

The Winter Queen, Sophia's mother, lived a long time. She was still alive in 1660, when her nephew Charles II was restored to the English throne and Sophia gave birth to her first child, a son named George. For some years there was little chance that George would inherit anything other than a relatively small German principality. The first hints of something greater appeared at the time of England's Exclusion Crisis, when opponents of James Duke of York tried to exclude him from succession to the crown on account of his Catholic faith. There were some 50 Catholics ahead of Sophia in the English succession, but if they were all excluded...

Settlement

Roman Catholics were not excluded – not then, at least. However, James's behaviour as king made his enemies wish he had been, and after three years on the throne he was driven into exile and replaced by his Protestant daughter Mary and her Dutch husband William. The couple were childless, making Mary's sister Anne heir to their throne. Anne herself was certainly not childless, although none of her constant stream of babies seemed capable of surviving into adulthood.

These were the circumstances under which Sophia held discussions with leading English politicians, who were initially unwilling to put her claim in writing. By the turn of the century matters were more serious and talks were resumed. This time, not wishing to appear over-eager on behalf of herself or her son George, Sophia played down her ambition and declared that the thought of depriving Prince James (the son of James II and Mary of Modena) of his birthright was hateful to her.

The fit of moral unselfishness did not last and the 1701 Act of Settlement declared Sophia and her issue (assuming they were Protestant) heirs to the English throne should William III have no children by a second marriage and all of Anne's children predecease her. Thereafter Sophia and her son George did not see eye to eye over what approach to take, he being far less keen than her on trying to press the Hanoverian link with England during Anne's lifetime. Events proved him right – Anne was deeply hurt by any talk of her mortality and shortly before her death sent a sharp letter to Sophia telling her to mind her own business.

The shock of Anne's rebuke may have hastened Sophia's death. Anne herself followed 53 days later. As William III had not remarried and none of Anne's children had survived, the provisions of the Act of Settlement took effect: George of Hanover collected his crown.

7

George I, 1714–27

Parents: Ernest Augustus,
  Elector of Hanover, and
  Sophia, Princess of the
  Palatinate
Born: 28 May 1660,
  Osnabrück, Saxony
Died: 11 June 1727,
  Osnabrück, Saxony
Marriage: Sophia-Dorothea of
  Celle, 1682 (divorced 1694)
Children: (i) George II, b.1683
       (ii) Sophia, b.1685

Friendship generally being a two-way process, George I and the British have rarely had anything good to say for each other. If George is remembered for anything (which he seldom is), it is for the false accusation that he could not even speak English. In turn, George regarded his newly acquired subjects as for the most part narrow-minded, bickering and superficial. He was prepared to tolerate them and their vagaries simply because their power enabled him to strengthen and secure Hanover, his beloved homeland. And if they did not like what he did, then they should not have invited him to become their king in the first place.

That said, the reign of George I marked a significant moment in British history. It ushered in years of peace, the fires of religious hatred began to burn themselves out, the Jacobite threat was negated, and ministers and the monarch developed ways of working together that were to endure through to the age of democracy. For some of this George was responsible, not necessarily deliberately or even consciously, but because of the man he was.

The Hanoverian

Unusual to relate, George had a happy childhood. Sophia devoted herself to her first-born, the blue-eyed, earnest little angel who tried his best to please her. There were firework parties and picnics, and not too much strenuous learning – the emphasis was mainly on languages, enabling the adult George to converse in French as well as his native German. He also knew Latin and a little Dutch and Italian. Oddly, given his mother's background, he picked up hardly a word of English. The arts, too, largely passed him by, although he enjoyed music and reading non-fiction. Towards the end of his life he showed himself sufficiently broad-minded (or anti-French) to shelter the radical philosopher Voltaire when he fell out with Versailles.

Louis XIV took up the reins of French government the year after George's birth, so by the time he was old enough to understand such matters, the squat Hanoverian realized that European Protestantism was under serious threat. While England was being neutralized with cash, French Catholic troops were seeking to overcome Holland. If the Dutch succumbed, who next? Hanover? Prussia? Perhaps even Denmark and Sweden? Although to modern eyes such fears seem wildly unrealistic, at the time they were very real and meant that before the art of peace George had to master that of war. He was just 15 when he first experienced battle and he was active on behalf of the Dutch in the campaigns of 1676, 1677 and 1678. When not fighting the French, in 1683–5 he was tackling the Turkish threat in Eastern Europe. By the time of Marlborough's wars (see p.110) his appetite for conflict had been assuaged (three of his brothers had been killed in action), although he was persuaded to act as nominal commander of the Emperor's army for a short time.

Military conflict was not the only friction in young George's life. At the age of 22 he was married to his cousin Sophia Dorothea of Celle, a sprightly, spoilt young lady of 16 who was technically illegitimate. (Her parents had been forbidden to marry for complex diplomatic reasons.) The marriage between George and Sophia Dorothea was not a success and provided Europe with one of its spiciest scandals for a generation.

Within a few years, after the birth of two children, George and his wife disliked each other intensely. He found comfort in the lean but affectionate arms of Melusine von der Schulenburg. Shortly afterwards Sophia Dorothea entered a dubious correspondence with count Philipp Christoph von Königsmarck. The dashing Swede was everything her matter-of-fact husband was not – romantic, poetic, impulsive. By 1692 Melusine had presented George with a daughter, and Sophia Dorothea and her count had become lovers. Tongues wagged, warnings were given.

It all ended in a Shakespearian-style tragedy made all the more heart-rending to modern ears by the cruelty of its double standards: neither George nor his Hanoverian courtiers had noticed the spirit of social tolerance seeping through Western Europe and which was evident in the comedies being performed on the London stage around this time. Either by design or accident Königsmarck was murdered and his body thrown in a lake. George and Sophia Dorothea were promptly divorced and she was confined to the palace of Ahlden in Celle for the remaining 32 years of her life. Contrary to rumour, her confinement was secure but not cruel or vindictive. Her ex-husband did not remarry, as he was entitled to do, and froze whenever the name of Sophia Dorothea was mentioned. Nevertheless, his image in England was not helped by the spread of neo-Gothic tales of a wronged wife kept chained up in a damp vault in the middle of a dark and impenetrable German forest.

To England

George I was loudly proclaimed King of Great Britain, France and Ireland the moment Anne died. Then, to everyone's surprise, silence. What was expected was some sort of Jacobite enterprise – a rising, perhaps, or even an invasion. But no. As we have seen, the Old Pretender was slow off the mark and George's accession went unchallenged for over a year.

For the 54-year-old elector it was a considerable jump in status. Instead of some 400,000 subjects he now had almost 9 million. Although this was not large by the standards of France or Austria, commercial enterprise had given Britain wealth out of all proportion to its size so that it now ranked as one of the great powers of Europe. Moreover, George had that most enviable status symbol of all – a crown. (At his coronation he had to make do with Queen Anne's as the traditional one had disappeared with James II.)

The new king had been given British citizenship some years before his arrival, but if anyone thought he would now slough off his German skin and remodel himself as a perfect English gentleman they were sadly mistaken. George was first and last a Hanoverian and he was too old to change. During his reign he returned home six times for a total of 33 months. He spent 85 per cent of his life in his electorate and its welfare was always his primary consideration when deciding foreign policy. With him to England came no less than 90 Hanoverians, including his son and heir George Augustus (now Prince of Wales) and his wife Caroline, their children and the influential advisors von Bothmer and von Bernstorff.

The English were fascinated by four other members of George's entourage. Mehemet and Mustapha were spoils of war, Turkish servants whom the young soldier had picked up while fighting in Eastern Europe. The other two were spoils of the bed chamber, the bony Baroness Melusine von der Schulenburg (still going strong at the age of 60 and now mother of three daughters) and the buxom Baroness Sophia Charlotte, the wife of George's master of horse. The king rewarded the former with the title Duchess of Kendal and made the latter Countess of Darlington. Most of his English subjects preferred the more tabloid soubriquets of the 'Maypole' and the 'Elephant'.

The new king, therefore, was an alien and remained so to the end of his life. Lacking any sense of theatre and disliking crowds, he was incapable of putting on the sort of public show that might have endeared him to his people. He was never popular – overweight, grumpy, middle-aged men rarely are – but he was tolerated for what he was not. He was not a Roman Catholic, he was not capricious, he was not inflated with a sense of his own importance, and he was not a proponent of the divine right of kings. He was a man of the world, blunt, straightforward and unpretentious. This was not much, but it was certainly better than the alternative lurking in Lorraine.

Whig government

George had not been brought over simply as a figurehead. The crown still had considerable powers which it was expected to exercise – indeed, government could not function unless it did. Foremost among these was the power of appointment. This meant not just fancy titles for the king's mistresses but filling the ministerial posts in the government. That done, all decisions were made in George's name and he could, and did, veto those he disagreed with. Despite difficulties presented by his poor English, he attended cabinet meetings, at least in the first part of his reign, and kept a watery eye on proceedings. In foreign affairs, where his beloved Hanover was concerned, he took the lead.

Whichever ministers George appointed, they had to operate through parliament. This limited his choice, of course. But eighteenth-century parliaments were more open to manipulation than their counterparts of the previous century. The crown could appoint to the Lords, as it always had done, to guarantee a majority there. It was in the Commons that tighter control was being exercised, largely though 'placemen'. These were MPs who held a salaried post in what we would call the civil service, or were in receipt of a royal pension. Since government had expanded considerably since the Restoration, the number of such placemen had multiplied. Unless their income had been guaranteed for life, they could generally be relied on to support the king and his ministers. As voting was a very public matter, the crown, large landowners and other men of wealth also exercised influence in boroughs whose numerically small electorates might be bribed or threatened at election time.

Traditionally the Tories had been the party most inclined to support the crown, but in George's eyes they had badly blotted their copybook by making approaches towards the Old

Pretender at the time of Anne's death and, even worse, during the 1715 rebellion. As a consequence, George came increasingly to rely on the Whigs, or rather on a certain segment of that party. By the 1720s, with Toryism in total disarray, the great majority of MPs regarded themselves as in some way Whig. The more independent-minded ('country') members were loath to toe any party line and so government and much of the opposition were nominally of the same party.

George's first leading minister was Charles Stanhope, Earl of Sunderland, whose foreign policy, based on peace with France, was pro-Hanover and thus much to the new king's liking. Insular MPs were less impressed, fearing that the country's interests were being ignored in favour of a petty German principality. In 1717 a new development shook up the political scene when George spectacularly fell out with the Prince of Wales. George Augustus moved out of St James's Palace and set up his own court in Leicester House. This became a centre of opposition for a time, attracting ex-ministers like Robert Walpole who had resigned over Stanhope's apparently unpatriotic manoeuvrings.

The king and his minister

An even greater shock came three years later when the South Sea Company, founded in 1711 to rival the Bank of England, went suddenly and dramatically bankrupt. Unwise speculation had pushed up shares in the dubious enterprise to ten times their original value. When the South Sea Bubble inevitably burst, many, including some at court, lost a great deal of money. The one man who seemed capable of managing the crisis was Robert Walpole. Recognizing this, George appointed him First Lord of the Treasury and Chancellor of the Exchequer. Walpole remained at the head of the ministry for the rest of the reign and beyond, justifiably earning him the accolade of Britain's first Prime Minister (although he rejected the title).

Walpole used his skill as a manager of the Commons to shelter the court from any scandal that might have followed the South Sea Bubble, and the king came to trust him further. Abroad, the 20-stone first minister kept the peace through alliance with France and Holland, while at home he ensured that minimum government proceeded with as little fuss and bother as possible – 'Let sleeping dogs lie' was his motto. It was just as George wanted: he headed the government, Walpole controlled it for him.

Thus a German king and his very English prime minister brought peace and stability to a land that had known little of either for a very long time. And under those favourable circumstances the economy, quickly getting over the South Sea business, boomed as never before. When George had a series of strokes and died during one of his visits to Germany, British society was more concerned with getting on the right side of the new king than with mourning the old. It was ungenerous behaviour towards one who had given them far more than they would ever realize.

8

George II, 1727–60

Parents: George I and Sophia
 Dorothea of Celle
Born: 30 October 1683,
 Hanover
Died: 26 October 1760,
 Kensington Palace, London
Marriage: Caroline of Ansbach,
 1705
Children: (i) Frederick, Prince
  of Wales, b.1707
 (ii) Anne, b.1709
 (iii) Amelia, b.1711
 (iv) Caroline, b.1713
 (v) George, b.1717
 (vi) William, Duke of
  Cumberland,
  b.1721
 (vii) Mary, b.1723
 (viii) Louise, b.1724

It is a popular sport among all but the most romantic historians to mock the monarchs of the House of Hanover, none of whom has come in for more scorn than George II. Nor is the ridicule the exclusive preserve of later generations: in his lifetime he was probably the subject of more malicious ribaldry than any other king or queen, before or since. For the most part the derision was justified.

The effect of all this was to expunge any lingering traces of majesty or mystery that still clung, cobweb-like, to the institution of monarchy. Queen Anne had occasionally 'touched' for the 'King's Evil' – laid hands on those suffering from scrofula in the belief that the royal fingers could bring healing. (Cardinal Henry is the last member of the royal family reported to have tried the trick.) The practice was left over from the days when the general populace viewed kings and queens, anointed by God, as somehow themselves semi-divine.

Less than 20 years after Anne's death, the thought of a monarch having any sort of mystical powers was palpably absurd. It was not just that the pragmatic importation of Hanoverians had broken the natural succession, either. The character and conduct of the second George brought the institution of which he was the living embodiment to an all-time low. George I's imperfections had been tolerated because he had got the nation out of a nasty hole. His son benefited from no such shield. Moreover, where the first Hanoverian had been simply blunt and boorish, the second was ox-head stupid. Scurrilous journalists and cartoonists, eager for a cheap penny, broadcast his foibles, weaknesses, errors and tantrums across the entire nation so that he who was supposed to be the glass wherein all dressed themselves, became instead the buffoon over whom all creased themselves.

Prince of Hanover

George was raised in Hanover. He loved the little electorate and always regarded it as his home, rather than England. Like his father, he returned there for long periods whenever he could and did his best to see that Hanoverian interests were given due weight in British foreign policy. Such demands were no more popular with his less European-minded British subjects than they had been in the previous reign.

George I and Sophia Dorothea of Celle, it will be recalled, had no love for each other after the first year or two of their marriage, and they divorced when their only son was 11. We do not know what effect his mother's subsequent forced removal from society had on the young George. It may partially explain his patent lack of confidence, although that may just as easily have been brought on by his father's bullying. Certainly the two together cannot have helped the child develop into a well-balanced adult.

The prince was given a strictly practical education similar to his father's. He was taught languages (including English which he spoke with a thick German accent), such history as would help him to understand the world of diplomacy, and certain military skills. He grew to love soldiering, setting great store by his immaculate guards and at the remarkable age of 59 becoming the last British monarch to lead his soldiers into battle (Dettingen, 1742). In all he did in his youth, George was watched over by a father suspicious of his son's character and untrusting of his abilities. One wonders whether he feared that the boy had too much of Sophia Dorothea in him?

Mother's child or not, George grew into an unpleasant adult. Physically unprepossessing, being short and squat with a heavy bovine face, his personality was equally unattractive. His best qualities were his determination (although easily turning to pig-headedness) and a computer-like memory: his obsession with facts, relevant and otherwise, would have made him an ideal member of a modern pub quiz team. The fixation with detail was linked to a passion for precision. Accustomed to visit the mistress of the day at nine o' clock each evening, he could often be found pacing up and down outside her room waiting for the chimes to strike the hour.

Less amusing were George's annoying pedantry, irritability, inflexibility (unless bullied) and insensitivity. The latter is exemplified in his reply to the request of his dying wife that he would not re-marry: no, he famously promised, henceforward he would make do with mistresses. With the notable exception of his patronage of the composer Handel, he showed little interest in the arts. He was not moved by either painting or poetry; had he been, the fifth-rate Colley Cibber would not have remained poet laureate for most of his reign.

Caroline

George was almost 20 when the War of Spanish Succession broke out and the young soldier was eager to display his prowess in the ranks of those resisting the expansionist ambitions of Louis XIV. His father would have none of it: what would become of Hanover if its only son and heir were slain in battle? Before he could get the whiff of gunpowder in his nostrils the prince had first to marry and produce a son. Once that was done, and only then, he might be permitted to go to war. The prince did as he was commanded and was eventually allowed to serve with Marlborough for one year.

The bride found for Prince George was the sensual and attractive Caroline of Ansbach. The couple were the same age and in crucial ways ideally suited: both had a no-nonsense approach to sex as a pleasurable basic instinct. It is no coincidence that they were in bed together when news came through of George I's death. Unusually, Caroline seemed content to share her husband with other women. When in Hanover in 1735, for example, he wrote her a detailed, blow-by-blow account of his seduction of the beautiful black-eyed Baroness Amalie von Walmoden. After the queen's death in 1737, Amalie divorced her husband and travelled to England to become the king's premier mistress and Countess of Yarmouth.

George's women were better than he deserved. Amalie was intelligent and well-read, as was his English mistress, the plain and slightly deaf Henrietta Howard. Queen Caroline's talents were by no means just physical, either. She had been well educated in the company of the philosopher Leibniz and was possessed of a clear and enquiring mind. In Britain she was at ease with such intellectuals as the poet Alexander Pope, and understood better than her husband the importance of keeping on the right side of key political managers. Through her instigation, improvements were made to the royal palaces of St James's and Kensington, and her death left a cultural vacuum at court that was never filled.

King of England

George I had taken steps to ensure that his son understood the British political system, letting him attend cabinet meetings and involving him in less important matters of policy. Even so, the king did not fully trust the prince and when away in Hanover he refused to name him Regent. He offered instead the ancient and convoluted title of Guardian of the Realm and Lieutenant, a snub that sent the Prince of Wales purple with rage.

Once at the helm himself, George II took a long time to grasp the political realities of his position. He began by ordering that Walpole be replaced by the amiable but only moderately talented Spencer Compton, a move that lasted just 24 hours before the queen tactfully negotiated its reversal. The king might choose whom he wished to head his ministry but that person had to be able to command a majority in the House of Commons if any business was to be done. Walpole, the first leading politician to refuse a seat in the House of Lords, promptly demonstrated how this worked by arranging for George's Civil List to be increased to £800,000 a year. Even then the message did not sink in. Almost 20 years later, in 1746, when George tried playing politics behind their backs, his Whig ministry resigned en bloc to force the king to stop his shenanigans.

Walpole remained in power until 1742, when old age reduced his powers and war (over the Austrian Succession) undermined his policies. Walpole's protégés, the Pelhams, (Henry and his brother Thomas, Duke of Newcastle) then more or less kept the system going until 1754, when the king again tried to circumvent the wishes of the Commons. Once more he was obliged to back down. The last years of his reign saw a ministry led by William Pitt the Elder. One of the king's bitterest foes who had once referred to Hanover as the 'despicable electorate', Pitt guided the country to unprecedented victories in Europe, India and North America during the Seven Years' War.

Except on those occasions when he tried to break the rules, George's management of the governmental system was adequate. The same cannot be said of the way he handled his own household, in particular Frederick Prince of Wales. As George I had denigrated and humiliated his son, so George II did the same to his. Frederick was kept in Hanover until 1728, when he was 21. Thereafter, until the prince's sudden and unexpected death in 1751, the father-son relationship varied between cold and downright murderous.

Following the previous generation's example, Frederick and his wife Augusta moved out of St James's Palace and established Leicester House as a base for opponents of the king and his ministers. George responded by banning his son from all the royal palaces. Among his admirers Frederick posed as a 'patriot', announcing that on his accession he would end the Whig monopoly of power and usher in an era of honest, incorrupt, non-party government. Such near-treasonous utterances filled George with apoplectic rage.

Surprisingly, Queen Caroline shared her husband's hatred of Frederick. 'If I was to see him in hell,' she is reported to have said, 'I should feel no more for him than I should for any other rogue that went there.'[27] The population at large followed the royal rages with delight – not for over a century had a king given his people so much to gossip about. It did not make him any more popular, though, and the news of his appropriately undignified death (of a heart attack while straining on the water closet) was met with delighted relief.

George III, 1760–1820

Parents: Frederick, Prince of Wales and Augusta of Saxe-Gotha-Altenburg

Born: 4 June 1738, St James's Square, London

Died: 29 January, 1820, Windsor Castle

Marriage: Charlotte of Mecklenburg-Strelitz, 1761

Children:
(i) George, Prince Regent & George IV, b.1762
(ii) Frederick, Duke of York, b.1763
(iii) William IV, b.1765
(iv) Charlotte, Princess Royal, b.1766
(v) Edward, Duke of Kent, b.1767
(vi) Augusta, b.1768
(vii) Elizabeth, b.1770
(viii) Ernest, King of Hanover, b.1771
(ix) Augustus, b.1773
(x) Adolphus, b.1774
(xi) Mary, b.1776
(xii) Sophia, b.1777
(xiii) Octavius, b.1779
(xiv) Alfred, b.1780
(xv) Amelia, b.1783

The accession of George III was greeted with much warmth throughout the British Isles. The English were particularly delighted. If Charles II and James II are discounted for their partly continental upbringing and their father for his Scottish birth, then George was the first born and bred adult Englishman to ascend the throne since Henry VIII.

The new king was British through and through, and proud of it. English was his first language and he delighted in the name of patriot. He was a stickler for duty: with him the country would always come first, before party, faction, family and certainly before Hanover. Those looking for auspicious omens noted that the date of his accession, 25 October, was the anniversary of the Battle of Agincourt – one of the most memorable dates in the Jingoist calendar. (The significance was reversed in the new-style Gregorian calendar – used in Britain and its colonies since September 1752 – in which the rather less auspicious Battle of Hastings occurred on 25 October.) With British arms recently triumphant in many corners of the world, great things were expected of the reign of George III.

Indeed, great things happened during the reign of George III. In many ways it was as monumental as that of any British monarch. It saw further progress towards constitutional monarchy, the appearance of an independent America, the beginning of Britain's second empire, the country's emergence as the leading global economic and commercial power, the defeat of the French Revolution and Napoleon, and the initial stages of a development that would alter the face of the entire globe: the Industrial Revolution.

Yet the king himself was closely involved with very little of this. American propaganda made sure he was blamed for the loss of the transatlantic mainland colonies, although the responsibility was hardly his alone (see below). Otherwise, the great changes of 1760–1820 – even the drift towards constitutional monarchy – took place either without George knowing or with his having little impact on them. This is the great sadness of his reign: glories predicted at his accession failed to materialize, while the unpredicted glories were none of his doing.

In the end, though, George's essential goodness and well-meaning won through. Politically, he made a terrible mess of his first years on the throne, and thereafter illness meant that only periodically was he in a fit state to participate effectively in matters of state. Yet he survived to become an increasingly fond symbol of a country bursting with nationalistic pride. Knowing he had their best interests at heart, however misguided his tactics, at the last his subjects forgave the folly of his younger years and, as was his wish, adopted him as the 'father of his people'.[28]

The Earl of Bute

On 6 March 1751 Frederick Prince of Wales, the estranged eldest son of George II, caught a cold. A fortnight later the 44-year-old prince suddenly died, leaving his son George heir to the throne of the leading Protestant state in Europe. George, just 12 years old, was a sensitive child. He was inclined to be passionate, and the responsibility of his inheritance weighed heavily on his underdeveloped mind. His mother Augusta, taught since her arrival in England from Germany that her sole purpose in life was to breed and not to guide her offspring once they had appeared, was able to offer her son little consolation or advice.

Unlike many of his family, George was no fool. He was not a scholar either: he picked up some French and German, a little basic Latin, and elementary maths, but was slow to learn and was happier with the straightforward and practical rather than the theoretical or pragmatic. This liking for the certain perhaps had its roots in an emotional insecurity that his father had been unwilling and his mother incapable of meeting. While the prince was still in his early teens the gap was filled by John Stuart, Earl of Bute, an attractive, knowledgeable man in his forties who became a cross between an elder brother and a father figure to the adolescent George. In 1756, when he came of age and was therefore able to make his own appointments, the boy immediately made Bute 'groom of the stole' – in effect, head of his household. Gossip said that Bute's elevation was due to the influence of the widowed Augusta, with whom Bute was wrapped in a clandestine affair.

The patriot

Bute had few influential friends and was not a politician. Like many viewing the political process of the eighteenth century from the outside, he was filled with disgust at the apparent corruption, scheming and unalloyed self-interest of the Whig politicians who had monopolized power since the Hanoverian accession. To some extent this criticism was justified, but more relevant (and interesting) was the fact that most people did not understand what was going on. Parliamentary rule through parties was only just emerging. We now know that one cannot function without the other, that parties are essential for organizing elections to and votes within an assembly. To the uninitiated eighteenth-century observer, however, particularly an excluded Tory, the sole function of party seemed to be to keep the Whigs in power and the Tories sidelined. In other words, 'political party' was a rather dirty phrase.

The high-minded made common cause with the ignorant in declaring that party should be an anathema to virtuous ministers in a wholesome government. This idea had been set out in the influential tract 'The Idea of the Patriot King', written in 1738 by Henry St John, Viscount Bolingbroke, a Tory leader from Queen Anne's reign whose career had been blighted by association with Jacobitism. The work's thesis was that a patriot king, using his prerogative power to appoint and dismiss ministers, should assemble a government of the most able men, regardless of party affiliation, who would manage the affairs of state with the true interests of the nation at heart.

Bolingbroke's idea appealed strongly to the Prince of Wales, whose personality displayed innocence and idealism in equal measure. Egged on by Bute, George decided that on ascending the throne he would be just such a monarch – a virtuous prince to raise his country from the scandalous and wretched mire of party politics and restore virtue to the heart of administration. The dream of Bute and his prince was beautiful, but flawed. They failed to realize that the Whigs would quickly label Tory promotions as Jacobitism. Even more damaging, the Whigs would condemn appointment on the basis of ability rather than parliamentary support as an attempt to restore the 'Stuart despotism' that the 1688–9 Glorious Revolution had supposedly ended for ever. The fatal weakness within the patriot king's idea was that it assumed the monarch to be wiser and more truthful than the political nation assembled in parliament. Such naïvety looked at best like arrogance – and at worst like tyranny.

Political apprenticeship

George's first act on hearing of his father's death was to consult with Bute. Master and pupil were quite apprehensive and neither had a clear idea for a programme of government. Nevertheless, they shared the view that all avenues should be open to men of talent. Strange sights appeared at court, country gentlemen and members of the aristocracy whose families had not been seen there for generations. Tories (or at least those who did not label themselves Whigs) got offices in church and state. In a short time the old Whig magnates, led for so long by the Pelham family, were in disarray and began to fight back. The 'Slaughter of the Pelhamite Innocents' was portrayed by its opponents in press and cartoon as a Jacobite-inspired attempt to take the country back to the days of James II.

The political leaders whom George had inherited, the Duke of Newcastle and William Pitt the Elder (Earl of Chatham, 1766) struggled to cope with Bute for a while before resigning over differences in foreign policy. Now, as First Lord of the Treasury, Bute was in effect Prime Minister and brought the Seven Years' War with France to a close (1763).

A prime minister needed to be able to steer his programme, particularly its financial aspects, through parliament, and this Bute could not do. There was no Tory party as such (just as there was no single Whig party in the modern sense of the word), and the collection of conservative country squires and king's placemen was never sufficient to give Bute a guaranteed majority in the Commons, especially as he was not there to manage matters himself. After a short period of impotent chaos, the royal favourite was obliged to resign. When the king continued to consult him in private ('behind the curtain'), the political establishment took umbrage and forced the deflated king to promise never again to confer with Bute on political matters.

Lord North

Over the next few years George went through a number of ministries, sometimes falling back on the old Whigs and at others trying again his new idea of a non-factional coalition. Eventually, in 1770, he came up with the amiable figure of Lord North around whom a stable administration could at last coalesce. Chubby, loud-voiced and seemingly imperturbable, the witty baronet remained as First Lord of the Treasury for 12 years. During this unfortunate administration George's reign reached its nadir.

The famous story is simply told. The Seven Years' War left Britain in control of much of North America. The administration of the colonies and their protection against the French and Indians was an expensive business, so the government in London tried to get the Americans to increase their contribution. The taxation was tactless, imposed by ministries that failed to realize the extent to which the Americans had developed their own political culture and sense of identity. (It is, however, too early to speak of American nationalism.) Colonial resistance only spurred the determination of London not to give way, until in 1775 the confrontation flared into open conflict.

When the Americans were not immediately defeated (with the exception of Marlborough's wars, the British had always been better at fighting on water than on land), Britain's European rivals, notably France, saw the transatlantic war as an ideal opportunity for revenge. They sent troops and equipment and for a time closed the sea routes between Britain and the war zone. Under such circumstances the British government had no choice but to accede to the Americans' demands and in 1783 it accepted the existence of the United States of America.

Lord North had sensed this ending long before it happened and made several attempts to resign. On each occasion he was dissuaded by the king, who remained determined never to surrender to rebels. When finally forced to do so, he wrote a declaration of abdication: 'His Majesty therefore with much sorrow finds that he can be of no further utility to his native country which drives him to the painful step of quitting it for ever.'[29] Shortly afterwards, for some reason he changed his mind.

Unfit ruler

The American position regarding the king had been straightforward. It found its clearest expression in the 1776 Declaration of Independence which stated in no uncertain terms that George III was single-handedly and personally responsible for all the ills that had befallen his American subjects. Having 'obstructed the administration of justice', for instance, 'plundered our seas, ravaged our coasts, [and] burnt our towns', it was clear that such a tyrant was 'unfit to be the ruler of a free people.'

This was clever politics. The colonial leaders knew full well that in certain British circles George's apparent high-handedness had already made him unpopular, as they also knew that to lay the blame for their woes at the foot of the entire parliament (as probably should have been done) would only have united the British political nation against them and considerably lessened their chances of success.

After the war the British sought a scapegoat for their loss. Their unfortunately naïve king fitted the bill excellently. After all, since he had set great store by his prerogative, especially the right to select and dismiss ministers, then he should be obliged to bear the ultimate responsibility when they proved inadequate to the tasks allotted to them. Moreover, in the age of imperialism that followed George's reign the loss of any colony, let alone an entire continent-full, was regarded as little short of treason. Not until after the Second World War, when losing overseas possessions had become a British habit, was it possible to view the events of 1774–83 dispassionately.

It was noticed that little evidence linked George personally to the 11 years of insensitive laws and pronouncements that followed the Peace of Paris (1763) and which eventually drove the Americans into rebellion. The king supported his ministers, it is true, but measures such as the infamous Stamp Act (a tax on legal transactions and printed material, 1765) were very much of their making, not the king's. He was far more concerned with matters nearer home, notably the tempestuous antics of John Wilkes.

Wilkes and liberty

John Wilkes was an ugly, anarchic rogue eager to prick pomposity and lay bare unwarranted privilege wherever he found it. As a young man he had married a wealthy heiress and mixed with the riotous aristocrats who patronized the pleasure-seeking Hell-Fire Club. In his more serious moments the fire-raiser wrote offensively of the king and his court in his *North Briton* newspaper. Arrested for seditious libel, he was let off on a technicality. By this time his cause had attracted opponents of the court and the attentions of the urban mob, which made a great nuisance of itself in the name of 'Wilkes and liberty'.

George's government struck back by getting hold of the sexually explicit 'Essay on Woman', a parody of Alexander Pope's 'Essay on Man', that Wilkes had helped write. Attacked in the Commons, scorned in the Lords by his former partner in sin the Earl of Sandwich (whose title survives in the filled bread snack he devised so he could eat while seated at the card table), and arraigned on charges of obscenity, Wilkes fled abroad. When he returned he was elected and re-elected several times for the county of Middlesex. On each occasion, the Commons refused to let him take his seat. Meanwhile, he and his supporters won a series of judgements in the courts that increased the freedom of the press and the rights of the individual over the government.

Wilkes also took up the cause of parliamentary reform. Furthermore, it came as little surprise to find that he held the cause of the dissident American colonists dear to his heart. Whether he had a heart or not, in fact, is open to question. George, innocent that he was, did not realize this and continued to take seriously a man whom most others recognized as a likeable but transparent scoundrel.

Black and white

With the king thus preoccupied, his ministers continued on their collision course with the Americans. However, once rebellion had broken out, might not the king have done more to avoid an irrevocable rift? Maybe, but only if George III's personality had been vastly different. He was not, never had been and never would be a politician. His world was black and white, good and evil, just and unjust. Compromise, finding the middle way, admitting that one's own position might not be the only one… were all concepts alien to his thinking.

George viewed rebellion by definition as wicked and wrong. Consequently accommodation with rebels was an impossibility. He had only to glance at names on the map to see how historically tied to monarchy the American colonies were, from Virginia and Jamestown, through New York, the Carolinas, Williamsburg, Princeton, Orange, Annapolis and, of course, Georgia. A more statesman-like prime minister than Lord North might have engineered a different outcome to the debacle, more able commanders might have engineered a military victory, a wiser head than George's might not have let the quarrel get out of control in the first place – but all these are improbable conditionals. The fact is that George was king and appointed the ministers and soldiers under whose provenance Britain divided from its American colonies. Apportioning blame is, at this distance, a largely irrelevant political exercise and not sensible history either.

Squire George

The sadness of George III is that he meant so well. Few monarchs have been as conscientious or have exhibited so strong a sense of duty. He took great pride in the remarkable developments in agriculture (earning the nickname 'Farmer George') and transport that were taking place in Britain. Unlike his Hanoverian predecessors, he made a point of patronizing native artists, such as the musician William Boyce. He supported the establishment of the Royal Academy, a national forum for the arts set up in 1768 with the painter Sir Joshua Reynolds as its first president. The king's huge and well-chosen personal book collection, now adorning the British Library, is hailed by scholars as a national treasure of inestimable worth.

George's private life, too, compared favourably with those of his German ancestors. He ate and drank sparingly, enjoying such simple pleasures as sea bathing (at Weymouth), watch repairing and book collecting. Unusually for the time and certainly for his family, he was faithful to his wife. Indeed, in the very act of marriage he displayed his extraordinary sense of what he ought rather than what he wanted to do. Around the time of his accession he had fallen madly in love with the pretty young Lady Sarah Lennox and would dearly have liked to marry her. Diplomacy dictated otherwise, and George, quite a handsome man, was obliged to renounce Sarah for the dim and tear-inducingly plain Charlotte Sophia of Mecklenburg-Strelitz. What began as duty, though, developed over time into a relationship of touching and enduring affection.

It was Charlotte who first guided her husband towards Windsor. The couple developed and refurbished the old castle, making it their favourite residence. The king particularly liked the informality of the place. Here, unlike in London, he could be the country squire. As the castle grounds were open to the public, many a schoolboy, farmer or local tradesman found himself stopped by a kindly old gentleman in an untidy blue coat and asked how he fared and what he thought of this or that. George frequently wandered into town to buy books, and took a personal interest in the welfare of nearby Eton College. What a shame that this George, the kindly benefactor who gave

£1,000 of his own money to see the streets of Windsor better paved, was not able to spend his entire life in such innocent activities but was obliged by birth to wrestle with matters beyond his comprehension and competence.

The Prince of Wales

There was one unfortunate Hanoverian tradition that George failed to abandon: a full-scale and bitter falling out between the king and his eldest son. As George I and George II had done, so George III not only rowed with the Prince of Wales but also found his son's hostility spilling over into politics.

As he would succeed his father as George IV, a more detailed account of George Prince of Wales, the Prince Regent, follows. All that really concerns us here is that his father might have inadvertently assisted the young George's wayward development by giving him his own household too early – at the tender age of eight – and entrusting the education of the high-spirited prince to a series of inadequate tutors who singularly failed either to inspire or to tame him.

By the age of 18 the Prince of Wales was running an unscrupulous mistress – Mary Robinson – and accumulating huge debts. (In agreeing to be paid off, Mary increased the latter by an extra £5,000, the sum she required not to hand over the prince's letters to the press.) Within another three years, in order to get money from them, the prince was associating with politicians opposed to his father. Stories of his debauchery and impossibly lavish spending were legion. Exaggerated and embellished, they titivated tables and taverns in just about every city of Europe, dragging the reputation of the Hanoverian monarchy to an all-time low. It was a very long way from the clean-cut and universally respected institution that George had planned with Bute a quarter of a century earlier.

Prerogative and riot

Of all European states, only Britain had the resources single-handedly to fight a war on the scale of the American War. (The enormous cost to France of participation in the campaigns helped precipitate revolution there in 1789.) Nevertheless, the demands of the conflict stretched Britain as never before and put the country's political and economic systems under great strain.

The eventual resignation of Lord North in 1782 led to a period of instability in which the king finally had to face up to reality and learn to live with ministers of whom he did not approve. He also had to accept the significant innovation of the prime minister (the Duke of Portland) selecting his junior ministers after he had taken up office. This development, together with losing control over the civil list and the right to dismiss judges, meant a significant reduction in the crown's political power.

The crown was far from impotent, however, as George demonstrated during the infamous Gordon riots of 1780. Two years previously, parliament had enacted a moderately tolerant Catholic Relief Act that did away with some of the more outdated features of anti-Catholic legislation left over from more bigoted times. In certain circles, though, the cry of 'no popery' could still rouse violent emotions. Lord George Gordon, the eccentric president of the Protestant Association, led a large street procession to parliament with a view to handing in a petition demanding the repeal of the Catholic Relief Act.

The situation rapidly got out of hand when the London mob – always a potential threat, especially in times of hardship – took the law into its own hands and started despoiling Catholic chapels. Soon private houses, taverns and even prisons were under attack. For more than a week the capital was in chaos. Through all of this King George remained remarkably calm and in the end it was he, not the government, who restored order. Using his power as commander-in-chief, he summoned 12,000 troops to London and told them to do whatever was necessary to quell the rioting. He made little distinction between the Gordon rioters and the Americans – both were rebels and law-breakers deserving of no mercy.

By the time order had returned to London's streets some 700 people had been killed, many more injured, and 450 arrested. Twenty-five were later executed. Gordon was tried for high treason and acquitted. He eventually died in prison on a charge of libel, having previously exchanged his once-beloved Protestantism for Judaism. The cause of religious toleration had been shaken but not halted.

Pitt and porphyria

George was rescued from the turmoil that followed defeat in America by William Pitt the Younger, son of Lord Chatham.

The king asked this remarkable young man to form a ministry at the end of 1783, when he was just 24 years old. Within a few months he had won over a majority of MPs, held a triumphant general election, and set himself up for one of the longest and more successful ministries in parliamentary history. He began with moderate reforms (regulating the government of India, for instance) and skilful management of the economy, and ended guiding the country through long wars with revolutionary France, 1793–1801.

Pitt and the king did not always see eye to eye, and it was a disagreement over further Catholic emancipation that brought about the prime minister's resignation in 1801. Thirteen years previously, however, their relationship had been altered in a way that few had predicted and certainly no one would have wished for. At the time it was widely reported that King George had gone mad.

George was not insane but suffered from an hereditary malady diagnosed in the later twentieth century as porphyria. This uncommon illness is in fact a group of related diseases associated with an excessive accumulation of porphyrins in the body. The most acute form of the disease may manifest itself in skin problems, increased sensitivity to touch, difficulty in walking, delusions, and loss of sight and hearing. With George the most alarming symptoms were the delusions. Stories – true and false – soon abounded of the antics of the unfortunate patient. It was said, for example, that he once ordered his carriage to halt in Windsor Great Park, descended and talked to an oak tree as if it were King Frederick the Great of Prussia.

The treatment given to the king, famously depicted in Alan Bennett's play *The Madness of George III* (later made into a film), was by modern standards horrific. At a time when mental illness was scarcely understood and scientific psychology unknown, unusual behaviour was commonly explained by the action of 'humours', by deliberate wilfulness on the part of the patient, or even by the malicious intervention of spirits. Under the guidance of the Willises, a celebrated family of doctors, George was subjected to intolerably cruel restraint in both straightjacket and upright chair. Other treatments included more traditional bleeding and cupping – raising blisters on the skin by placing inverted hot metal cups on the body's soft tissue. Such remedies, as well as enforced separation from the queen and other loved ones, made no impact on the disease but imposed a mental torture just as painful as the physical one.

The 1788 outbreak of illness eventually passed, leaving the king exhausted in body and mind and deeply humiliated. The horror returned in 1801 and 1804 and by 1810 his incapacity was clearly permanent. The Prince of Wales, who with the passage of time had grown closer to his father, was given the powers of regent the following year. Thereafter the king lived in a world of his own, deaf, blind and unable to recognize anyone he met on his shufflings around Windsor Castle. Even the queen, officially responsible for his welfare until her death, was a stranger to him. When this melancholy existence finally came to an end on 29 January 1820, it was a blessed release for George and all who cared for him.

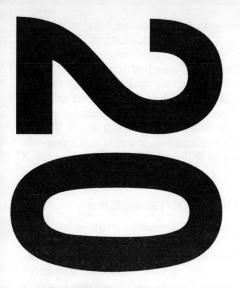

20 George IV, 1820–30

Parents: George III and
  Charlotte of Mecklenburg-
  Strelitz
Born: 12 August 1762,
  St James's Palace
Died: 26 June 1830, Windsor
  Castle
Marriages and children:
1 Maria Fitzherbert, 1785
  No children
2 Caroline of Brunswick, 1795
  Child: Charlotte, b.1796

The late-eighteenth century was not a good time for monarchy. First the Americans threw off the institution, then the French. Catching the revolutionary fervour, a number of European states followed suit and declared themselves republics. That the British monarchy survived was due less to the popularity of the royal family than to the fervent nationalism bred of military success on land and sea. The crown, for all its weaknesses and silliness, was included beneath the broad blanket of the 'British way of life' and thereby given protection it might not otherwise have been afforded and which it did precious little to deserve.

George III's troublesome sons

Europe was beset with war and domestic turmoil of every description from the outbreak of the French Revolution (1789) onwards. Serious talk of revolution, reaction and reform was everywhere matched by equally serious action. Everywhere? Not quite. Within their gilded palaces and pavilions Britain's kings, princes and princesses appeared uniquely out of touch with the earnest mood of the age. As a consequence, with George III apparently insane (1810–20) and his sons, for the large part acting like overgrown and very spoilt schoolboys, the reputation of the monarchy fell to a desperately low ebb.

Adolphus Duke of Cambridge, the youngest of George III's sons to live to adulthood, was the least troublesome. A grim man, he spent most of his time in Hanover and managed, exceptionally, to live within his means and father only legitimate offspring. The next youngest, the genial Augustus Duke of Sussex, made two illegal marriages and ran up vast debts. His elder brother Ernest, Duke of Cumberland, was the worst of a grim bunch: George III's wicked-looking and devious fifth son was reputed (inaccurately) to have committed murder and incest. He was certainly tyrannical, perverted and violently reactionary, while his German wife, Princess Frederica of Mecklenburg-Strelitz, was very much of the same ilk. Twice widowed, it was whispered that she had murdered both her previous husbands.

There was nothing very genial about the next brother, either. Edward Duke of Kent was hated by the Prince of Wales for his hypocrisy and radical views, and by the army for his sadistic taste in punishment. After living with Madame Julie de St Laurent for 27 years, he ditched her at the age of 51 for a formal marriage with the 32-year-old Princess Victoria of Leiningen. Their only child became Queen Victoria.

William Duke of Clarence, the future William IV, is dealt with later (see p.168) which leaves Frederick Duke of York and George Prince of Wales. York was a military man. As the nursery rhyme 'The grand old Duke of York' suggests, he was better at giving parade ground orders than directing troops in battle. He was relieved of active command after a series of disasters and the revelation that his mistress was making her fortune by selling commissions. Thereafter, he devoted himself to army administration (at which he showed some ability), accumulating the traditional family debts, and chasing unsuitable women.

George Prince of Wales, for all his glaring faults, was at least fun. The House of Hanover is not renowned for its sense of humour, although it was frequently a source of mirth in others. George I managed an occasional grim smile, and his son a coarse laugh, while the tragic life of George III provided little to laugh or smile about. George IV – 'Prinny' as he was nicknamed when Prince Regent – was the witty one of the family. He was clever, too, and possessed a sharp if sometimes unreliable eye for artistic beauty. Everything about him, from his own body to his architectural projects, was large, and many of the country's most famous tourist sights owe their provenance to his lavish imagination. Sadly, though, he lacked judgement. He misjudged individuals and crowds, physical objects and abstract ideas.

Finally, George misjudged himself, specifically the ability of his body to take the continual punishment to which a life of riotous living had subjected it. As a defender of the sovereign's rights he was a failure; nor did he offer much in the way of moral or social justification for the institution he represented. Yet he brought colour and art and humour to an area of national life that had long been a drab tapestry of the earnest, boorish or boring. For all his folly, therefore, the country was the poorer for Prinny's passing.

Prince of Whales

George reacted with gusto to the strict, humourless education stipulated by his father. Where papa urged moderation, duty and chastity, the son pursued over-indulgence, irresponsibility and licentiousness. He was spectacularly profligate, accumulating debts that even by today's standards are considerable. Within two years of running his own household, with a budget of £6,000 per annum, they touched £200,000. Within a few years they soared to well over half a million and were still around that figure as late as 1811, when the prince was made regent and a special sinking fund had for years been attempting to reduce his debt mountain.

Where did all this money go? A great deal went on a lifestyle the like of which had not been seen in the household of a British ruler since the time of Henry VIII. Feasts, wines, gifts, china, silver, furniture – all were of the highest quality and on the most lavish scale. Like Henry VIII, George paid the price. His florid good looks were soon submerged beneath a corpulence that earned him the nickname 'Prince of Whales'. In middle age his obesity became disabling. For public appearances, which he adored, he did his best to disguise his bulk within crippling corsets and cunningly designed outfits. The truth was too broad to be hidden, however, and the cruel caricaturists of the day found in the prince, regent and king a never-ending source of amusement.

Maria and marriage

George had many lovers. He was not an athletic man and sought comfort in his women rather than carnality, which frightened him. The majority of the girlfriends were experienced wives, mothers or, preferably, grandmothers. The great love of his life was Maria Anne Fitzherbert, a twice-widowed Roman Catholic six years his senior. By 1784 the prince was totally obsessed with her – he never did anything by halves – and she was certainly fond of him. Yet she was a lady of principle and refused to become his mistress. Almost out of his mind, the prince begged, blubbered and even arranged a fake suicide, but his beloved was adamant: marriage must proceed consummation of their passion.

Marriage it was then, a service conducted according to Anglican rites shortly before Christmas, 1785. Romantic the secret ceremony might have been, but it was also political dynamite. Even George realized this, refraining from mentioning it to his political friend and ally, the radical Whig MP Charles James Fox. Royal marriages required the consent of the sovereign to be legal, and George III (sane at the time) refused such consent point blank. The illegality of the union saved the prince from another pitfall – the stipulation of the Act of Settlement that an English monarch might not be married to a Roman Catholic.

The prince was not naturally monogamous and he and Maria had grown apart by 1794. They were reconciled a few years later, when she was heartened to hear from Pope Pius VI that, whatever English law said, the Church regarded her marriage as legal. The couple drifted apart again when George became regent, although her 'husband' and the British government ensured that she never wanted for money for the rest of her life.

The beast from Brunswick

Maria might have had enough cash, but George never had. This was partly why he decided to obey his father's wish and, in 1795, engage in a regular royal marriage. The union was also intended to produce a legitimate heir to the throne. Sadly for George, his aversion to homework saddled him with about the least suitable partner in all Europe. At 27, the eccentric Caroline of Brunswick was at the height of her considerable earthly powers. She was everything her groom was not: uncouth, vulgar, lusty, foul-mouthed, unromantic and rough. Where he delighted in fine fashions and delicate scents, she dressed with the taste of a fishwife and refused to wash either her body or her underclothes. On first meeting her the prince was so overwhelmed by the smell that he had to be restored with a glass of medicinal brandy.

Caroline was at her coquettish best for the wedding. George, green and anaesthetized with drink, tried not to believe it was happening. He found what followed even more distasteful. But somehow, despite the alcohol and the revulsion, he managed: with impeccable timing he got his wife pregnant at the first – and last – attempt. By the time Princess Charlotte was born nine months later the couple were at each other's throats. He found consolation in the wise, grandmotherly arms of Lady Jersey; his wife was subjected to a discrete government investigation into charges of adultery. When nothing concrete could be established, she went abroad. Here she pursued her tasteless ways until news came of her father-in-law's death – she was queen at last! Posing as the wronged wife before a mob that despised her husband, she made a triumphant return to the capital. Not since it had greeted Charles II at his restoration had London welcomed anyone with such ardour. Public warmth failed to melt George's heart, however. When Caroline made her way to Westminster Abbey for his coronation, she found the doors closed in her face. Her sudden death shortly afterwards brought the sordid saga to a welcome close.

Politics

George was not a political animal. As a young man he had favoured the Whigs as he admired their leader, Charles James Fox, and hoped they would help him out of his financial difficulties. Moreover, he had no intention of assisting his father by showing favour to the Tories. On coming to the throne he reversed his position, turning his back on the Whigs and maintaining the Tory ministry.

Thereafter George exerted less influence on affairs than any previous adult monarch. He was obliged to accept Canning as foreign secretary, although he hated the man. A few years later, finding Canning a good deal more acceptable than he had imagined, he chose him as prime minister over the Duke of Wellington. Otherwise George had to do largely as he was bidden, even accepting further Catholic emancipation, which he detested. His efforts to embarrass the government by conducting Hanover's foreign policy independently of Britain's were pitiful rather than seriously troublesome. Every foreign head of state in their right mind knew where the real power lay.

George's heritage

Beneath all this bluster and buffoonery, George IV was an essentially honest man. He also possessed a most unusual quality in a British monarch – a sincere admiration for the arts. He read and appreciated Jane Austen and Walter Scott, surrounded himself with beautiful furniture and works of art, and built like no other monarch before or since. Without his patronage, extravagant though it might have been, we would not have the exotic oriental pavilion at Brighton, the Royal Lodge and rebuilt castle at Windsor, and a whole host of London streets, crescents and other monuments, including Buckingham Palace, Regent Street, Regent's Park and Carlton House Terrace.

Nor were George's creations all static. His coronation introduced new pageantry, and he made flamboyant visits to Wales, Ireland and Scotland. The latter, which saw him parading down Princes Street ridiculously swaddled in plaid, laid the foundations for the royal family's sentimental love affair with the northern kingdom that persists to this day. By the time of his death, his combination of ostentation and incompetence had brought parliamentary monarchy almost to a close and prepared the way for the crowned figurehead.

21
William IV, 1830–7

Parents: George III and
  Charlotte of Mecklenburg-
  Strelitz
Born: 21 August 1765,
  Buckingham House, London
Died: 20 June 1837,
  Windsor Castle
Marriage: Adelaide of
  Saxe-Meiningen, 1818
Children: (i) Charlotte, b.1819
             (ii) Elizabeth, b.1820

It is difficult to get excited about William IV nowadays, although during his lifetime a number of women managed it and for a short time he was probably more popular than any Hanoverian had been. Looking back, his reign has an end of era feeling to it. It was not just that he was the last of the House of Hanover (a province his family now ruled not as mere electors but as kings in their own right) but that by the time of his death the monarch's vain and inept political interferences were increasingly out of place. (Technically speaking, Queen Victoria was a Hanovarian although she is nearly always referred to as belonging to her husband's Saxe-Coburg-Gotha family.)

The country and its leadership had moved on, avoiding revolution by accepting gradual development. William, like most of his family, did not like change and found it difficult to recognize it around him. When he scorned his people's good will, as he did after a short time on the throne, he did not realize that popular respect was something monarchs needed to cultivate. It was on the way to becoming their life blood, their very *raison d'être*. In modern parlance, it went with the job.

Sailor Bill

The third son of George III, William was sent into the navy at the age of 13 and remained at sea for about ten years. He saw some active service, made friends with Horatio Nelson and annoyed most other officer colleagues with his arrogant eccentricity, philandering and air-headed ways. Orders meant nothing to him – he did what he wanted and sailed his ship where he wished.

Created Duke of Clarence in 1789, with an annual allowance of £12,000, the eccentric William swapped active participation in the Senior Service for a more leisured life ashore. Still officially a naval man, he was later elevated to the Gilbertian-sounding ranks of Admiral of the Fleet and, three years before he became king, Lord High Admiral (a title specially revived for him). The siren that kept him off the water was the Irish actress Dorothea Jordan, an attractive woman of talent and intelligence. The happy couple set up house together and produced ten children, the 'Fitzclarences'. The longest lived of the brood, Augusta, was still around late in the third decade of Queen Victoria's reign.

Like his brothers, William always spent more than he had, obliging him to draw on the long-suffering Dorothea's earnings to make ends meet. However, unlike most of the royal family, he was surprisingly popular with the public. People warmed to his transparent honesty, lack of pretension, earthy language and genuine eccentricity – there was always a good story when Duke William was around for he was rarely predictable and never made any attempt to excuse or hide his transgressions. Perhaps fortunately, he did not carry though his dream of one day becoming an MP.

The duke's relationship with Dorothea ended in 1811 when he realized that his legitimate heirs, if he were to have any, might one day inherit the crown. After failing to secure an English wife, in 1818 he married the 26-year-old German Princess, Adelaide of Saxe-Meiningen. The couple's children were either still-born or died in infancy.

Political toils

Had he not inherited the crown, William might have been remembered with affection. Unfortunately, though, he became heir presumptive on the death of the Prince Regent's only daughter in 1817 and ascended the throne 13 years later. It was not a position to which he was well suited by either temperament or education.

Things went admirably for a short time. At first, the new king was more popular than ever when he insisted on celebrating his accession by careering round London in an open carriage, raising his hat to the crowds and stopping to offer lifts to astounded bystanders. A cut-price coronation, one tenth as expensive as that of his predecessor, also raised his status in the eyes of the masses. It was when the political situation grew tricky that things started to go wrong.

Reform was the watchword of the day. The prime focus of attention was on the corrupt, antiquated and thoroughly unrepresentative House of Commons. Demographic changes since medieval times, for example, meant that several constituencies had only a handful of electors. The Tories, who dominated the House of Lords, believed a system that had stood the test of centuries should not be interfered with. Led by Lord Grey, the Whigs were pledged to moderate reform. William was a Tory at heart, despite flirtation with the Whigs in earlier years. Reform meant change and he therefore opposed it.

William inherited a Tory government led by the Duke of Wellington. This was defeated in the 1830 general election, obliging the king to ask Grey to form a ministry. Grey did so and set about trying to get a Reform Bill through parliament. After much turmoil it became clear that the Lords would never accept the Bill. The only chance was to alter its composition by the creation of sufficient Whig peers (perhaps as many as 80) to give Grey a majority in both Houses. Appointment to the peerage was still very much a royal prerogative and William refused to play ball. Instead, he asked the Duke of Wellington to form another Tory administration.

Wise Tories, noticing the way the wind was blowing, declined to back Wellington for fear of a popular uprising. That left the king in a very embarrassing position. With his tail between his legs, he had to accept Grey back as prime minister and agree to appoint as many Whigs as were necessary to get the Reform Bill through the Lords. Rather than humiliate their sovereign, the Lords voted the Bill through and the king signed it into law.

At a stroke, William had swung from being the darling of the people to their enemy: the king who had tried to thwart his subjects' will. He was proud of the new abuse, he declared, because he had earned it for sticking to his principles. He had not of course. Although he had damaged the royal prerogative, he had stopped short of endangering the institution of monarchy itself. He never forgave Grey, though, and delighted when the new Whig leader, Lord Melbourne, gave him an opportunity to dismiss his ministry in 1834. This eccentric action was already anachronistic. It proved to be the last occasion on which a sovereign, not parliament, decided whether or not a ministry should continue in office.

After Melbourne's dismissal, William invited the Tories, now led by Sir Robert Peel, to have another go at forming a government. Peel's efforts came to little and for the rest of his reign William was forced to go along with a string of Whig reforms to which he heartily objected. (His savage brother, the Duke of Cumberland, even talked darkly of launching a military coup.) When William died of pneumonia in 1837, he left virtually no monument to his brief reign. His surviving children were all illegitimate, he had not been a builder like his brother, and his political machinations, such as they were, had all come to nothing.

part four

Saxe-Coburg-Gotha/ Windsor (1840–)

The death in 1817 of Charlotte, Princess of Wales, the only child of the Prince Regent and Caroline of Brunswick, sent a thrill of dismay through the British political establishment. There was a very real possibility that the enormous family of George III, who was now no more than a senile shadow in Windsor Castle, faced extinction. The old king's five surviving daughters were unmarried or childless. Only three of his seven living sons – the Prince Regent, the Duke of York and the Duke of Cumberland – were legally married. York's marriage was childless, as was the Regent's on Charlotte's demise. To date the Duke of Cumberland and his sinister partner had failed to procreate, although they did manage it later.

Consequently, parliament let it be known that by fathering only illegitimate children the four unmarried dukes were letting down the nation. It was also made clear that if they should mend their ways and marry, their allowances would be generously reviewed. Driven by the double spur of funds and the hope of fathering a future monarch, the Dukes of Cambridge, Clarence and Kent entered a sort of breeding race. Only the Duke of Sussex, deeply attached to his long-standing mistress, refused to join in.

The result of this outburst of royal lust was a bumper crop of new little Hanoverians. The key birth as far as the British monarchy was concerned was the first and only child, a daughter, of Edward Duke of Kent and Princess Victoria of Saxe-Coburg. Eighteen years later the child would accede to the British throne as Queen Victoria. Three years after that she married her first cousin, Prince Albert of Saxe-Coburg-Gotha. He was the son of Victoria's mother's brother, Prince Ernest of Saxe-Saafeld-Coburg. Technically speaking, the marriage brought Victoria into the house of Saxe-Coburg-Gotha (also her mother's family) and thus ended Hanoverian rule. (For those interested in genealogical detail, the Gotha connection came from the first marriage of Albert's father, Ernest, to Louise of Saxe-Gotha-Altenburg. Albert's mother, Princess Marie of Württemberg, was Ernest's second wife.)

The alteration in family name was not important and one may include the reigns of Victoria and her son, Edward VII, under the Hanoverian label. Those opting for Saxe-Coburg-Gotha (sometimes simplified as just Saxe-Coburg) generally do so in recognition that Victoria's reign marked a distinct break with the past. Whether Hanoverian or Saxe-Coburg-Gotha, during the First World War the German name was changed to the more patriotic-sounding Windsor (see p.200) – which it retains to this day.

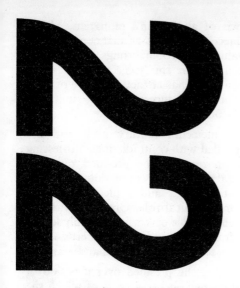

22 Victoria, 1837–1901

Parents: Edward, Duke of Kent and Princess Victoria of Leiningen

Born: 24 May 1819, Kensington Palace

Died: 22 January, 1901, Osborne House, Isle of Wight

Marriage: Albert of Saxe-Coburg, 1840

Children:
- (i) Victoria, Princess Royal, b.1840
- (ii) King Edward VII, b.1841
- (iii) Alice, b.1843
- (iv) Alfred, Duke of Edinburgh, b.1844
- (v) Helena, b.1846
- (vi) Louise, b.1848
- (vii) Arthur, Duke of Connaught, b.1850
- (viii) Leopold, Duke of Albany, b.1853
- (ix) Beatrice, b.1857

Victoria is the best-known of all Britain's monarchs. She is recalled every day in subjects as diverse as manners, railway stations, plums, moral values, bathroom fittings, architecture and gallantry. Her life has been the subject of countless biographies and more recently she has attracted the eye of film-makers and TV documentary producers. Perhaps uniquely, Victoria is the undisputed icon of her age.

Yet the queen, like the nineteenth century itself and her relationship with it, was riddled with contradictions. Professing to uphold her inherited prerogative, she presided over the emergence of a constitutional monarchy. Bent on doing her duty, for years she hid from the world and neglected to fulfil important aspects of her monarchical role. Obsessed with her husband and with setting an example of Christian family living, she did not much care for babies and after Albert's death allowed herself to become besotted with a tipsy manservant.

Similarly, in the wider picture, she presided over a period of unparalleled technological change on key aspects of which she turned her back. Telephones, for instance, were never fitted in the living quarters of her palaces and other residences. The professed servant of her people, she knew little about how most of them lived nor did she make much effort to find out. Charity was fine but structural change to the system alarmed her. Yet it was this change, in the form of legislation on such matters as the franchise, housing and local government, that enabled the British monarchical constitution to survive the painful and often violent birth-pangs of European democracy.

There were three strands to Victoria's success as a monarch. One was under her own control – her honest, transparently well-meaning yet forthright personality. The other two were provided by circumstance: her longevity, and the coincidence of her reign with Britain's period of unprecedented power and influence. Unwittingly and at times unwillingly she became the focus of an intense patriotic pride, an indomitable symbol of power and wealth that was widely believed to stem from traditional Protestant virtues. She was the mother of the nation, its empire and all its citizens. By the end of her reign the image of Britannia on one side of the penny coin and the bust of the venerable queen on the other had become virtually interchangeable.

Princess Alexandrina

Victoria was not really Victoria at all. Rather, the name which she assumed at her coronation was not the primary one given at her christening and certainly not that intended at birth. Her parents wanted her to be Georgiana, followed by four other names, the last of which was Victoria. The Prince Regent, her godfather, decreed otherwise: he would not have a feminized form of his name bestowed upon a possible future queen, nor would he allow his late daughter's names to be used. Far more dignified, he suggested, would be the name of the child's other godfather, Tsar Alexander of Russia. With that could go her mother's name. So it was: the baby was finally baptized Alexandrina Victoria.

The Duke of Kent died shortly after his daughter's birth, leaving the infant very much under her mother's influence. Within her Kensington Palace home, the child was generally known as 'Drina', although her German-born mother generally stuck to 'Victoria'. Other key figures in the household were Uncle Leopold (who left England to become King of the Belgians in 1831), Drina's half-sister Féodore, her governess Louise Lehzen, and Sir John Conroy, her mother's ambitious Irish advisor.

On Conroy's advice, the heiress was given a strange, sheltered upbringing. Sir John had persuaded the Duchess that Victoria's uncles were eager to see the child perish so the throne could pass to their offspring. To prevent this, Victoria was cut off from her own family, escorted even when she walked up a stairway, and rarely left alone. Conroy's aim was to get mastery over Victoria so when she became queen he would have access to real power. Alternatively, if William IV died before Victoria's eighteenth birthday, Conroy believed he could impose himself as her secretary and mentor.

'I will be good'

The Duchess and Conroy misjudged their intended victim. William IV died a convenient 27 days after Victoria came of age. Choosing the name Victoria over Alexandrina, the 18-year-old queen sought and obtained the support of Louise Lehzen to exert her independence. Before long she had demanded and got her own rooms and banished her mother to the far end of Buckingham Palace. Conroy, whose relationship with the

Duchess had attracted the predictable rumours, was given a generous pension and told to go away.

It is said that Victoria, on discovering her proximity to the throne by accident during a history lesson, had reacted by declaring, 'I will be good.' The childish pronouncement was certainly well-intended, although during her first years on the throne 'wilful' or 'tactless' might have been more apt adjectives. There was a good deal of awkward Hanoverian blood in the little queen's young veins. Her graceful demeanour, musical voice and innocent blue eyes belied the capricious strength beneath. As one whose favourite study was history, she knew what it meant to be a monarch – even though she had not fully grasped the subtle realities of the crown's position in early nineteenth-century Britain – and she was not going to let anyone take advantage of her.

Lord Melbourne, the prime minister at Victoria's accession, might not have taken advantage of the queen but he certainly had a considerable impact on her. A widower in his fifties, he adopted a guardian-father role, spending many hours each day advising his protégé on the powers of the crown and the current political situation. Very much an old-school Whig, he had not approved of the Great Reform Bill of 1832 (though he had reluctantly voted for it) and believed the crown should remain politically significant. (The Great Reform Bill had redistributed some Commons' seats to reflect population changes and widened the franchise to include more middle-class voters. Although only moderate in scope, it had demonstrated the Establishment's willingness to change.) The impressionable queen drank in every word the 'good, kind-hearted' Melbourne told her, even when he warned her not to read *Oliver Twist* because of the unpleasant characters and scenes it contained. The suffering of the masses, he explained, had been greatly exaggerated and agitation on their behalf was led by a few unprincipled malcontents.

At the time of her coronation, June 1838, the pretty young queen was as popular a monarch as anyone could remember. Only a year later, Melbourne's teaching bore bitter fruit and Victoria's estimation in the eyes of her subjects plummeted. First, she impulsively accused Lady Flora Hastings, a maid-of-honour with Tory inclinations, of no longer being a maid, and crudely insisted that the poor girl have a medical examination to prove her virginity. The suspected bounder was none other than Sir John Conroy. When the royal doctor was unable to support the queen's accusations, popular sympathy for Lady Flora swelled. Victoria came in for even more criticism later in the year when the reason for Flora's distended stomach was diagnosed as fatal cancer of the liver, a disease the initial examination had missed.

Meanwhile, Melbourne had resigned after losing the support of the House of Commons, and Sir Robert Peel, a Tory, prepared to take over as prime minister. Now a confirmed Whig, Victoria could just about accept a Tory ministry. What she would not do was obey Peel's quite reasonable and customary request that she replace her Whig-inclined ladies-of-the-bedchamber with women of a Tory persuasion. Peel promptly refused to take office, leaving the triumphant queen to re-appoint Melbourne.

Such open and high-handed involvement in politics, appearing to circumvent the wish of the elected House of Commons, was a very dangerous game indeed. It brought the popularity of the monarchy back to Hanoverian levels – the queen was hissed in public and pursued by ironic cries of 'Mrs Melbourne!' Had she continued in the same headstrong vein the monarchy might even have been done away with altogether. Certainly she might have been: in 1840 she survived the first of several assassination attempts. (The shooting only served to raise public sympathy for the queen, who survived six further assassination attempts: 1842 (twice), 1849, 1850, 1872 and 1882.) Fortunately for her and the institution she represented, at this moment a white knight appeared over the horizon, rescued the floundering queen and escorted her to safer pastures. The knight's name was Albert.

The royal family

Victoria had met her tall, pale first cousin when they were both 16. They had got on well but not spectacularly so; Albert in particular had reservations about Victoria's obstinacy and apparent delight in trivia. When they next met, in 1839, his doubts melted before her obvious attractiveness and passion for him. She proposed, as etiquette demanded, he accepted, love deepened and so was born one of the few royal marriages of genuine and long-lasting devotion.

In advertisements, Christmas cards, second-rate Hollywood movies and pulp fiction the sentimental template of family life that the royal couple set persists in the western world to this day: united in romantic love, the mother and father surround themselves with dear, contented offspring in a tableau of domestic bliss around the family meal table in a room that overlooks green countryside. Compared with all that had gone before – the mistresses, cruelties, adulteries, rows, orgies, beheadings, scandals – it was a stunning development. What made it all the more unusual was its affinity with the ideals of the burgeoning middle classes, not with the notoriously anarchic carryings on of the aristocracy with whom the royal family supposedly had closest links.

This new bond between the top rung of society and the third one down would prove to be one of the monarchy's greatest assets – and in the next century one of the hardest to maintain. The image of even the original Victorian family was something of a fantasy. The bond between the queen and her husband was steadfast enough, but both parents were disappointed in their elder son, and Victoria had to put up with workaholic Albert's many absences and distractions. Moreover, although apparently relishing the business that initiated babies, Victoria hated being pregnant and dreaded giving birth. Infants and young children did not much interest her.

The Prince Consort

Prince Albert of Saxe-Coburg-Gotha, a university-educated man of considerable intellectual ability, brought a new seriousness to the royal family. Blessed (or cursed) with a Germanic dislike of frivolity, he was deadly earnest in all he did. Whether preparing papers for the cabinet, arranging the Prince of Wales's education, planning improvements at the couple's country retreats at Balmoral, Scotland (chosen because its setting reminded Albert of Germany) or Osborne (Isle of Wight), or inspiring a wonderful exhibition of the country's commercial and industrial wealth (the Great Exhibition, 1851, held in Hyde Park in a gigantic Crystal Palace of glass and iron), he threw himself unsparingly into each project, checking the details and seeing that his wishes were carried out to the letter.

In the political sphere Albert's influence was considerable. The development was a gradual one as at first the queen was reluctant to surrender prerogative functions to her husband, however much she loved him. In time her constant preoccupation with pregnancy and birth, coupled to an acknowledgement of his superior intellect, brought about a change in her views that allowed him to become, unofficially, the senior political partner. He, for example, wrote papers and then presented them to her for signature. She described him as her 'permanent minister'; modern historians go further and talk of an 'Albertine monarchy'. The novelist politician Benjamin Disraeli remarked sardonically that if Albert were ever king he would happily re-introduce a personal absolutism.

As an outsider, Albert had a clearer view than his wife of the way the British political system was developing, and he advised her against becoming too obviously partisan in party matters. At the same time, being conservative by nature, he also weaned her from the Whigs (then developing into the Liberals) and inclined her towards the Tories (transmogrifying into the Conservatives). This was not an immutable position: he preferred the Liberal William Gladstone to the Conservative Benjamin Disraeli, whom he thought something of a parvenu spiv.

The middle of the nineteenth century is reckoned to be the golden age of the back-bench MP, when an individual gentleman might follow his principles and conscience without jeopardizing his parliamentary career. In this atmosphere, before the advent of the rigid two-party system, the crown's power was still considerable – indeed, its position as referee was sometimes essential for the formation of a cabinet. In 1854, for instance, when incompetent handling of the Crimean War (1854–5) brought down the government of Lord Aberdeen, Albert (assisted by Victoria) played an important part in enabling Lord Palmerston to construct a stable administration in its place.

It was always Victoria's regret that the British people as a whole never took to her intensely well-meaning husband. Over the previous 125 years they had had their bellyful of German princes. There was also a feeling that the Queen of Great Britain deserved better than a penniless European princeling. Albert's puritanical obsession with work and duty seemed too good to be true. He lacked the British capacity to let his hair down and laugh at himself – an insight into his unpopularity can be gained by asking how such a cold, sober, driven neurotic might have been handled by Charles Dickens, the most popular novelist of the time. In today's parlance, Albert was just too Victorian for his own good. Consequently, he was never allowed to become king (as Victoria had wanted), nor was he even given a peerage. The best he received was the title 'Prince Consort', awarded 17 years after his marriage. (Even that was better than Prince Philip got when he married Elizabeth II in the next century.)

Grandmother of all Europe

Victoria and Albert had nine children. A quick glance over the preceding pages shows that there was nothing unusual in that. What was unprecedented was that, thanks to developments in health and medicine, they all survived into adulthood and beyond. Furthermore, through carefully planned marriages they came to form a Europe-wide net of royalty. At the centre of this web, like some ancient and venerable spider, sat the world's most influential woman.

The queen's first-born and favourite, Princess Victoria ('Vicky'), married the liberal-minded Prince Frederick of Prussia. When he eventually came to the throne in 1888 it was as Emperor of Germany, a new entity with Prussia at its heart. Although he died of throat cancer shortly after his accession, by then Empress Vicky had a large family of her own. The eldest inherited his father's crown as Emperor William II of Germany ('Kaiser Bill'), while Princess Sophie married Constantine ('Tino'), a future King of Greece.

That was but one strand of the Victorian web. Through her uncle, Victoria already had links with Belgium (see p.175). Her second son, Edward Prince of Wales ('Bertie'), was married to Princess Alexandra of Denmark. Their children included the future George V and a Queen of Norway. Victoria's third child, Alice, also married a German prince. Her children included Alexandra, the future Empress of Russia, and a Russian grand duke. (Unknown to her, Queen Victoria was a carrier of haemophilia. The condition was inherited by Tsarevich Alexis, the son of the last tsar of Russia, through his mother.) Duke Alfred of Edinburgh, Victoria's fourth child, married a Russian and fathered a future Queen of Romania. A daughter of Victoria's third son married a King of Sweden, and her last child, Princess Beatrice, bore Queen Victoria Eugenie of Spain. By the end of the century there was hardly a royal house in Europe that was not related in some way to the ancient widow of Windsor.

Victoria's position in foreign affairs had been eased by her ineligibility, as a woman, to inherit the crown of Hanover. That millstone passed to her creepy Uncle Ernest. Nevertheless, tradition and her vast mesh of family contacts encouraged her belief that in foreign affairs her power was less circumscribed than at home. This led to some unpleasant confrontations, most notably with the high-handed Lord Palmerston and later over

Prussian designs on Schleswig-Holstein. By the end of her reign, however, her participation even in foreign affairs had been reduced largely to exhortations and admonitions – and awarding the Victoria Cross for exceptional gallantry overseas. (She had instituted the Victoria Cross, Britain's highest award for bravery in action, during the Crimean War.)

The widow

Having done much by example and moderate behaviour to restore the prestige of the monarchy that her uncles had done their best to dissipate, in the middle of her reign Victoria came close to undoing all she had achieved. The cause was the sudden death of her dearest Albert, probably from typhoid fever, in 1861. The queen was more than distraught – she became profoundly, pathologically depressed. For the rest of her life she wore nothing but black. She erected a vast hall and monument to his memory in west London, she was photographed with his bust looming over her, his rooms were untouched and every morning she had hot water for shaving brought to his dressing room just as when he had been alive.

The general public saw little of the queen's heart-rending, obsessive grief because they saw precious little of her. For years she withdrew almost completely from public view, spending months on end at Balmoral or on the Isle of Wight. She deigned twice to open parliament but in the pre-television days that brought her into contact only with the elite. A whole generation grew up to whom she was little more than a name and an image on coins and postage stamps. Her eldest son Bertie suffered, too. His easy-going, genial personality had always jarred with Albert and shortly before his death the Prince Consort had visited his son at Cambridge to confront him over a liaison the young man had been conducting with an Irish actress. As Albert had returned ill from the meeting and subsequently died, in her distress Victoria blamed Bertie for abetting his father's demise.

Being the sort of person she was, Victoria still insisted that she was shown government papers and that ministers came to her for personal meetings. When she was in Scotland, both actions necessitated long, tiring and time-wasting journeys. After a brief period of sympathy for their queen's bereavement, ministers began to tire of her behaviour. The public at large were less tolerant – why should the queen be paid £385,000 per annum from public funds when she did next to nothing for it? A substantial republican movement grew up with branches in many large towns. Its most powerful advocate was Charles Bradlaugh, editor of the *National Reformer* and radical MP for Northampton who was prevented from taking his seat in the Commons on account of his publicly declared atheism.

In her darkest hour Victoria turned to an outspoken Balmoral gillie (attendant) for support. John Brown, once a favourite of Albert's, now became his wife's trusted companion. He was summoned from the Highlands to the Isle of Wight, where he waited upon her, drove her about in her pony carriage, helped her mount and dismount her horse, and generally made himself useful – and remarkably familiar. When Brown came into the royal presence tipsy and reeking of tobacco the queen forgot her strong disapproval of inebriation and smoking.

Rumours began, of course, and the queen was lampooned as 'Mrs Brown'. Some talked in hushed tones of a sexual side to the relationship, others said the couple had been secretly married in Switzerland. The former is highly unlikely (although Victoria appreciated strong arms about her when being helped from the saddle), the latter virtually impossible. Brown's death in 1883, though it rekindled the queen's unhappiness, removed a powerful source of harm to her image and public standing. She had his room, like Albert's, made into a sort of shrine but contrary to the film *Mrs Brown* she had not broken protocol by visiting him on his deathbed.

Empress of India

With the assistance of family and certain politicians, by the mid-1870s Victoria had managed to lift herself out of her deepest gloom. She was fortunate that by this time, following a further widening of the franchise in 1867, a two-party system was establishing itself. This further removed the crown from politics because the choice of prime minister was made for it – the post went automatically to the leader of the party with the most seats in the House of Commons after a general election.

Depressed or not, the queen did not surrender her power graciously. When the Liberals won the 1868 election, for example, she was extremely loath to invite the party's leader, William Gladstone, to form a government. Unlike Albert (and it is surprising how many of her ex-husband's views she came to reject) she disliked the man, believing him to be a hypocrite. She frowned upon Gladstone's radical reforming policies, too. With no other option, however, she did her duty and accepted as her first minister the man who, she complained, addressed her like a 'public meeting'. Great and open was her delight when the Liberals were defeated six years later.

The overthrow of the Liberals was engineered by one who became Victoria's favourite politician of all, Benjamin Disraeli. He was everything she wanted: charming, witty, considerate, flattering and not dedicated (at least not in her presence) to social reform. On top of all that, he was an empire man after her own heart. He got the government to buy shares in the newly-built Suez canal and presented the waterway to her almost as a gift. In 1878 he risked war to thwart Russian ambitions and returned home from the crisis conference proudly bearing 'peace with honour'. Victoria was thrilled. In some ways even more exciting, two years earlier Disraeli had his sovereign officially proclaimed 'Empress of India'. The move charmed the ageing queen, not least because she had beaten her eldest daughter to the supreme accolade: Vicky did not become Empress of Germany until 1888. When Disraeli died (1881) Victoria confessed to crying for days on end.

Constitutional monarchy

By the time she was 60 the queen had become a national institution. Since her empire – which had doubled in size during her reign and on which the sun never set – extended right around the world, it could be said that she had grown into a global institution. From northern Canada to the Falkland Isles, St Kitts to Hong Kong, she was toasted, respected, revered for all that she stood for: imperial power, tradition, duty, authority, morality. In an almost mysterious way the British people elevated her into a talisman, a totem. When she celebrated Golden and Diamond Jubilees in 1887 and 1897, and hundreds of thousands thronged the streets of London to cheer her, in a way it was themselves and their achievements they were applauding, not the little old lady with a grumpy face who trotted by in a gilded coach.

The jubilees symbolized the way the monarchy had slowly changed under Victoria. They were shows, displays of theatrical pageantry in which the monarch played the lead role, but they were in no way related to the real issues with which the country was wrestling at the time: socialism, Irish home rule, votes for women (which Victoria strongly disapproved of), trade union power, the growing threats to Britain's commercial supremacy, and imperial conflicts. Prime ministers and cabinets came and went, policies changed, but all of this now happened largely out of the queen's reach. True, she still kept abreast of official business, sitting at her memento-strewn desk reading and signing papers as Albert had taught her. Yet much of this was formality, habit passed down from a previous age.

The political writer Walter Bagehot had summed up the crown's new position in his book *The English Constitution* (1867). Here he had distinguished between the 'efficient' (power-wielding) and 'dignified' parts of government. The crown and the House of Lords he placed in the latter. England (and we must assume the rest of Britain) was a disguised republic in which the monarch had only three rights: to be consulted, to encourage and to warn. The main function of the dignified sector of government was to add prestige and legitimacy to the efficient side, hence its largely ceremonial role.

In practice Victoria came to accept this situation. Although she remained reclusive, she did finally stir herself to make a number of state visits at home and abroad. The most notable were to Ireland, whose problems she neither fully understood nor recognized, and to France. The cross-Channel venture in particular, the first visit to those shores by a reigning British monarch since the unfortunate Henry VI had gone there for his French coronation of 1431, signalled how the monarchy would develop in the next century.

End of an era

Queen Victoria died on 22 January 1901. She had enjoyed an extraordinary reign, perhaps the most extraordinary in all British monarchical history. First of all, it was the longest. More importantly, at her accession the crown had been a threatened, much reviled institution of uncertain powers; at her death these powers had been clarified, the monarchy's position secured and its prestige restored. Some of this had been Victoria's doing, some Albert's and some had been simply a by-product of wider political changes. Whatever the reasons, the reign of Queen Victoria had enabled the British monarchy to survive.

This is all the more remarkable because the queen herself had rarely directed change. Normally she had resisted it, letting go of her prerogative only reluctantly and rejecting much of the new world springing up around her. As a result, the Victorian era died long before the woman who gave it its name.

Nevertheless, after her marriage to Albert, Victoria had rarely let her petulant, reactionary instincts get the better of her. She was aware of her own stormy nature and strove to contain it, often through prayer. It was this most human of traits that proved to be her most endearing. Like most of us, but unlike many of her predecessors, she understood her faults and tried to mend them. For that she has been remembered ever since with surprising but genuine affection.

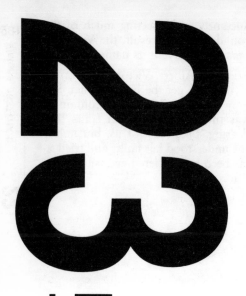

23 Edward VII, 1901–10

Parents: Queen Victoria and Prince Albert

Born: 9 November 1841, Buckingham Palace

Died: 6 May 1910, Buckingham Palace

Marriage: Princess Alexandra of Denmark, 1863

Children:
(i) Albert, Duke of Clarence, b.1864
(ii) King George V, b.1865
(iii) Louise, Princess Royal, b.1867
(iv) Victoria, b.1868
(v) Maud, Queen of Norway, b.1869
(vi) John, b.1871

Edward VII is often said, correctly, to have been Britain's first truly constitutional monarch. The accolade – if that is what it is – cannot be given to his mother. Victoria might have ended her life as the apex of the ceremonial side of the constitution, but that had not been her intention at accession. Edward took things on from where Victoria had left them, relishing the theatrical aspect of monarchy far more than she had done. Nevertheless, he still exercised some political influence, especially in foreign affairs, and once or twice during his reign his role was crucial (see p.191). These intrusions, though veering towards unconstitutionality, caused little resentment because their effects were generally beneficial. Moreover, it was difficult to take against so warm-hearted a man as Edward.

The British had come to like Queen Victoria largely for what she represented; her son they liked for what he was. Edward VII was indeed the most genial of monarchs. With the passage of time his weaknesses – a fondness for food, wine and sex – have become less heinous, while his good qualities – essential kindness, sociability and an unwillingness to pre-judge – have gained in appeal. He has not changed but the yardstick by which he is measured has. Fat and frankly pleasure-seeking, Edward is more at home in the late twentieth century than he had been in his own more censorious era.

The rebel

British monarchs had for centuries specialized in making their children's lives a misery, and Victoria, thanks in large part to her husband, continued the tradition with her eldest son. To be fair to both parents, the problem was more than simply poor parenting. The difficulty of raising a royal child in the modern age persists to this day. In earlier times, when the institution of monarchy was largely unchallenged and instruction by governesses and private tutors was the norm among the upper classes, the education of a member of the royal family was comparatively straightforward. Princes and, if they were lucky, princesses were educated in a similar manner to other members of their social strata.

By the later nineteenth century, those planning the education of the next generation of royalty faced a difficult dilemma: how to teach a future monarch about the more egalitarian world while at the same time preventing them from becoming immersed in it. The mystery of monarchy had to be preserved alongside a sensitivity to the subjects' needs and aspirations. Not sending royal children to school helped maintain their distance but left them out of touch with reality; sending them to school brought them more into touch with reality but drew back the curtain covering their exclusivity. Educating royal children at elitist private schools partly solved the problem, but it was at best a compromise.

There was no compromise in the education planned for the future Edward VII. Prince Albert knew that the crown's influence depended on the degree to which it was respected and admired, and he set out to make his son the most respected and admired young man in Europe, if not the whole world. The anxious, well-meaning father forgot that a carving, no matter how carefully shaped, will always reflect the stone from which it has been hewn, and Edward was made of very different material from his father. He picked up languages easily enough (though he always spoke English with a German accent), for he had a good ear and memory. But the sensitive child loathed the long hours spent sitting alone at a table listening to the earnest dronings of his tutor. Perhaps suffering from ADHD (Attention-Deficit Hyperactivity Disorder), he reacted with tantrums and wild fits of temper. He was beaten and subjected to other cruelties intended to tame his 'selfishness', all to no effect. Already Victoria was harshly labelling her disappointing first born 'weak' and 'idle'.

After the tortures of the schoolroom, from which he was permitted only occasional forays into the outside world – carefully chaperoned by older men of unsullied virtue – Edward was given spells at both Oxford and Cambridge Universities, and a time in the army. It was during the latter, based in Ireland, that a group of fellow officers introduced him to the accommodating actress Nellie Clifden. News of their son's 'fall' rocked Victoria and Albert to their puritanical cores, and led to the queen blaming Edward for hastening his father's death.

Tum Tum

Marriage, Victoria decided, was the only way to keep the errant Bertie on the straight and narrow. Holy matrimony had proved such a delight for her dear departed Albert and herself, so surely it would be the same for her son and stop him wandering off after further Nellie Clifdens? With the help of her eldest daughter Vicky, now resident in Germany, the queen scoured Europe for a suitable Protestant princess. The Prince of Wales, who insisted that he marry 'for love', was permitted a say in the matter too.

The eventual choice was Princess Alexandra (Alix) of Denmark. The couple met, clearly felt attracted to each other, and the marriage was duly celebrated with spectacular pomp and exuberance in March 1863. The 18-year-old Alix became pregnant almost immediately and over the next seven years presented her husband with three sons and three daughters. Everyone agreed that the Princess of Wales was a charming young woman, pretty yet elegant and demure. The queen took to her immediately. Unfortunately, Edward's passion for his new wife did not endure as Victoria had hoped it would. Alix was good looking but neither lively nor bright – some even thought her intellectually retarded. Moreover, she was lamentably deaf. Before too long her zestful husband was drawn to more sparkling pastures.

Having failed to live up to his parents' expectations of him, Edward had decided that he might as well enjoy himself. He ate five hearty meals a day, many of them comprising numerous courses, and was soon swelling embarrassingly around the middle. Behind his back his friends referred to him as 'Tum Tum'. The prince tried to make a virtue of his girth by starting the fashion of leaving the bottom button of the waistcoat undone. Fine wines always adorned his table and brandy and other spirits were never far from reach, although Bertie himself was never regarded as an inordinately heavy drinker. Tobacco, on the other hand, he could not do without: ten or so of the fattest Havana cigars and twenty cigarettes a day was his normal ration.

Bertie's more active pleasures included the theatre, with which he was obsessed, and shooting, which he enjoyed immensely. When paying a state visit to Egypt he was far happier taking pot shots at Nile crocodiles than traipsing around ancient ruins. He also loved good clothes, horse racing, yachting, cards and all forms of gambling. Then there were his women. The list of his amours reads like a roll call at a girls' school and will probably never be finalized. It includes the famous actress Sarah Bernhardt, the lovely and ambitious Lillie Langtry, the radical aristocrat Daisy Brooke, the easy-going Cora Pearl and Edward's final haven, the wise, sympathetic Alice Keppel. Sexual and other adventures twice brought 'Edward the Caresser' (as Lytton Strachey dubbed him) into court, and he was implicated in a number of divorce cases. The less respectable press, to the horror of the prince's ancient mother, had great fun with his peccadilloes: between the Prince of Wales and Lillie Langtry, ran one quip, there was absolutely nothing – not even a sheet.

At first glance all this self-indulgence looks distinctly Hanoverian, as if Edward had fallen into just the sort of life his father had so patently wished to protect him from. But Edward was different from his uncouth ancestors. He was civilized, gentlemanly, discrete, loyal and acutely aware of the changing world in which he lived. Although paternalist in outlook and certainly no political ally of the socialists, he had slept with some of them and knew what they were on about. 'Tax motors,' he once said, 'tax the rich, but never the poor. Never tax the poor man's food.'[30]

Ambassador royal

Victoria kept her son on the fringes of domestic government until her very last years. Edward served on Royal Commissions but he never saw cabinet papers. He did, however, find an enjoyable role for himself as a roving ambassador for his country. His first visit, to the US and Canada, was a great success. In the States he adopted the name 'Lord Renfrew' in order not to draw attention to himself. No one was deceived. Travelling in luxury trains specially provided by the federal government, he passed through Chicago (from where he went shooting), St Louis and Baltimore on his way to Washington DC, where he met President James Buchanan and his very pretty niece. In New York he drove down a Broadway thronged with cheering crowds. Finally, after quick visits to Bunker's Hill and Harvard, he set sail for home. Even Victoria was impressed, writing to her eldest daughter that Bertie, 'was immensely popular everywhere he went and really deserves the highest praise.'[31]

The North American visit set the tone for further popular tours to the Near East, Ireland (several times), India, Germany (twice), Greece (twice), Russia, Scandinavia, Portugal, Italy (including a controversial call on the Vatican) and, momentously, France. As well as these formal visits the Prince frequently cruised the Mediterranean and took annual holidays in Biarritz.

The greatest triumph, and the one political act for which Edward is remembered, was his visit to France in 1903. Anglo-

French relations had been at a dangerously low ebb for some time. Five years previously, when forces from the two countries confronted each other at Fashoda on the upper reaches of the Nile and neither was prepared to stand aside, there was a distinct possibility of armed conflict. Edward, now in the third year of his reign, knew this. On arrival he delivered a speech (in good French) that was full of admiration for his hosts, their country and its glorious traditions. It had long been his desire, he continued, to see a warm friendship established between France and his own country.

The words were noted with approval, but the ordinary Parisians had yet to be convinced. When Edward entered the capital voices in the crowd yelled 'Vive Fashoda!' at his carriage. There were even cries of 'Vive Jeanne d'Arc!' Unruffled, 'bon Edouard' smiled and waved back. At the theatre that evening the king broke more ice with his generous attention to a famous French actress whom he had seen in London. Parisian society was impressed. Further public appearances and utterances followed, each one more warmly received than the last until the crowds were gleefully shouting 'Vive Teddy!' whenever the royal party drove by. None of Edward's illustrious ancestors had conquered France so swiftly, so cheaply or so easily as he did on the famous visit of 1903.

The royal triumph led to the compact known as the 'Entente Cordiale'. By its terms Britain and France agreed to settle their colonial differences. Further talks and arrangements followed, tying the two countries closer together in what looked increasingly like a military alliance. In recent years, studying the causes of the First World War which broke out in 1914, scholars have questioned the wisdom of Edward's French wooing. By drawing Britain and France closer together, they point out, the king was adding to Germany's feeling of nervous isolation. (Edward did not get on with his nephew, the German Emperor William II.) Within ten years the German people's fears had assumed such a proportion that they were prepared to risk war rather than be gradually suffocated, as they saw it, by the overwhelming might of France, Russia and Britain.

King at last

Edward was almost 60 when he finally inherited his mother's crown. His accession brought a sense of relief, the old queen having had too much of a cloying past about her, and Edward seized his chance with an energy that belied his bulk and age. He brought glamour and a sense of fun to his position. The dull but worthy monarchy had given way to a bright but distinctly less moral one, and the change was welcome. The king adored his starring role, always acting royal even if he did not behave so. He was producer and set-builder, too, reinstating a lavish state opening of parliament, widening the Mall, rebuilding Admiralty Arch and tidying up Buckingham Palace.

As king Edward continued his life much as before, travelling abroad and moving regularly around his palaces and stately homes, he took a close interest in domestic politics as well as foreign affairs. Two matters in particular, both military, benefited from his support. Against opposition from conservatives and those keen to reduce the armed forces' budget, he supported Viscount Haldane's army reforms and the reorganization of the Royal Navy by Sir John Fisher. Both left Britain better prepared for war in 1914 than it might otherwise have been.

Edward did not welcome the Liberal landslide victory of 1906, nor did he approve of the string of reforming measures the subsequent government introduced. He was distinctly unimpressed by Chancellor of the Exchequer David Lloyd George's 'People's Budget' of 1909. When the House of Lords dusted down its constitutional rights and refused to pass the budget into law (it was ages since the Lords had dared reject a financial bill), Prime Minister Herbert Asquith asked the king to create sufficient Liberal peers to allow the bill to pass. Edward refused.

It looked like 1832 all over again (see p.172). There was, however, a key difference. While William IV had been obliged to back down over the Great Reform Bill, Edward VII never took so firm a stand as his predecessor. He did not say he would never create sufficient Liberal peers, only that he would not do so immediately. First, he demanded, Asquith should seek re-election on so major an issue. If the electorate backed the government in its struggle with the upper house, the king would do his duty and back it too. It was not an unreasonable line to take.

Edward did not live to see the outcome of the confrontation. On the afternoon of 6 May 1906 he suffered a series of heart attacks at Buckingham Palace and was carried to an armchair. In this position, with the queen's permission, he was visited by close friends. Among them was Mrs Keppel. He uttered his last, delightfully appropriate words on being told that one of his horses had just won at Kempton Park: 'I am very glad'.[32] A few hours later he was dead. His funeral, the final pageant of a dying era, was attended by no less than nine kings.

24

George V, 1910–36

Parents: Edward VII and
  Alexandra of Denmark
Born: 3 June 1865,
  Marlborough House, London
Died: 20 January 1936,
  Sandringham, Norfolk
Marriage: Mary of Teck, 1893
Children: (i) King Edward VIII,
          b.1894
        (ii) King George VI,
          b.1895
        (iii) Mary, Princess
          Royal, b.1897
        (iv) Henry, Duke of
          Gloucester,
          b.1900
        (v) George, Duke of
          Kent, b.1902
        (vi) John, b.1905

George V established the style of twentieth-century British monarchy. Like most of his subjects, he was a simple person caught up in troubled times. He struggled, along with millions of others, to make sense of what was going on: the wars and revolutions, strikes and depression, technological transformation and social upheaval. Seeking security, he clung to what he had been brought up to recognize as right and decent, setting an example of middle-class virtues which millions found quietly reassuring.

George's lifestyle reconstructed the 'domestic' or 'family' monarchy initiated by Victoria and Albert, in which the role of the crown was as much social as political. In important parliamentary and constitutional matters the king made little effort to press his own views but rather attempted to tune in to the conservative consensus and see that it prevailed. He encouraged people to think of the 'royal family' rather than just the monarch. This reflected the rising status of women, the increasing attention being paid to children (as birth control made each one more precious), and the media-fed obsession with a near-mythical family life.

This new monarchy brought difficulties of its own. The twentieth-century middle-class family was a private institution whose activities went on largely behind closed doors. In accordance with this view, the British press (with the fawning BBC following suit) was far more respectful of royalty than it had been a century earlier. Paradoxically, therefore, the royal family become more remote as it became less exalted. Furthermore, George and his queen established a form of monarchy that others could not or would not follow. His son and heir opted out altogether; his second son managed to stay on the straight and narrow, as did his granddaughter Elizabeth, although her family did not. Thus by the end of the century Queen Elizabeth II was living according to precepts – her grandfather's – that those around her were unwilling or unable to uphold. It was not a happy situation.

At sea

George was the second son of Edward Prince of Wales and Princess Alexandra. His elder brother was Albert Victor, known to everyone but his mother as 'Eddie'. The two boys had little in common. Where George was dutiful, Eddie was wayward; where George was diligent, Eddie was slothful; where George was short ('the sprat'), Eddie was tall (the 'herring'). It would be hard to conceive of two such different boys – and conception may be the explanation.

Although few words have been uttered against the virtue of Alexandra Princess of Wales, it might not be mere coincidence that the Waleses were staying in Elsinore, Denmark at the time of George's conception (September 1864). They were there to meet the Russian Grand Duke Nicholas, brother of the future Tsar Nicholas II, who was getting engaged to Alexandra's sister. If Alexandra and the Grand Duke had indeed slept together, it would explain the uncanny likeness of George V to Tsar Nicholas II.

Reacting to his own harsh upbringing, the Prince of Wales paid little heed to his sons' early education. Alexandra was more than happy to concur with their happy idleness. Victoria, however, was not. The moment their grandma heard that Eddie and George were not being brought up properly – i.e. rigorously – she demanded that an earnest tutor be hired and the boys set to task. George, the dutiful one, knuckled under and made a model (if not too gifted) pupil. Eddie, lazy, awkward and remarkably dim, was a teacher's nightmare.

In 1877 the boy's father ended the ignominy of the inkwell by sending both boys – George to keep an eye on Eddie – to the naval training ship *HMS Britannia*. Here and in their subsequent naval careers they were supposed to be treated like ordinary recruits – a far-sighted request for the day. Needless to say, they were not. They were protected from the cruelties and discomforts of Victorian naval life, and George was promoted more rapidly than was usual and far more rapidly than his modest talents deserved. Eddie, meanwhile, left the service to continue his education as heir apparent. It proved fruitless as, on 14 January 1892, he died suddenly of pneumonia. (That was the official line, anyway. Another option, since disproved, was that he had died of gonorrhoea contracted while in the Navy. Far more sinister, it has also been suggested that he was poisoned to prevent so hopeless an individual coming to the throne.)

The death that saved the monarchy from acute embarrassment filled George with energy-sapping trepidation. Gone in a trice were his dreams of a quiet life afloat, showing the flag in exotic locations and enjoying jolly larks with his sailor friends. In their place was the daunting prospect of being King of Great Britain and Emperor of India. The thought of the responsibility that accompanied the crown still encircling the stern and daunting brows of his grandmother was enough to make a man ill. George was sent to the South of France to recover.

A pillar of support

Although he compared favourably with the deceased Eddie, George was by no means over-endowed with traditional kingly qualities. He was not imaginative nor in any way academically gifted; he would be the first monolingual British monarch since Plantagenet times. As a public speaker he was competent but no more, nor did his dinner-party conversation sparkle. His humour was schoolboyish. An attractive personality might have compensated for these shortcomings, but unfortunately George scored below average on the charisma scale too.

As it turned out, George's lack of fizz did not much matter as by the twentieth century the sovereign's role had become almost entirely ceremonial. It was not important whether or not he understood the subtleties of cabinet papers and other documents. All that was required was that he read them, which he always did, and when appropriate add his signature on the dotted line. In fact, the qualities that George possessed in abundance – diligence, dignity and a sense of duty – were ideal for his position. A bit more wit might have helped. Too much, though, like too much intelligence or imagination, might easily have spoilt his aptitude for what had become for the most part an exceedingly tedious job.

Besides, George had a useful ally to interpret where he did not understand and hold his hand when he felt everything was getting too much for him. She was his wife, Queen Mary. Physically bigger than her husband but still frightened of him, Mary (universally known as 'May') was a great-granddaughter of George III. She had been raised in Britain as a minor member of the royal family, but had spent several years touring Europe after mounting debts had forced her parents to move abroad for a while. At the age of 24 she became engaged to the lethargic Prince Eddie, only to lose him six weeks later. After a suitable interval the practical young woman let it be known that she would be happy to exchange one brother for another. George proposed in 1893 and the couple were married at a ceremony of glorious splendour on 6 July.

May fitted perfectly into George's concept of what the monarchy should be. Physically impressive, her shyness and lack of warmth made her appear all the more regal on state occasions. She was a good organizer and a more perceptive reader than her husband, although by no means intellectual. Her gaffes could be painful – she once asked slum dwellers from the East End of London why on earth they lived where they did – or just embarrassing: she was heard to ask a Tory candidate at election time how 'we' were doing. Also embarrassing was her passion for jewels and other objets d'art. When visiting a country house she would take favoured pieces away with her when she left, apparently in all innocence. Many years later Queen Elizabeth II made a point of returning as much of this royal loot as she could. For all her frigidity and dottiness, May adored her George and offered him a pillar of support that was sometimes sensible and always affectionate.

Sadly, this affection was not readily shown towards the couple's children. George could be quick tempered and harsh. His cool, lofty wife had little time for mewling infants and only slightly more for them when they were older. The eldest child, the future Edward VIII, emerged as an insecure child-man whose behaviour shook the institution he represented right down to its Anglo-Saxon roots. Alfred Frederick, the future George VI, matured into a shy, stammering man of little confidence or consequence. His brothers Henry and George were, respectively, a drunken wastrel and a cocaine addict. The youngest boy, Prince John, suffered from epilepsy and was kept away from public view until his early death.

Baptism of fire

Following the death of Queen Victoria, George and May were duly created Prince and Princess of Wales. In this capacity their most notable contribution to the royal tapestry was making state visits. They began with Australia and New Zealand, proceeded to Vienna after Edward VII's coronation, then sailed off to India in 1905. They returned via Egypt and Corfu, and were off again shortly after arriving home, this time to Norway. The trips were regarded as successes, the prince behaving with admirable decorum and tact, his wife with elegant puissance. The year after he became king, George made his most spectacular overseas visit when he sailed to India, donned a new £60,000 crown, and was crowned emperor in a 'Durbar' (reception) of unsurpassed magnificence. Nevertheless, George always said he disliked foreign trips. A stickler for detail and routine, he found travel unsettling. He was much happier sitting at home with his stamp collection or ploughing meticulously through his copy of *The Times*, printed on linen specially for him.

The death of Edward VII was hardly a shock – given his lifestyle, the wonder was that he had lived so long. That said, he could hardly have died at a less fortunate moment. Inexperienced and lacking in confidence, the 45-year-old George V took over the throne in the middle of a most serious constitutional crisis. There was no way the new sovereign could sidestep the issue, either (see p.192). After the House of Lords' rejection of Lloyd George's 'People's Budget', the Liberal party resolved to curb the power of the upper chamber by statute. To do so it needed to get its Parliament Bill through the Conservative Lords. This would require more Liberal peers. Edward VII had said he was prepared to create those peers if the Liberals won a general election in which Lords reform was the central issue. His son, taking careful advice, agreed to do the same.

The result of the second election of 1910 (the first had been fought on the issue of the budget) was not conclusive. The Conservative Party won the most votes but the Liberals got the same number of seats. This might have put the king in an impossible position had not the Irish Nationalist and Labour Parties also declared in favour of the Bill, giving the pro-reformers a substantial majority. In these circumstances the king, convinced that he was acting as his father would have done, declared himself willing to create 250 new Liberal peers. Rather than embarrass their monarch, the Conservatives backed down and the Bill went through both houses.

War

George's baptism of fire over the House of Lords' reform was but the first of many extremely taxing problems he faced during his reign. A more forceful man might have mishandled them, but on each one George took advice, effaced his own opinions and did what he believed was his duty to the nation as a whole. It was exemplary constitutional monarchy.

The First World War brought the crown into the political arena on a number of issues. To do his bit for morale, the king made hundreds of visits to hospitals and factories at home and crossed to the front in France on several occasions. Although safely out of the reach of enemy artillery, on one trip he managed to break his pelvis when he fell from his horse. Queen May did her bit for the war effort too, supporting charities and women's war work. It was also announced that in order to help in the wartime economy drive the king had become teetotal. In fact he was known to warm himself with the occasional tipple after meals. His unflinching backing for General Haig was more controversial and it may have helped keep in power a man whose tactics and judgement have been seriously challenged. Both Haig and the king were deeply Christian, the former believing he had a God-given mission to lead his country to victory.

The global conflict brought further vexations. The first concerned the royal family's name, Saxe-Coburg-Gotha. A more German-sounding appellation would be harder to imagine and it raised more than a few eyebrows the moment war broke out. George was slow to realize that his heritage (he had scarcely a drop of British blood in his body) caused suspicion and irritation, and when it was pointed out to him he was equally slow to do anything about it. Indeed, throughout the war the royal family maintained clandestine contacts with their relatives on the other side of no-man's land. Appearances had to be kept up, though, and in 1917 the king heeded advice and changed his family name. The preferred option was 'Windsor', after the favoured royal residence in Berkshire.

Shortly afterwards an equally tricky issue arose when the Russian tsar Nicholas II was forced to abdicate and, a few months later, the Bolsheviks (communists) seized power. Nicholas asked for asylum in Britain. George and May wanted to grant it but Lloyd George, now prime minister, told them that such a move would not go down well with the Labour Party and its working-class supporters. The labouring masses, who made up the bulk of British soldiers at the front, were broadly sympathetic to the Bolshevik cause. The tsar's request was therefore turned down. When the Russian royal family were murdered the following year, George was smitten with guilt and feebly regretted not taking a firmer line with his prime minister on such a personal matter.

Crisis after crisis

Peace did not end George's difficulties. First, he had to accept the independence of the Irish Republic (Eire). On the death of Conservative Prime Minister, Bonar Law, the king had to chose his successor because the Conservatives had no internal mechanism for doing so. In 1924 George shook hands with Ramsay Macdonald, the first Labour prime minister, and found to his surprise that he liked the man and found him 'quite straight'. Two years later George may have drawn on his experience with Macdonald when he asked the Conservative government of Stanley Baldwin not to overreact to the General Strike. Baldwin was well advised and the strike eventually ended without notable violence.

After a bout of very serious illness in 1928, when it was feared he would die, the king welcomed Ramsay Macdonald back to Downing Street the following spring. Two years later, with the country ravaged by the Great Depression, George begged Macdonald not to resign but to form a National Government with the Liberals and Conservatives. This he duly did, though it met with little success in tackling the nation's troubles. It is worth noting that governments of all persuasions were remarkably generous to George over financial matters. The civil list was enhanced and the Crown allowed to operate on an almost tax-free basis for the first time

Also in the early 1930s the king gave his assent to the Bill that removed Westminster's powers over the Dominions. This gave the sovereign a new and unique role as the only formal link between the Commonwealth's self-governing nations and the mother country. Later George signed the Government of India Act, granting that country a degree of self-government. It is a measure of the brevity of British imperial grandeur that a man born before Victoria had been created Empress of India should at the end of his life have accepted the necessity of loosening Britain's grasp on the jewel in its imperial crown.

Sunset

George had never fully recovered from his illness of 1928. Now well into his sixties, he spent much of his time on the famous royal stamp collection (largely British Empire, of course) and worrying about his wayward eldest son, Edward Prince of Wales. At Christmas 1932 he established a tradition by delivering a Christmas wireless message to his subjects. The first was written for him by Rudyard Kipling. In this as in so many other ways the fledgling BBC proved an invaluable ally of the monarchy in its wish to convey an image of probity, sobriety, patriotism, dignity, duty and sound family values. Three years later 'Grandpa England', as his granddaughter Elizabeth called him, celebrated his Silver Jubilee. The wildly expensive pageant, although heavily retrospective, was well received even by a country in the depths of depression.

Depression overcame the king, too, at the end of 1934 when he heard of the death of his favourite sister Victoria. The following January he caught pneumonia. At this stage, with an extraordinary disregard of the law, even the king's death was stage-managed. When it was clear the end was nigh, his doctor, Lord Dawson, administered a lethal injection that terminated the king's life in time for his demise to be announced in the morning papers rather than the less prestigious evening editions. Thus Dawson could make his famous announcement with perfect certainty: 'The King's life is moving peacefully towards its close.'[33] His Majesty's last words were also carefully chosen – 'How goes the Empire?' – although the more prosaic, 'Bugger Bognor!' is probably more accurate. The queen, too, joined in the charade of Victorian sentimentality when she wrote in her diary: 'At five to twelve my darling husband passed peacefully away...The sunset of his death tinged the whole sky.'[34]

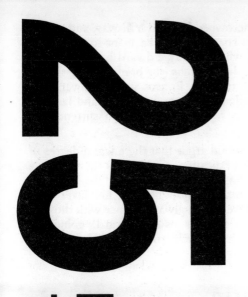

25 Edward VIII, 1936

Parents: George V and
 Mary of Teck
Born: 23 June 1894, White
 Lodge, Richmond, Surrey
Died: 28 May 1972, Paris
Marriage: Wallis Simpson
 (née Warfield), 1937
No children

The brief reign of the uncrowned Edward VIII was, and still is, a source of great drama. The only adult bachelor to ascend the throne since William II, who was gay, Edward had the second shortest reign of all English monarchs (the briefest being that of Edward V, the elder of the two Princes in the Tower) and became the first voluntarily to abdicate. Richard II and James II are generally agreed to have been coerced into surrendering their crowns.

Yet there are those who would argue that there was a degree of coercion about Edward's abdication, too. Nor is that the only point of controversy. It has been suggested that the king had become *persona non grata* because he and his lover held political sympathies that were strongly at variance with those of the government. Whatever the reasons for Edward's going, the incident brought the British monarchy to its lowest point in the twentieth century.

A people's prince?

It is reported that George V once said, 'My father was frightened of his mother; I was frightened of my father, and I am damned well going to see to it that my children are frightened of me.'[35] As it turned out, the future Edward VIII was not particularly frightened of his father, but the remark is an alarming indication of George V's limitations as a parent: if Edward did not fear him, he did not like him much either. Thus the eldest son of an aloof, aggressive father and a cool, distant mother came almost inevitably to perpetuate the royal family's notoriously sad dysfunctionality.

Prince Edward, who cried whenever taken into the daunting presence of his great-grandmother (much to her annoyance), was the first heir to the throne to be sent to school unchaparoned. From the naval training establishment at Osborne he went to France to learn the language then to Oxford to be introduced to the world of scholarship. He did not much care for it. By this time, aged 18, his distinctive personality was apparent.

If George V was beginning to look very much like a relic from the Victorian past, his eldest son was a pointer to the future. His style was relaxed and obtrusively casual. He liked fast cars and fast women – nothing very unusual in that – but he also seemed to take interest in ordinary people. He talked sympathetically with them and said he wanted to do what he could to help them. During the Depression he even floated a paternalistic back-to-work scheme. Some of his ill-thought-out remarks about the plight of the poor and unemployed implied criticism of the government.

This is where opinion on Edward divides. The traditional line is that his head was turned by the adulation his good looks and easy manner attracted at home and abroad, so that he came to believe the applause was for him personally rather than for the attractive representative of an institution. This had a disastrous effect on his damaged personality: raised in cold neglect, he had such low self-esteem that he was known to cry out in an anguish of self-loathing, 'I do feel such a bloody little shit!'[36] Grasping at adulation as a child does chocolate, he formed a distorted idea of his own importance and influence. Perhaps, somewhere at the back of his mind, he believed he might be able to do for Britain what Adolf Hitler was doing for Germany.

The alternative view of Edward is kinder, more sentimental even. His popularity and dislike of the establishment were genuine signs that here, at last, was a member of the royal family who thought as the masses thought, someone who as king would be able to develop the monarchy into a thoroughly modern institution, shorn of all its pomp, snobbery and aloofness. His abdication, forced upon him by those determined to preserve the status quo, left the royal family stuck half a century behind the rest of the nation.

'The Fort'

When war broke out in 1914 Edward asked to see active service. The opportunity was denied him because, it was explained, his capture would give the enemy an invaluable bargaining counter. Thwarted, the prince had to make do with staff jobs in the Grenadier Guards. During the 1920s, on Lloyd George's suggestion, he made numerous state visits to Australia, New Zealand, Canada, the USA, India and the Caribbean. Everywhere he went he was greeted by rapturous crowds and press coverage far more flattering than anything his parents had received on their more staid overseas tours. Thus was born the first British royal media star.

Edward was a fine sportsman. He rode in steeplechases, until George V forbade it after a nasty fall, and he became the first royal to learn to fly. In 1930, his father gave him Fort Belvedere, an estate near Sunningdale, Berkshire, that had been in the crown's possession for years. The prince developed the grounds, tidied the neglected gardens and took an interest in rose growing. He also made 'the Fort' a humming hub of fast and fashionable society. Among the most frequent visitors were Ernest and Wallis Simpson. Ernest was a well-dressed, well-balanced but somewhat dull Harvard graduate who had come to live in England. The plain but lively Wallis was a well-known socialite who had worked her way up the social ladder from what were later wickedly referred to as, 'much seduced circumstances.'[37] She was Ernest's second wife, and he her second husband. By 1935 she was considering taking a third.

Wallis Simpson

In accordance with his wish to be remembered as 'Edward the Innovator', one of Edward VIII's first acts on becoming king was to order economies on the royal estates. After that innovation went not much further than being infuriatingly irresponsible with governing papers, not bothering to look at them and leaving them lying about the Fort, and making sympathetic remarks when visiting the depressed steel and coal communities of South Wales. The public, however, were little bothered. Fed the usual sycophantic diet of royal half-truths and trivia from the BBC and the press, they were more interested in the king's person. He was 41 and still unmarried, and since he was known to be fond of the ladies many of his subjects speculated innocently that he might shortly marry and start a family.

In 1936 the news from abroad was worrying. The previous year Adolf Hitler, the German Chancellor, had broken the Treaty of Versailles by reintroducing conscription for an army of half a million men. His Nazi Party had also intensified its racist campaign against the Jews. Hitler now went further. He again overrode Versailles by sending troops into the demilitarized Rhineland and used the Berlin Olympics to broadcast the supposed glories of Nazism. Towards the end of the year he allied with Mussolini, the fascist dictator of Italy. At the time both were assisting the right-wing General Franco in Spain's bloody civil war. Britain's National Government, headed by Stanley Baldwin, responded to the fascist threat by instigating moderate rearmament.

It was against this gloomy background that news broke of the king's wish to marry Wallis Simpson, with whom he was completely obsessed. The relationship was a complex one: an intriguing liaison between a feeble man of little body hair who feared he was infertile as a result of childhood mumps, and a powerful, dominating woman whom lesbians found highly alluring. In Wallis the king found both a mother and a dominatrix, whose toe nails he delighted to paint and to whom he wrote childish notes. The lop-sided affair was also tinged with masochism – if he annoyed her, she would make him cry. It is possible that Edward was telling the truth when he said that he did not make love with Wallis until after they were married; one wonders just how much he did thereafter, too.

Wallis's interest in Edward is difficult to fathom. Whatever her motives, she was interested enough in him and bored enough with her husband to be in the midst of divorce proceedings. The government had known of the royal affair for some time but had, with a combination of threats and pleadings, persuaded the British media not to mention it. Overseas, where Baldwin's censorship could not reach, the story had been common knowledge for months. The prime minister, his government, the great majority of MPs, the Archbishop of Canterbury (Edward was Supreme Governor of the Church of England), and leading figures in several of the Dominions were strongly opposed to their king marrying Mrs Simpson.

Compromise was suggested in the form of a morganatic marriage (where the wife, of lower rank than the husband, forfeits for herself and her children all right to inherit his titles and so forth) but rejected when it became clear that the necessary legislation would almost certainly not be forthcoming. How could the king, head of the Anglican communion, marry a twice divorced woman when his church did not sanction divorce? It soon became obvious to Edward that he had to choose between his crown and marriage to Wallis Simpson. It was also clear that a decision needed to be made quickly to halt the almost daily erosion of the crown's prestige.

Edward had always had reservations about being king. It is possible that subconsciously he saw his love for Wallis as a means of escape from the stuffy life into which he was being inexorably dragged. Thus, on 11 December 1936, less than a year after his accession, he delivered these famous words (touched up by Winston Churchill) to his astounded, divided people:

> A few hours ago I discharged my last duty as King and Emperor, and now that I have been succeeded by my

brother, the Duke of York, my first words must be to declare my allegiance to him. This I do with all my heart.

...you must believe me when I tell you that I have found it impossible to carry the heavy burden of responsibility and to discharge my duties as King as I would wish to do without the help and support of the woman I love.[38]

The Duke and Duchess of Windsor

Ever since that momentous day there has been much speculation about what really happened. The king was still popular and parliament sovereign – between them they could have overcome all obstacles and reached a solution that did not involve abdication. The fact is the government did not want to reach an accommodation: they wanted Wallis Simpson and Edward Windsor out. Why?

To begin with, the king had already annoyed the political establishment. His handling of confidential papers had been scandalous. He never read and rarely listened. With his remarks on unemployment and fascism, which he openly admired, he had overstepped the mark of what was acceptable from a constitutional monarch. His own private secretary had written frankly, 'The best thing that could happen to him would be for him to break his neck.'[39]

Wallis Simpson was an equally serious liability. Baldwin had evidence that even before the abdication she had tired of the obsessive, fawning attentions of the king. She had other sexual relationships, with a car mechanic and a duke. She was also friendly with the German Ambassador to Britain, Joachim von Ribbentrop. Much of the evidence against Wallis did not come into the public domain until long after her death and a good deal remains to be uncovered. From what we do know, however, it is obvious why Baldwin and others in the know regarded the prospect of King Edward and Queen Wallis with nothing short of horror.

Edward and Wallis were created Duke and Duchess of Windsor, given a handsome pension and went to live in France. Here they were married in 1937. The couple then travelled extensively, on one occasion meeting Hitler and the rest of the Nazi hierarchy. Their relations were cordial. The Duke did himself no favours being photographed giving the Nazi salute. Later, when contemplating the invasion and conquest of Britain, the Führer drew up plans for Edward to be puppet king of his cross-Channel province. Marriage did not divert Wallis from her unwise ways. She tormented her lap-dog husband with infidelity and during the war was once again in communication with von Ribbentrop.

When France fell in 1940, the Windsors moved to Madrid then Lisbon. Winston Churchill, uneasy about what he was learning of their Nazi sympathies, made Edward Governor of the Bahamas and insisted that he and his wife take up residence there. After the war they returned to Paris. Here they continued their sad, empty existence, haunted by memories and regrets. As Wallis had come to realize too late, 'You can't abdicate and eat it.'[40]

The couple made a few, strained visits to England, notably for the funerals of King George VI and the Duke's mother, Queen Mary. In 1967 they were invited for the first time to make a public appearance when a memorial to Queen Mary was unveiled in the capital. Edward died in 1972 and Wallis 14 years later. At Frogmore, within the grounds of Windsor Castle, they were laid to rest beside each other. Eternal proximity was thought a fitting punishment for breaking the rules.

26

George VI, 1936–52

Parents: George V and
Queen Mary of Teck
Born: 14 December 1895,
Sandringham, Norfolk
Died: 6 February 1962,
Sandringham, Norfolk
Marriage: Elizabeth
Bowes-Lyon, 1923
Children: (i) Elizabeth II,
b.1926
  (ii) Princess
Margaret, b.1930

The abdication of Edward VIII struck at the heart of the British monarchy. It demonstrated in the brightest possible colours the flaw in its key principal, hereditary succession. It was left to George VI to pick up the pieces and, with an enormous amount of help from his wife, the government and the media, he did manage to get the institution back on its feet again. The Second World War, with its inevitable upsurge in patriotism, also helped.

The trouble was, the monarchy that George salvaged was that of his father: he rebuilt the neo-Gothic institution, brick by brick, as it had been at the time of the Great War. The result was an imposing and impressive edifice – but by the second half of the twentieth century one that was desperately out of date.

Bottom of the class

Queen Victoria did not immediately take to her great-grandson Albert Frederick Arthur George, the future George VI, because his birthday was the anniversary of the death of her long-lamented Albert. The child's name stood him in good stead, however, and by the time of her death the old queen had decided that the child with a long face and sticking out ears had broken the spell that had for so long hung over the date. The Empress of India was the last person little 'Bertie' managed to charm for a very long time.

Raised in the same strict regime as his wayward elder brother Edward, the sickly Bertie wilted. Nature had given him few talents, and those he had were soon belittled and bruised. Naturally left-handed, he was forced to write with his right. His knock-knees were painfully straightened by binding his legs in splints. His father's furious bellowings and obsession with tedious detail left him battered and bewildered.

The boy did try, however. He did his best to conform and strove most diligently for some academic or sporting recognition. It was desperately tough going: at Osborne he once came a notorious 68/68 in his year. At a time when the Royal Navy did not attract the brightest stars in the firmament, that was quite an achievement. Moreover, as was the tradition in boys' schools, dim pupils with no compensating talent were mercilessly bullied. Bertie was no exception. He was nicknamed 'bat lugs' because of his ears and pricked to see whether his blood really was blue. By his late teens he was a shy, twitching, stammering wreck with tissue-thin confidence.

Ill-treatment and failure drew out a less attractive side of Bertie's personality. Like his father and grandfather, with whom he shared a frustration at being unable to keep up with the quick minds he inevitably encountered, he had a furious temper. He shouted at servants and, later in life, would even hit his wife.[41] None of this, of course, got into the press.

Psychosomatic illness kept Bertie ashore for the early years of the First World War. He recovered in time to see action on *HMS Collingwood* during the Battle of Jutland, before joining the Royal Naval Air Service and then the newly-formed Royal Air force. He did not qualify as a pilot quickly enough to take part in wartime missions. As might be expected, neither did he win any prizes during the year he spent at Cambridge University with his brother Harry.

Duke of York

Bertie, like his father, was saved by his marriage. It was a close run thing. He first pursued Helen 'Poppy' Baring, a bright spark who was reputed to have slept with most of his brothers. A curt telegram from the queen soon put a stop to that one. The next object of his affection was Lady Elizabeth Bowes-Lyon, the attractive daughter of the Earl of Strathmore of Glamis Castle. The stuttering prince proposed to her twice before, on his third attempt, she finally accepted him. It is not clear why she did so. Marrying into the royal family had its obvious attractions, but Bertie was not everyone's dream husband. Perhaps it was the man's very vulnerability that drew Elizabeth to him? She was everything he was not: lively, quick, charming and good-looking – ideal for the 'power-behind-the-throne' role that she would play with such skill and relish. It is interesting, too, that Edward Prince of Wales had urged Elizabeth to accept his younger brother, perhaps recognizing that the couple would make more suitable occupants of what he called 'Buck House' than he himself.

The wedding of Bertie and Elizabeth in 1923 broke new ground. For fear of raising republican sentiment with displays of lavish expenditure, nineteenth-century royal weddings had been relatively low-key affairs. The Prince's was a deliberately spectacular exercise in pageantry. It took place in Westminster Abbey and was filmed for distribution around the Empire. (The Archbishop of Canterbury refused to let it be broadcast live lest the service be heard by those in inappropriate circumstances –

the wireless, after all, could be listened to while lying in bed, or worse.) The ceremony and its attendant procession attracted crowds numbering over a million, an early example of the British people's twentieth-century obsession with manufactured fairytale.

While Edward was around there was no chance of Bertie making much of a mark, even with Elizabeth at his side. He undertook the expected overseas tours and performed many routine tasks at home. His numerous visits to factories and similar enterprises, together with his position as president of the Industrial Welfare Society, earned him the unflattering soubriquet of 'the Industrial Duke'. Paradoxically for one at the apex of the class system, he sought to weaken Britain's mountainous social barriers by establishing the Duke of York's Summer Camps for boys from all walks of life. Where he was concerned, the barriers remained secure enough: his camp tent was equipped with a four-poster bed!

Albert becomes George

'I never wanted this to happen,' sobbed Bertie when it was clear he would have to take over the crown from his brother.[42] Perhaps no king ever ascended a throne more unwillingly or with a greater sense of his own unpreparedness and unworthiness than did the unfortunate Duke of York. He did not even have the confidence to be crowned in his own name. 'Bertie' all his life, in an attempt to recapture the monarchy of his father he took the throne as 'George'. He also made the change out of deference to Queen Victoria who, since her Albert had not been allowed the title of king, had insisted that no other Albert should be. Thus did Bertie defer to two dead hands even before his coronation. It was not an auspicious start.

The continued popularity in some quarters of Edward, the 'King Over the Water', did not make George's lot any easier. Nor did his brother's unhelpful advice, which he continued to telephone from abroad. Having endured the long, stuffy reign of George V, the British people had been eagerly looking forward to a bit of sparkle on the throne. That hope had been dashed almost as soon as it had been fulfilled and they were left with George V Mark Two: the same rigidity, formality and conservativeness. In some ways it was even worse – at least the king's father had been able to give a speech and had carried himself with dignity. George VI, sallow and nervous, could not even act the part of king.

Things could only get better, and they did. The coronation of George VI and the first British-born queen since Catherine Parr cost twice that of George V and May, and was excellently received. The Australian speech therapist Lionel Logue assisted the king with his stammer. The queen's vivacity and easy manner helped divert attention from her husband's deficiencies. Their two children, the Princesses Elizabeth and Margaret, enabled George to been presented as a decent family man, part of a happy yet dutiful team. Then came the war.

Recovery

George liked Neville Chamberlain and strongly and openly, perhaps too openly, endorsed his policy of appeasement. He was doubly sorry, therefore, when Chamberlain was forced to resign in May 1940. Churchill was not a welcome replacement and the king made it clear that he would have preferred Lord Halifax, even though he was a peer. George felt threatened by Churchill's forceful personality and was suspicious of his maverick career. Churchill had also blotted his copybook in George's eyes by supporting Edward VIII when he wished to marry Wallis Simpson. Churchill it was, though, and in a short time the king came to recognize that the choice had been the correct one.

Cowardice was not among George's faults. When invasion threatened in the summer of 1940 he announced that the royal family would not flee abroad but would stay in Britain and share the country's fate. Declaring himself prepared to fight to the end, he took out his service revolver for a few practice shots. While the two princesses moved between Balmoral and Windsor for their safety, the public was told that the king and queen would remain in Buckingham Palace. The loyal press trumpeted the significance of the gesture when the Palace received its first of several hits by enemy bombs, in September 1939. In fact the couple had been in no danger. Taking two cars, one for themselves and the official, armoured one for the queen's luggage, they drove to Windsor every evening. Similarly undermining of their fortitude was the revelation, made long after the war, that an escape route via Liverpool to the United States was always kept open for them in case Britain were invaded.

George had already crossed to France to review the British forces there (1939) and when the bombing started at home he made a point of touring the areas that had been hit. On their first visit to the East End of London after a raid, the King and Queen were subjected to a barrage of boos and jeers. The locality had suffered heavy casualties the previous night, partly as a result of the inadequate provision of air-raid shelters. Feelings ran high: how dare the king and queen, who had spent the night secure beneath a shield of concrete, come mincing around the rubble expressing lah-di-dah regret and telling people to bear up?

The outburst of popular discontent was not made public for years. Instead, the more favourable opinion of the king, which gradually developed as the war progressed, was said to have been there from its outbreak. There was no point in trying to elevate the king above Churchill, who usurped the traditional role of the monarch as the symbol of the nation. Instead, the press, the BBC and film deliberately cultivated the idea of the king and his family as being the living embodiment of high civilian morale. George was said to keep a pig to help with his family's food rations, for instance. (Although the royal family were declared to be on the same rations as their subjects, there is no evidence that this was adhered to. Meals at royal palaces remained substantial, and when the clothes ration was reduced to 48 points, the queen's remained at 1,277.) He provided photo opportunities to back up his resolute image, visiting North Africa in 1943 and the Normandy beaches ten days after D-Day. He also instituted the George Cross and George Medal for civilian gallantry. It was quite to be expected, therefore, that London's victory celebrations in 1945 centred around the balcony of Buckingham Palace.

Post war

George was not happy with post-war developments. He disliked the Labour Government of 1945 with its egalitarian principles, nationalization and high taxation. He was sad to see India go, depriving him of his title of emperor. It was with some relief, therefore, that he went on a tour to South Africa in 1947. In a new development, he was accompanied by Queen Elizabeth and their two daughters, then aged 21 and 17. This was the first time a royal overseas visit had been undertaken by an entire royal family.

It used to be said that the war effort had exhausted the king, leaving him weak and ill. In fact, the strain of the war had been no greater for George than it had been for anyone else –

considerably less than for many. What really undermined his health, precarious at the best of times, was cigarette smoking. Like his father and grandfather, he was hopelessly addicted to nicotine. He had a cancerous lung removed in 1952 and died the following year at the age of 56. After paying him respect for a dutiful reign, the nation turned eagerly to the future in expectation of a second and equally glorious Elizabeth Age.

27

Elizabeth II, 1952–

Parents: George VI and
Elizabeth Bowes-Lyon
Born: 21 April 1926,
Mayfair, London
Marriage: Philip Mountbatten,
Duke of Edinburgh, 1947
Children: (i) Charles, Prince
of Wales, b.1948
(ii) Anne, Princess
Royal, b.1950
(iii) Andrew, Duke of
York, b.1960
(iv) Edward, Earl of
Wessex, b.1964

Throughout the twentieth century the British monarchy made a virtue of being old-fashioned. This instinctive position was upheld by circumstance and inclination: the institution itself was time-encrusted, and upbringing and education ensured that its incumbents were all deeply conservative. They looked and behaved like hologram museum exhibits. It was their role, their very *raison d'être* to be living links with the past, icons of tradition and continuity. A forward-looking constitutional monarchy was a contradiction in terms.

Two world wars enhanced the sovereign's other function: acting as the focal point of patriotism. The very words of the national anthem – 'God Save the King/Queen' – reinforced the crown as the nation's rallying point in times of danger. Even Churchill in all his glory was relegated to a transitory flower beside the royal rose when he was voted out of office in 1945. For many millions the monarch was a proud nation personified.

This symbolic function was a relatively new development. It had arisen during the reign of Queen Victoria because the only logical alternative would have been abolition of the monarchy altogether. In other words, as it had done since the days of Henry VIII, the crown had mutated to suit its environment. Like any species, its survival depended on its ability to adapt.

New Britain

By the last quarter of the twentieth century Britain was changing rapidly. The monarchy, however, failed to react; or, when it tried to do so, it got it badly wrong. As a consequence the crown was mocked more viciously than at any time since William IV, and criticized more heavily than at any time since Victoria's prolonged depression over a century earlier.

The explanation for the nation and its monarchy getting out of kilter lay partly in the personalities of the leading members of the royal family, which are dealt with below, and partly in the way British society had moved on. First, the country was much more diverse as Scots, Welsh and Irish spun away from England and the whole racial and cultural mix was spiced with large-scale immigration from former colonies. Second, Britain had gradually shrugged off its imperial past and was edging towards a post-nationalist identity as a vigorous, semi-European nation of anarchic eccentricity. The old Britain delighted in brave and well-spoken young airmen attacking Germany with bouncing bombs; the new one revelled in Monty Python mocking tweedy upper-class twits.

The third way in which Britain had changed was linked to the second: many of the age-old class barriers based on breeding had been pulled down. Their meritocratic, plutocratic or even celebrocratic replacements were not necessarily any more appealing, but by the end of the century the national disease of cringing deferentiality had all but died out. Predictably, the interface between the old monarchy and this new, informal Britain was confused, messy and at times downright nasty.

Princess Lilibet

As had been the custom for royal ladies since time immemorial, Princess Elizabeth (known within the family as 'Lilibet') and her sister Margaret Rose were educated at home. Until she was 11, private tutors gave Lilibet only one-and-a-half hours of academic teaching per day, the rest of her time being taken up with the arts, rest and recreation. The first made little impact on her matter-of-fact mind. When the princess became heir-presumptive at the age of ten, Queen Mary tried to make good her granddaughter's educational deficiencies by arranging a few extra classes. Even so, the king and queen's determination that their daughter would not become a blue-stocking meant that her intellectual education, even by the standards of the day, was seriously lacking.

By not attending school Lilibet was also deprived of experiences that could have proved invaluable to her later on. Isolated in palaces, castles and country houses, she met no ordinary people in ordinary situations. She did not go shopping, fill in a form, pay a bill or even handle money. All the little things of everyday life were done for her. What she knew of rationing, voting, budgeting, cleaning, cooking, saving, spending and planning was all second-hand. Like a princess in a fairy tale, she lived on a royal island in the middle of a lake of wealth and privilege that separated her from the real world beyond.

Nor was this situation an accident. The golden rule of monarchy that had served since William IV's time had been the need to preserve a degree of distance between crown and subject. The elderly Sir Frederick Ponsonby had pompously tried to point this out to Edward VIII:

The Monarchy must always retain an element of mystery. A Prince should not show himself too much. The Monarchy must remain on a pedestal...If you bring it down to the people, it will lose its mystery and influence.

Edward had not agreed, pointing out to Sir Frederick that 'times are changing.'[43] Everyone in the royal household knew what had become of Edward. His brief reign and attitude was held up as an object lesson to them all: it was folly to question the maxims that had served for the better part of a century.

There were modest gestures toward modernization, of course, as there always had been. During the war, for instance, Elizabeth was allowed to join the ATS (Auxiliary Territorial Service – a woman's branch of the Army), but the workshops where she was supposed to learn vehicle maintenance were scrubbed spotless before her arrival and her fellow 'new recruits' were in fact hand-picked instructors in disguise. The nearest Elizabeth got to her people was on VE night, 8 May 1945, when, escorted only by her spinster teacher and a few officers, she was allowed to mingle with the ecstatic London crowds.

Philip

Elizabeth did not appear unduly daunted by the prospect of one day wearing the crown. She was carefully weaned into the job, making her first broadcast at the age of 14 and two years later carrying out her first public engagement: inspecting the Grenadier Guards. By 1944 she was regularly accompanying her parents on their tours around their war-torn kingdom. She also received and replied to an address from the House of Commons. All these occasions she managed with an aplomb that belied her age. What she handled far less well were informal gatherings, such as debutante dances, where she was expected to relax in the company of people of her own age and make small talk.

It was already clear that the future queen was tough, serious-minded and devoted to the task to which she had been called. Her example and mentor was her father. She noted with approval his neatness; she was fascinated by his punctiliousness; his reserve she fully understood; his sense of duty she found thoroughly inspiring. This man, she decided, would to be the pattern for a life of dutiful work that she intended to be a model for the entire nation.

Firm-minded though the princess was, she was also flesh and blood. From her early teens she had set her heart on Philip of Schleswig-Holstein-Sonderburg-Glucksburg, a fellow descendant of Queen Victoria. This energetic, good-looking and somewhat raffish naval officer responded by finding a place in his heart for the wholesomely pretty Elizabeth. After her parents' reservations had been set aside, the pair were married in a fairly restrained ceremony at the end of 1947.

Philip changed his name to the less Germanic-sounding Mountbatten and was created Duke of Edinburgh. However, much to his chagrin, he was offered no prospect of the crown or of being Prince Consort, as Victoria's Albert had been. His bride did not even adopt his family name. Only much later (1960) did Elizabeth agree that lesser royals might call themselves Mountbatten-Windsor. Philip was a man of boundless energy and was hurt and frustrated at the way he had been by-passed: 'I'm just a bloody amoeba!' he fumed.[44]

The Duke of Edinburgh

Opinion was strongly divided over the marriage of Elizabeth and Philip. Most agreed that it started well, helped by the strong physical bond between them. Only on their honeymoon did they share a bedroom, however, and ever since the 1950s there have been almost continual rumours of Philip's philandering. The wife of one of his friends, Mike Parker, said that the Duke and he would slip out of Buckingham Palace for a night on the town as 'Murgatroyd and Winterbottom'.[45] Gossip-mongers suggested he was involved in the early 1960s sex-and-spy scandal that centred around the Tory War Minister John Profumo. Philip himself, in his brusque matter-of-fact way, has always dismissed these and other such stories as nonsense. His friends support his denials.

That said, the royal couple did occasionally have rows in public, and more frequently the queen would show obvious annoyance at her husband's impatience or tactlessness. From the opposite camp came the retort that all marriages had difficult moments, and Elizabeth and Philip's was no exception; the only difference between them and everyone else was that, because of their jobs, the tiffs were public property. Royalists added that if further evidence of a loving relationship were needed, then it was surely there in the form of their children. The births of Charles (1948) and Anne (1950) were to be expected; those of Andrew and Edward, born ten and 14 years later respectively, were not. They had to be proof of a basically happy marriage.

Faithful to his wife or not, the Duke of Edinburgh was always good for a story. Where Elizabeth would never put a foot wrong, asking the right questions, making the appropriate tactful remarks, and doing her best to appear interested in whatever function she was attending, her husband was far more transparent. When bored with an official visit – which he easily was – he would suggest in a loud voice that they leave. He swore, made gaffes of a racist and politically partisan nature, and spoke his mind. When French Canadians questioned the need for a royal visit to their country, he snapped, 'Look, we don't come here for our health. We can think of better ways of enjoying ourselves…'[46] It was almost Hanoverian in its tactless honesty. On one occasion the Duke sat in the gallery of the House of Commons and by his expression made clear his views on the matter under debate – he never took his seat there again.

Philip was easily parodied. His service manner and liking for field sports clashed with the lifestyle of most journalists, who made easy copy by mocking it. During the 1960s and 1970s his straight-talking endorsement of self-reliance, competition and physical toughness was very much at variance with the prevailing liberal culture. By the 1990s, though, his approach was coming back into fashion and, while continuing to pick up on his tactlessness, the media began to treat him more kindly. His age helped, too – the follies of old men tend to evoke more sympathy than criticism.

There was a good deal to thank the Duke for. The World Wildlife Fund, one of the many charities he presided over, pioneered the conservation movement. The Duke of Edinburgh's Award Scheme, his finest creation, gave millions of youngsters in many countries a genuine sense of achievement and self-worth. His attempts to bring up to date the institution into which he had married rarely achieved the desired results: hoary flunkies fled before him when he stormed around Buckingham Palace on an early modernization programme, only to slip back into their old ways after he had gone. Nevertheless, he did try. Wherever he went there was a certain frisson, an energy and excitement that people did not experience in the presence of his diligent but slightly humdrum wife.

Margaret

During the first part of her reign the queen was presented as a near-perfect phenomenon. Hardly a syllable of personal criticism was to be heard, even in areas of the media traditionally critical of the royal family. The gossip columnists, ever eager for a royal story, looked elsewhere. There was mileage in the antics of the Duke of Edinburgh, as long as those reporting them remained within the bounds of propriety. More tangible (and publishable) were the activities of the queen's younger sister Margaret.

Margaret was everything her sister was not: beautiful, vivacious, creative, witty, volatile, unreliable and sexy. She had the talent and sparkle to have enjoyed a career in the arts, except for a royal princess of the House of Windsor that was then unthinkable. So, too, was the possibility of marriage with Group Captain Peter Townsend. A divorced equerry of her father's, Townsend had been around the Palace since 1944. He was 15 years older than Margaret and had watched her growing up until, in coronation year, rumours began to circulate of a clandestine love affair.

Townsend was sent away to a post in Brussels. When he returned two years later, the couple's ardour burned undimmed. Brows furrowed. The Tory government stepped in, declaring that as a marriage between Margaret and the RAF officer would not be recognized by the Church of England on account of his status as a divorcee, the union would damage the crown. The heart v duty drama had been played out only 20 years before, and everyone knew how the star of that show had turned out. Cornered, Margaret was urged not to follow her reviled uncle Edward. She surrendered, and the Townsend affair came to a tearful end.

Romantics say Margaret never recovered. Five years later she married Anthony Armstrong-Jones. After the birth of two children the marriage faltered and ended in divorce. The princess, who had never been exactly enthusiastic in carrying out her royal duties, virtually dropped out. Her popularity plummeted. Condemned as a frivolous extravagance on the public purse, she was the subject of spicy, sad tales of Caribbean hideaways, men friends, over-indulgence and high-living. Her death in 2002, after a long period of ill heath, finally brought one of the reign's several royal tragedies to its inevitable conclusion.

Opening the door

Ironically, Elizabeth was served well by the peccadilloes of her husband and sister. They gave her family a slightly more human face and, by way of contrast, raised her still higher above the common herd. Almost beyond criticism, for 15 years the queen single-handedly upheld, even enhanced the traditional monarchy of her ancestors.

The televized coronation brought royal pageantry to a new pitch. A series of overseas visits, beginning with a round-the-world tour of the Commonwealth in 1953–4, were well covered and enthusiastically received. With Philip dutifully but reluctantly walking behind her, she made the expected round of hospitals, factories and other sites. She opened parliaments, launched ships, entertained visiting dignitaries and delivered annual Christmas broadcasts (by now televized) to her subjects all around the world. Press releases and selected photographs showed her children developing into young adults with the occasional teenage difficulties that every family experienced. It was all just as grandpa George would have wanted: domestic, dignified, distant.

Unfortunately for the queen, domestic, dignified and distant was precisely what 1960s Britain was not. Divorce, the pill, drugs, the Beatles, Carnaby Street, hippies – these were the icons of a 'Swinging Britain' seeking a new identity. The Empire had gone, or was going, and few but the queen cared much for its ersatz replacement, the Commonwealth. The past and all its hitherto sacred traditions were mercilessly mocked in the magazine *Private Eye* and the satirical TV show *That Was The Week That Was*. Deference, that keystone of hereditary monarchy, wilted terminally. This was never more sharply demonstrated than when the Beatles smoked cannabis in a Buckingham Palace bathroom when collecting their MBEs.

Almost before anyone had realized what was happening, the royal family found itself stuck in a backwater, miles from the mainstream of British life. It was out of touch and painfully out of date. Like the tweeds it wore and the strangulated accents with which it spoke, among the young and the forward-thinking it inspired laughter, not awe. Something had to be done.

The queen was urged, with little success, to moderate her high-pitched, nasal voice and unbend a little in public. In the late 1960s she gave permission for a documentary to be made about her life and work. *The Royal Family*, which showed Elizabeth going about her monarchical duties and cooking a family barbecue, was viewed by many millions around the world and regarded as an outstanding success. It was never shown again, however, and copies were subsequently impossible to get hold of. Someone had realized that perhaps it had not been such a good idea after all: as every stripper knows, the more one shows, the more the audience wants.

Prince Charles

Although relations between the nation and the monarchy continued to deteriorate during the 1970s, the reservoir of goodwill towards the queen personally was still deep enough for her Silver Jubilee in 1977 to be celebrated with genuine and widespread enthusiasm. That aside, all was not going well. Margaret was divorced, with her sister's support, the following year. In a sense that did not matter too much because the queen's sister was now some distance from the succession. The Prince of Wales, however, was not, and it was around him that the vultures were circling.

Charles was definitely a disappointment to his father and probably, though she might not admit it even to herself, also to his mother. He had grown up into a gentle, ineffectual man who was constantly trying to be someone else. The first heir to the throne to earn a degree, he was no fool. What he lacked was confidence, a core of emotional security. A brusque, hectoring father, a pre-occupied mother incapable of expressing love, and some pretty unpromising genes probably accounted for his confused make-up.

Philip wanted a tough, no-nonsense son in his own mould. He got one in his daughter Anne, the Olympic horsewoman, but not in his eldest son. Charles played polo, jumped through the expected military hoops, and always dressed like a country gentleman. His father suspected, quite rightly, that the young man's heart was not always in the traditional role he was playing. He talked to plants; he liked acting, painting, writing and the arts. These were not the sort of things that had wasted the time of any previous Windsor – except Margaret, of course, and Philip certainly did not see her as a pattern for future sovereignty. By 1977 Charles and his father were not talking to each other.

It's a Knockout

Things began to go seriously wrong for 'the Firm' (the royal family's private name for themselves) in the 1980s. To begin with the decade was dominated by a prime minister whom the queen did not get on with – Margaret Thatcher. Quite simply, there was no room for two queens on one small island. Then, one by one, the royal marriages began to unravel. Margaret had led the way at the end of the previous decade. In 1973 Princess Anne had fallen in love with and married Captain Mark Phillips, a shy, not-too-bright Dragoon Guards officer whom the royal family, not themselves masterminds, nicknamed 'Fog'. After producing the regulatory two children, the couple drifted apart and separated in 1989.

Andrew, a hearty young man who had seen active service as a helicopter pilot during the Falklands War (1982), married the equally hearty redhead Sarah Ferguson in 1986. Although they too managed to produce a pair of children, it was not long before the tabloid newspapers – long since shorn of hang-ups about reporting royal misdemeanours – were carrying stories and pictures of the couple's infidelities. They separated officially in 1992.

A few years before this, the younger royals, with 'Fergie' prominent among them, had cast aside any last vestige of dignity attached to their branch of the monarchy by taking part in a futile TV game show, *It's A Royal Knockout*. Organized by Edward, now a would-be film producer, it was not only in toe-curling bad taste, but Edward walked out of the post-show press conference when this was suggested. Horrified, the older members of the royal family and their entourage prayed for the earth to open and swallow them up before they were subjected to further embarrassing idiocy. Their prayers went unheeded.

The Queen of Hearts

Charles married in 1981. His bride was Lady Diana Spencer, a young and innocent woman of strikingly good looks. The wedding, celebrated in St Paul's Cathedral, was perhaps the greatest royal pageant of the age. It also confirmed the status of the new Princess of Wales as a natural star, brighter even than Margaret had been and with plenty more opportunity to let her light been seen. Through the spontaneous, open and alluring Diana, it looked as if the royal family's dour public image might finally be set aside.

The marriage between Charles and Diana was a disaster. Each sought from it what the other could not provide. The prince wanted a companionable, unthreatening mother figure who would boost his shaky self-confidence. That was never Diana. The princess wanted an understanding, strong and reliable man who would tolerate her weaknesses, applaud her strengths and be her rock in life's inevitable storms. That was certainly not Charles. Thus two damaged personalities, like frightened swimmers in deep water, clutched at each other in vain. Hope turned to disappointment, disillusionment, bitterness and eventually to scorn. The fall-out of the marriage's spectacular collapse brought the monarchy to its lowest point since the abdication of Edward VIII.

If Charles had ever been in love with Diana, the fire had burned out even before the wedding. In its place an old flame was rekindled, his affection for Camilla Shand, now Mrs Parker-Bowles. Older than Charles and wiser, Camilla had first met the prince in 1973. They had then gone their separate ways before reuniting, secretly and most passionately, in 1979. By then Diana was already featuring on Charles's radar. Shortly after his marriage, he returned to Camilla's motherly arms and plain but worldly-wise face. Diana knew.

Insecure and now betrayed, after the birth of her first son, Prince William, Diana went off the rails. She still managed to captivate each time she made a public appearance but behind the scenes the picture was altogether more distressing. She suffered from eating disorders, had sharp words with her mother-in-law, and indulged in inappropriate and ill-concealed love affairs. A number of observers commented that her second son, Prince Harry, resembled Charles hardly at all. After living separate lives for some time, the couple accepted the formal dissolution of their marriage in 1996. The next year, in the company of her current boyfriend, Diana was killed in a high-speed car crash in a Parisian underpass.

Strength in adversity

Meanwhile, the aura of perfection surrounding the queen was fading fast. In 1992 her fortieth year on the throne was celebrated by a well-made documentary, *Elizabeth R*. The public's attention, however, was elsewhere – on Charles and Diana, Andrew and Fergie. Later that year the queen herself was rudely brought back to centre stage. There was an upsurge of anger at her tax-free private income (perhaps £18 million per annum) and at a gigantic civil list (£600,000 per annum going to the Queen Mother alone) that was guaranteed to rise by 7 per cent a year, whatever the rate of inflation. The Secretary of State for National Heritage then made matters a good deal worse by announcing that the government would foot the bill for an estimated £60 millions worth of fire damage done to an uninsured Windsor Castle. Fed by stories of Charles's treatment of Diana and Fergie's undignified frolicking, murmurs of criticism swelled to angry jeers. Elizabeth caught the mood when she honestly declared 1992 to have been not the *annus mirabilis* she had hoped for after 40 years of service to the nation but an *annus horribilis*.

The crown back-pedalled hard. It agreed to pay tax on its private income and to meet the expenses of members of the family. It also accepted, with much bitterness, the decision to scrap the royal yacht *Britannia* and not to build a replacement. The royal train would go too. Whatever good those moves did, it was undermined in 1997 when the queen dramatically failed to catch the national mood over the death of Diana.

The princess had won the hearts of the British people because of her looks, her openness, her vulnerability. She was a type everyone recognized: the attractive but fragile girl, let down in love, who had subsequently made a mess of her life. There was one in every family, every street. When the news of her death came through, the royal family were enjoying their summer break at Balmoral. They decided to stay there. The royal standard flying above them was not lowered, nor was one hoisted to half mast on Buckingham Palace. Among the royal household there were those who suggested that Diana's death was like the removal of a cancer.

The public was horrified at this apparent lack of sympathy or respect for their sweetheart. How could the Windsors continue their holidays while the nation mourned for the 'People's Princess'? Too late the queen realized what a serious misjudgement she had made. She came south with her family, inspected the 15,000 tons of flowers heaped against the railings of Buckingham Palace and ordered the Palace flag to be flown at half mast. Watched by 2.5 billion television viewers world-wide, she even bowed her royal head in respect as Diana's coffin passed her. The funeral was the centrepiece of an unprecedented bout of national mourning that defied all reason. Throughout the service, even when subjected to implicit criticism by Diana's brother, the queen sat unmoving, inscrutable. Right or wrong, at that moment she showed an inner strength that was almost beyond belief.

Recovery

It would take more than the death of a well-loved princess and the carping of the press owned by a republican-inclined Australian to bring down the monarchy. Guided by palace officials and encouraged by the monarchist Labour prime minister Tony Blair, the ageing queen made further efforts to appear less remote, less cold. Her garden parties embraced a wider selection of guests and she was even photographed visiting a pub.

The death of the Queen Mother in Golden Jubilee year (2002) helped boost the re-awakening sympathy for the hard-working queen. The Queen Mother, who had undertaken royal duties until the very end of her long life, had always been the most popular member of the royal family. Her passing caused the public to look again at the queen and transfer to her some of the affection and respect previously reserved for her mother. Respect, in fact, was the key. Whether royalist or republican, there were few who did not admire a woman who had stuck to her task so diligently for half a century. At the height of the Golden Jubilee celebrations a crowd of one million flooded the Mall to show their appreciation.

So, to the surprise of many, the British monarchy survived into the twenty-first century. Its anachronistic nature became even more obvious when hereditary peers lost their automatic seats in the House of Lords. There was ongoing criticism, too, on account of its cost and when individual members of the royal family said or did something unwise. Yet opinions polls regularly showed that monarchy was still what the people wanted. This remarkable resilience continued to confound commentators of all persuasions. It stemmed from Britain's unusually powerful attachment to its heritage, from the crown's ability to change and, most importantly, from the willingness of sovereigns to serve to the best of their ability. Heredity being an unreliable means of selection, however, only time will show whether that tradition is maintained.

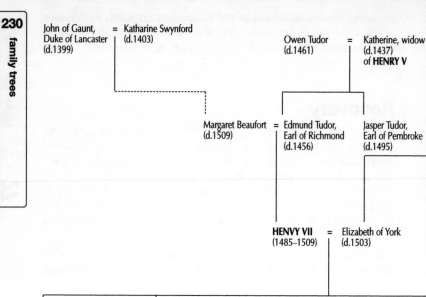

John of Gaunt, = Katharine Swynford
Duke of Lancaster | (d.1403)
(d.1399)

Owen Tudor = Katherine, widow
(d.1461) (d.1437)
of **HENRY V**

Margaret Beaufort = Edmund Tudor, Jasper Tudor,
(d.1509) Earl of Richmond Earl of Pembroke
(d.1456) (d.1495)

HENVY VII = Elizabeth of York
(1485–1509) (d.1503)

Arthur, = Catherine of (1) = **HENRY VIII** = (2) Anne Boleyn = (3) Jane Seymour = (4) Anne of Cleves
Prince Aragon (1509–47) (d.1536) (d.1537) (d.1557)
of Wales (d. 1536)
(d. 1502) = (5) Catherine Howard
(d.1542)

= (6) Catherine Parr
(d.1548)

PHILIP II, = **MARY I** **ELIZABETH I** **EDWARD VI**
King of Spain (1553–58) (1558–1603) (1547–53)
(d.1598)

The Tudors

EDWARD IV = Elizabeth Woodville
(1461–83)   (d.1492)

EDWARD V   Richard, Duke of York
(1485)   (d. 1455)

Margaret   =   **JAMES IV,**   Mary   =   (1) LOUIS XII, King of France
(d.1541)   King of Scotland   (d.1533)   (d.1515)
               (1488–1513)   =   (2) Charles, Duke of Suffolk
                                                 (d.1545)

Madeline, (1) = **JAMES V,** = (2) Mary of Guise   Frances   = Henry Grey,
of France   King of Scotland   (d.1560)   (d.1559)   Duke of Suffolk
(d.1537)   (1513–42)   (d.1554)

FRANCIS II,   (1) = **MARY,**   = (2) Henry, Lord   Lady Jane Grey
King of France   Queen   Darnley   (d.1554)
(d.1560)   of Scots   (d.1567)
                    (1542–67,
                    d.1587)

                              = James, Earl of (3)
                              Bothwell
                              (d.1578)

JAMES VI OF SCOTLAND   = Anne of Denmark
(1567–1625)   (d.1619)
AND I OF ENGLAND
(1603–25)

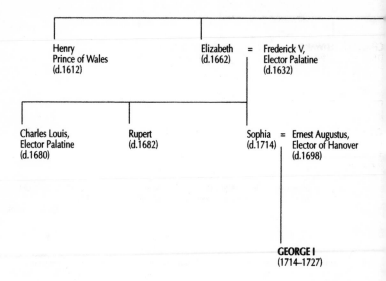

Henry
Prince of Wales
(d.1612)

Elizabeth   =   Frederick V,
(d.1662)   Elector Palatine
                 (d.1632)

Charles Louis,   Rupert
Elector Palatine   (d.1682)
(d.1680)

Sophia   =   Ernest Augustus,
(d.1714)   Elector of Hanover
               (d.1698)

GEORGE I
(1714–1727)

The Stuarts

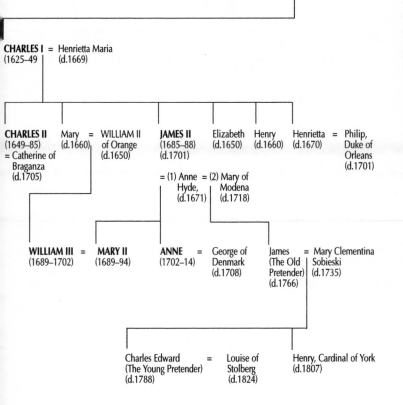

JAMES VI OF SCOTLAND = Anne of
(1567–1625)   Denmark
AND I OF ENGLAND   (d.1619)
(1603–25)

CHARLES I = Henrietta Maria
(1625–49) | (d.1669)

CHARLES II   Mary = WILLIAM II   JAMES II   Elizabeth   Henry   Henrietta = Philip,
(1649–85)   (d.1660) of Orange   (1685–88) (d.1650)   (d.1660) (d.1670)   Duke of
= Catherine of   (d.1650)   (d.1701)   Orleans
Braganza   (d.1701)
(d.1705)
                                  = (1) Anne = (2) Mary of
                                     Hyde,   Modena
                                     (d.1671)   (d.1718)

WILLIAM III = MARY II   ANNE   = George of   James   = Mary Clementina
(1689–1702)   (1689–94) (1702–14) Denmark   (The Old   Sobieski
                                    (d.1708)   Pretender)   (d.1735)
                                                 (d.1766)

                    Charles Edward   =   Louise of   Henry, Cardinal of York
                    (The Young Pretender)   Stolberg   (d.1807)
                    (d.1788)   (d.1824)

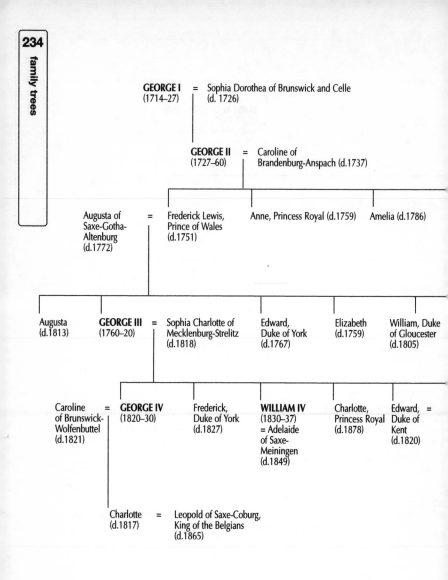

GEORGE I = Sophia Dorothea of Brunswick and Celle
(1714–27)   (d. 1726)

GEORGE II = Caroline of
(1727–60)   Brandenburg-Anspach (d.1737)

Augusta of = Frederick Lewis,   Anne, Princess Royal (d.1759)   Amelia (d.1786)
Saxe-Gotha- Prince of Wales
Altenburg   (d.1751)
(d.1772)

Augusta   GEORGE III = Sophia Charlotte of   Edward,   Elizabeth   William, Duke
(d.1813)   (1760–20)   Mecklenburg-Strelitz   Duke of York   (d.1759)   of Gloucester
                         (d.1818)   (d.1767)   (d.1805)

Caroline   = GEORGE IV   Frederick,   WILLIAM IV   Charlotte,   Edward, =
of Brunswick- (1820–30)   Duke of York   (1830–37)   Princess Royal   Duke of
Wolfenbuttel   (d.1827)   = Adelaide   (d.1878)   Kent
(d.1821)   of Saxe-   (d.1820)
                                        Meiningen
                                        (d.1849)

Charlotte   = Leopold of Saxe-Coburg,
(d.1817)   King of the Belgians
            (d.1865)

The Hanoverians

William, Duke   Caroline (d.1757)   Mary (d.1772)   Louisa (d.1751)
of Cumberland
(d.1765)

Henry, Duke   Louisa   Frederick   Caroline
of Cumberland   (d.1768)   (d.1765)   (d.1775)
(d.1790)

Victoria   Augusta   Elizabeth   Ernest Augustus,   Augustus,   Adolphus,   Mary   Sophia
of Saxe-   (d.1840)   (d.1840)   Duke of   Duke of   Duke of   (d.1857)   (d.1898)   Amelia
Coburg   Cumberland   Sussex   Cambridge   (d.1810)
(d.1861)   (King of   (d.1843)   (d.1850)
                                      Hanover)
                                      (d.1851)

VICTORIA
(1837–1901)

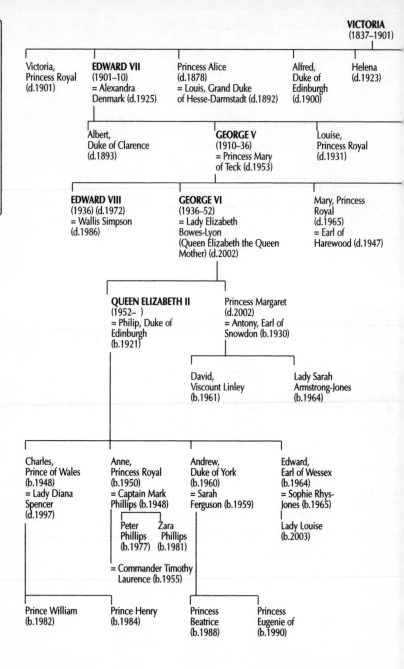

The Saxe-Coburg-Gotha/Windsors

= Prince Albert of Saxe-Coburg-Gotha (Prince Consort) (d.1861)

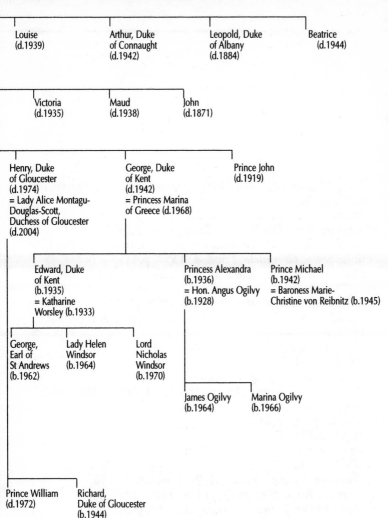

Louise
(d.1939)

Arthur, Duke
of Connaught
(d.1942)

Leopold, Duke
of Albany
(d.1884)

Beatrice
(d.1944)

Victoria
(d.1935)

Maud
(d.1938)

John
(d.1871)

Henry, Duke
of Gloucester
(d.1974)
= Lady Alice Montagu-
Douglas-Scott,
Duchess of Gloucester
(d.2004)

George, Duke
of Kent
(d.1942)
= Princess Marina
of Greece (d.1968)

Prince John
(d.1919)

Edward, Duke
of Kent
(b.1935)
= Katharine
Worsley (b.1933)

Princess Alexandra
(b.1936)
= Hon. Angus Ogilvy
(b.1928)

Prince Michael
(b.1942)
= Baroness Marie-
Christine von Reibnitz (b.1945)

George,
Earl of
St Andrews
(b.1962)

Lady Helen
Windsor
(b.1964)

Lord
Nicholas
Windsor
(b.1970)

James Ogilvy
(b.1964)

Marina Ogilvy
(b.1966)

Prince William
(d.1972)

Richard,
Duke of Gloucester
(b.1944)

endnotes

[1] Greg Walker, ed., *John Skelton, Selected Poems*, Everyman, 1997, p.95.

[2] Shakespeare, *Richard II*, II, i.

[3] Richard Rex, *The Tudors*, Tempus, 2002, p.129.

[4] W. Nicholson, ed., *Grindal's Remains*, Cambridge, 1843.

[5] John Stow, *Chronicle*, London, 1598, p.415.

[6] Wallace MacCaffrey, *Elizabeth I*, Edward Arnold, 1993, p.371.

[7] J. E. Neale, *Elizabeth I*, Penguin, 1961, p.397.

[8] Stewart Ross, *The Stewart Dynasty*, Thomas and Lochar, 1993, p.202.

[9] *Ibid.*, Ross, p.219.

[10] *Ibid.*, p.231.

[11] Widely cited, e.g. *Ibid.*, p.230.

[12] H. R. Trevor-Roper, *Archbishop Laud*, Macmillan, 1965, p.56.

[13] Ross, *op.cit.*, p.245.

[14] *Ibid.*, p.255.

[15] *Ibid.*, p.256.

[16] *Ibid.*, p.256.

[17] Maurice Ashley, *Charles II*, Panther, 1973, p.46.

[18] Stewart Ross, *History in Hiding*, Hale, 1991, p.93.

[19] John Miller, *James II*, Methuen, 1991, p.21.

[20] Ross, *op.cit.*, p.279.

[21] Julian Hoppit, *A Land of Liberty? England 1689–1727*, Oxford, 2000, p.135.

[22] Edward Gregg, *Queen Anne*, Routledge & Kegal, Paul, 1980. p.35.

[23] 1714, Canto 3, I.7. The word 'tea' was then pronounced the French way, *thé*.

[24] Ross, *op.cit.*, p.282.

[25]*Ibid.*, p.345.

[26]*Ibid.*, p.297.

[27]Lord John Hervey, *Memoirs*, (ed. Sidgewick), 3 vols, London, 1931, III, pp.812–3.

[28]Mrs Arbuthnot's diary, quoted in John Brooke, *George III*, Panther, 1974, p.607.

[29]Brook, supra, p.356.

[30]Cited on www.spartacus.schoolnet.co.uk/MOedwardVII

[31]Philip Magnus, *King Edward the Seventh*, John Murray, London, 1964, p.41.

[32]*Ibid.*, p.456.

[33]Piers Brendon and Philip Whitehead, *The Windsors*, Pimlico, 2000, p.64.

[34]Cited on www.geocites.com/jesusib/GeorgeV

[35]Frances Donaldson, *Edward VIII*, Futura, 1976, p.10.

[36]Brendon and Whitehead, *op.cit.*, p.36.

[37]*Ibid.*, p.60.

[38]Donaldson, *op.cit.*, p.295.

[39]Cited on http://news.bbc.co.uk/1/hi/uk/2701965.stm

[40]Cited on http://news.bbc.co.uk/1/hi/uk/2699035.stm

[41]Mentioned in Brendon and Whitehead, *op.cit.*, p.90.

[42]John W. Wheeler-Bennett, *King George VI*, Macmillan, London, 1958, p.293.

[43]Cited from Edward VIII's autobiography, *A King's Story*, in Gyles Brandreth, *Philip and Elizabth, Portrait of a Marriage*, Century, 2004, p.89.

[44]Brendon and Whitehead, *op.cit.*, p.131.

[45]Nicholas Davies, *Elizabeth: Behind Palace Doors*, Mainstream, 2000, p.133.

[46]Brendon and Whitehead, *op.cit.*, p.176.

taking it further

Selected biographies and other reading

Alison Weir, *Britain's Royal Families: The Complete Genealogy*, Pimlico, 2002

Richard Rex, *The Tudors*, Tempus, 2002

S. B. Chrimes, *Henry VII*, Methuen, 1972

J. J. Scarisbrick, *Henry VIII*, Methuen, 1968

David Starkey, *Six Wives: the Queens of Henry VIII*, Vintage, 2004

Jennifer Loach, *Edward VI*, Yale, 2002

Wallace MacCaffrey, *Elizabeth I*, Edward Arnold, 1993

J. E. Neale, *Elizabeth I*, Penguin, 1961

Stewart Ross, *The Stewart Dynasty*, Thomas and Lochar, 1993

John Miller, *The Stuarts*, Hambledon and London, 2004

Maurice Lee, *Great Britain's Solomon: James VI and I in His Three Kingdoms*, University of Illinois, 1990

Charles Carlton, *Charles I*, Routledge, 1983

P. Gregg, *Charles I*, Dent, 1981

Maurice Ashley, *Charles II*, Panther, 1973

John Miller, *Charles II*, Weidenfeld and Nicholson, 1991

John Miller, *James II*, New Haven, 2000

Bryan Beven, *William III*, Rubicon, 1997

Edward Gregg, *Queen Anne*, Routledge & Kegan, Paul, 1980

Ragnild Hatton, *George I*, Thames and Hudson, 1978

John Van Der Kiste, *George II and Queen Caroline*, Sutton, 1997

John Brooke, *George III*, Panther, 1974

E. A. Smith, *George IV*, Yale, 1999

Anne Somerset, *The Life and Times of William IV*, Weidenfeld and Nicholson, 1993

Elizabeth Longford, *Victoria, RI*, Weidenfeld and Nicholson, 1964

Monica Charlot, *Victoria the Young Queen*, Blackwell, 1991

Philip Magnus, *King Edward the Seventh*, John Murray, London, 1964

Kenneth Rose, *George V*, Macmillan, 1983

Piers Brendon and Philip Whitehead, *The Windsors*, Pimlico, 2000

Frances Donaldson, *Edward VIII*, Futura, 1976

Frances Donaldson, *George VI and Queen Elizabeth*, Weidenfeld and Nicholson, 1977

Sarah Bradford, *George VI*, Penguin, 2002

Gyles Brandreth, *Philip and Elizabeth: Portrait of a Marriage*, Century, 2004

Nicholas Davies, *Elizabeth: Behind Palace Doors*, Mainstream, 2000

Selected websites

http://www.royalist.info
http://www.bbc.co.uk/history/historic_figures
http://www.royal.gov.uk
http://www.britannia.com/history
http://www.tudors.crispen.org
http://www.great-britain.co.uk/history

Places to visit

Sites associated with the modern British monarchy are, of course, legion. An interested visitor might begin with those listed below. Opening times are often limited – please check locally.

London

Tower of London
Banqueting House, Whitehall
Houses of Parliament
Westminster Hall
Westminster Abbey
Hampton Court
Buckingham Palace

Outside London

Caernarfon Castle, North Wales
Windsor Castle and Chapel, Berkshire
Holyrood House, Scotland
Edinburgh Castle, Scotland
Sandringham House, Norfolk
Balmoral Castle, Scottish Highlands
Osborne House, Isle of Wight
Royal Pavilion, Brighton
Stirling Castle, Scotland

index

Why not try another book from
the **teach yourself** series?
Read on to sample a
chapter from **The First World War**

teach yourself

the first world war

goal
sample another book

category
history

content
- explore the events of this harsh and costly war
- understand the impact on all those involved
- discover the details of this powerful story

be where you want to be with **teach yourself**

teach
yourself

12 'keep the home fires burning' – the home front

This chapter will cover:
- the British reaction to the war
- the problems that faced the British government
- the Easter Rebellion in Ireland
- the issue of conscription
- the extent to which the war affected the everyday lives of the British people.

'Keep the home fires burning
  While your hearts are yearning
Though your lads are far away,
  They dream of home.'

(A popular song, *Keep the Home Fires Burning*,
written by Ivor Novello, 1893–1951)

Britain at the start of the war

In 1914, at the outbreak of war, Britain had a Liberal
government led by Herbert Asquith. Other leading members of
the government included David Lloyd George, Chancellor of the
Exchequer, Sir Edward Grey, Foreign Secretary, and Winston
Churchill, First Lord of the Admiralty whilst Lord Kitchener
was appointed Secretary for War. The declaration of war led to
a wave of anti-German feeling that sometimes turned to
mindless hysteria. People with German-sounding names had
their windows smashed and their businesses ransacked, lecturers
of German or Austrian origin were abused by their students
even if they had long been naturalized British citizens. Many,
even though they were old and infirm, were interned and some
were even driven to suicide. The writer D. H. Lawrence was
insulted because his wife was a member of the Richthofen
family; Prince Louis of Battenberg, forced to resign from the
Royal Navy because of his German connections, changed his
family name to Mountbatten. The Royal Automobile Club
(RAC) banned members of German or Austrian origin and it
was even considered unpatriotic to own a dachshund dog. In his
magazine *John Bull*, Horatio Bottomley advised his readers, 'if
one day in a restaurant you are being served by a German
waiter, you will throw your soup in his foul face; if you find
yourself sitting next to a German clerk, you will spill the inkpot
over his foul head'. At the same time the country was affected
by spy mania and much of this was caused by the appearance of
Erskine Childers's espionage novel, *The Riddle of the Sands*
(1900), and the irresponsible writing of William Le Queux.

To cope with the situation, the government passed the Defence
of the Realm Act (DORA) which allowed the use of an extensive
range of emergency powers. For serious crimes, civilians became
liable to trial by courts martial and for lesser crimes, by
summary trial and punishment. Whilst steps were taken to
protect railways and ports from acts of espionage, the
censorship of all outward-bound overseas mail was introduced
to prevent people communicating with the enemy. Censorship of

the press was also introduced and action taken to control the sale of alcohol. Measures were also taken to prevent the spread of false rumours and powers were granted to the government to requisition factories and workshops and turn them to wartime production.

Early problems

The appointment of Lord Kitchener as Secretary for War created problems. The choice of the hero of the Battle of Omdurman and the Boer War was intended to provide a boost to the morale of the British people and to his credit, he recognized that it would be a prolonged war and his famous 'Your country needs you' poster inspired thousands to volunteer to serve in the forces. An aloof man who resented criticism, he proved difficult to work with since he held the view that he should be allowed to run the war by himself without interference or a need to consult his Cabinet colleagues. He refused to delegate responsibility, treated his subordinates with contempt and was even at loggerheads with Lloyd George. As far as the nation was concerned, his untimely death in 1916 was regarded as a tragedy but as one observer commented, 'it was not so much regretted in government and by his friends, not at all, for he never had any.' Margot Asquith, the Prime Minister's wife said of Kitchener's death, 'if he was not a great man, he was a great poster'.

In 1915, Field Marshal Sir John French let it be known in *The Times* newspaper that the main reason for his lack of success on the Western Front was an acute shortage of shells. This disclosure led to public disquiet, open criticism of the government, a crisis of confidence and the end of the Liberal government. In its place, Asquith set up a coalition government with a Cabinet consisting of Liberals, Conservatives and the leader of the Labour Party, Arthur Henderson. David Lloyd George was appointed Minister of Munitions. The mercurial Welshman took control of all munitions factories and, against considerable trade-union opposition, used his persuasive skills to do away with a range of restrictive practices and encouraged the employment of women. More inclined to use businessmen than civil servants to run the factories, Lloyd George's management of the munitions industry was impressive. Earlier, Kitchener had commented that four machine guns per battalion would be sufficient and anything more a luxury. Lloyd George, determined to exceed this, famously said, 'Take Kitchener's figure. Square it.

Multiply by two. Then double it again for luck.' A. J. P. Taylor (1954) summed up his achievement, 'The army began the war with 1,330 machine guns. During the war 240,506 were manufactured – thanks to Lloyd George.' Lloyd George was also responsible for a range of measures taken to combat absenteeism due to drunkenness by reducing licensing hours, diluting the strength of beer and imposing heavier taxes on alcoholic drinks. King George gave his campaign a boost by banning the consumption of alcohol in the royal household but the Houses of Parliament declined to follow the sovereign's example.

Women go to war

British trade-union leaders feared that the permanent employment of women in the workplace might bring about the dilution of industry and lead to unemployment when servicemen were demobilized at the end of the war. Some also feared the consequences of the additional independence women might gain by having their own pay packets. Women were not just employed in the manufacture of munitions but in many other positions vacated by men serving at the front. In the munitions factories, girls worked 12-hour shifts, seven days a week for a wage of £2.20, just half that paid to men doing the same work but nearly three times that paid to soldiers serving in the trenches. The task of filling shell cases with explosives was not without its dangers and the powder turned the faces of the girls bright yellow and earned them the nickname 'canary girls'. There were also major disasters when an explosion at a munitions works at Chilwell in Nottinghamshire killed 250 and another at Silvertown in London's East End claimed over 300 lives. The idea of them being a 'gentle sex' was abandoned as women worked in a range of heavy industries, delivered coal, collected refuse, operated buses and trains and were employed in agriculture as Land Girls. Many volunteered to become nurses and towards the end of the war they were allowed to enrol in the services as uniformed auxiliaries. Altogether 92,000 joined the Women's Army Auxiliary Corps (WAAC), the Women's Royal Naval Service (WRNS) and the Women's Royal Air Force (WRAF). With many young girls living away from home in hostels, the employment of women on such a large scale created social problems and there was concern about their moral welfare. The work of such organizations as the Women's Patrol and the Women's League of Honour failed to prevent a

30 per cent increase in the illegitimacy rate of children born during the war years. Living away from their homes and their parents allowed girls a greater freedom that brought with it changes in their attitudes and outlook. The wearing of cosmetics and smoking became widespread as did drinking in public houses whilst dress-wise, the wearing of long skirts and camisoles gave way to short skirts and brassieres. Some young women also used language that would have shocked their parents and grandparents. It is estimated that in the final year of the war over 1.3 million women were in employment with over half of them doing jobs previously done by men.

The Easter Rebellion of 1916

In 1914, it seemed that the long-standing Irish demand for home rule was about to be granted but when the war started Asquith's government declared that the issue would have to be suspended until the conflict was over. In the event, both those who favoured home rule, the Irish Nationalists, and those against, the Unionists, declared their support for Britain in her war 'for the freedom of small nations' and some 80,000 Irishmen volunteered to serve in the British army. Many of them were Irish Nationalists only too pleased to fight for the independence of largely Catholic Belgium but home in Ireland there were still those who resented the British government's decision to suspend the granting of home rule.

Amongst a group known as the Irish Volunteers were men who regarded the coming of war as an opportunity to force the hand of the British government since they believed that 'England's difficulty was Ireland's opportunity'. The leaders of these men, Patrick Pearse, Sean McDermott and James Connolly, set about planning a rebellion against continued British rule. Their cause was helped by the fact that the British government was considering the introduction of conscription and this would have meant that Irishmen would have been forced to serve in the British armed forces. As preparations were made for the rebellion, so the Irish Volunteers paraded openly, collected money to buy weapons from Germany and tried to recruit men for a Citizens' Army. The rebellion was planned to take place on Easter Sunday 1916 when men would take over strategic points in the centre of Dublin and surround the British army barracks in Dublin Castle. The rebel headquarters was to be the General Post Office in Sackville Street, now known as O'Connell Street.

The uprising got off to a bad start when a German gun-running ship was intercepted by the Royal Navy. Even so, events went ahead as planned and on Easter Sunday morning people watched as the rebels ran up the Irish green orange and white tricolour over the post office and Pearse read a proclamation declaring the establishment of an Irish Republic. With none of the promised German assistance forthcoming, the rebels were hopelessly outnumbered and one by one their strongholds were overrun by British troops. From Dublin Bay, salvos (gunfire from ships) from a Royal Navy gunboat reduced the centre of the city to rubble and a mass of flames. On 29 April, the Irish Volunteers surrendered unconditionally.

The rebellion, which cost the lives of 550 people and left over 2,500 wounded, also caused damage to buildings and property at an estimated cost of £3 million. Arrests followed and although 90 people were sentenced to death only 15 were actually executed. One of those put on trial was a former British diplomat who had earlier been awarded a knighthood, Sir Roger Casement. In spite of his Protestant Ulster origins, he sympathized with the aims of the Irish Nationalist movement and had gone as far as to travel to Germany to win support for the rebellion and urge Irish prisoners of war to form a brigade to fight against the British. His mission proved a failure and he returned to Ireland to try and prevent the uprising that he was now convinced was doomed to failure. Soon after he was put ashore from a German submarine in Tralee Bay, Casement was arrested and sent for trial at the Old Bailey in London charged with treason. At his trial, he presented his case well but the appearance of his diaries containing details of his homosexual activities proved decisive. He was found guilty and hanged in Pentonville prison. To this day, the authenticity of Casement's diaries remains disputed and to the Irish, he is considered a patriot and martyr to the cause of their independence.

The bulk of the Irish people had not supported the rebellion and they were angry that their lives had been put at risk and their homes destroyed because of it. However, when it became known that British soldiers had shot some prisoners out of hand, imprisoned many blameless men and that James Connolly, too weak to stand, had been tied to a chair to face his executioners, sympathy for the rebels increased. Because of his American birth and half-Spanish parentage, one of the leaders of the rebellion to survive was Eamonn de Valera who was later to become Prime Minister and then President of an independent Ireland.

The issue of conscription

In September 1914, Herbert Asquith told the House of Commons that 439,000 men had already volunteered for military service. By the end of that month, this had risen to 750,000 and afterwards the monthly average was 125,000. To some extent these figures were a response to Kitchener's poster but other more subtle methods were also used to encourage men to enlist. Even so, as people became aware of the carnage on the Western Front and the horrific nature of trench warfare, the recruiting posters lost their appeal and ceased to have the same effect. With no longer a rush to enlist, the number of volunteers declined and this meant that the government had to give some thought to the idea of conscripting men for the army.

It was the Earl of Derby who first suggested a scheme by which men were invited to voluntarily register for military service on the understanding that married men would only be called up after all single men on the register. The 'Derby Scheme' failed because whilst married men registered in large numbers few bachelors came forward. Early in 1916, the Military Service Act introduced conscription for all bachelors aged between 18 and 41 and four months later this was extended to all men in that age group. The decision to introduce conscription led to uproar in the House of Commons with a number of Liberal Members of Parliament (MPs) voting against and some senior members of the Cabinet threatening to resign. Across the country branches of a Non-Conscription Fellowship, a movement founded by the Labour MP Fenner Brockway and supported by such notables as Bertrand Russell, Lytton Strachey and Virginia Woolf, were set up. Opposition was based on the fear that conscription would 'militarize the nation' and that it impinged on personal freedom. By the end of the war, conscription had been extended to include men up to the age of 50.

Conscientious objectors

The Military Service Act made provision for men who, for reasons of conscience, were opposed to being conscripted for military service to register as conscientious objectors. Such men, whose objection was usually based on either moral or religious grounds, fell into two categories – alternativists and absolutists. Alternativists were prepared to serve providing they would not be involved in the shedding of blood; the absolutists refused to engage in any form of military service or put on uniform. The alternativists were allowed to join a Non-Combatant Corps and many of them served with distinction in the front line as medical orderlies and lost their lives, but dealing with the absolutists proved a far more difficult matter. Ridiculed as 'conchies' or 'won't fight funks', they had to appear before tribunals usually made up of people who had no sympathy with their viewpoint whatsoever. The questioning was intended to trap men into saying that in certain circumstances they would resort to violence – 'What would you do if a criminal assaulted your mother?' 'What would you do if a stranger attempted to rape your wife?' were typical. The Non-Conscription Fellowship and Quakers offered to coach young men awaiting their tribunals in the art of handling such questioning. Considered cowards, very few succeeded in convincing the tribunals of the validity of their reasons and if they persisted with their objection, they were arrested and sent to prison to serve indeterminate sentences with hard labour. Some were even held in solitary confinement and placed on a diet of bread and water. There were instances when men were forcibly put into uniform and sent to army units in France and, now subject to military law, they were liable to be shot if they refused an order. Although there were rumours, there is no evidence that any conscientious objectors were actually executed.

The effects of the war on the everyday lives of the British people

As a result of towns along the East Coast being shelled by German warships and Zeppelins, and Gotha bombers bombing London and other towns and cities, some 1,500 people had been killed and 3,000 injured by enemy action. Even so, for the vast majority of the people, the war presented no immediate threat to their safety.

During the war it became necessary to ration certain foodstuffs. In spite of the success of the German U-boat campaign, there was never any acute shortage of food and rationing was introduced more to avoid queuing and to assure the people that come what may, everyone would get a fair share of the food available. Even so, sugar was rationed in 1917, meat, butter and tea in 1918 and housewives had to adapt in order to feed their families. In rural areas, food was usually quite plentiful but in the towns and cities a flourishing black market provided extra food and scarce luxuries for those who could afford to pay extra for them. Where foods were in short supply, alternatives had to be found. Margarine replaced butter, white bread became a rarity, horsemeat was eaten and new ways of preserving food used. It was discovered that the dried roots of dandelions provided a powder that tasted something like coffee and that rye bread was not so bad after all. Unfortunately, a tragedy occurred when a housewife decided to cook not only the stalks but also the leaves of rhubarb and succeeded in poisoning her family. In addition, families were encouraged to have meatless days, use government recommended 'war recipes' and above all to avoid wastage. Everyone was encouraged to grow as much food as they could in their gardens and allotments. Fuel and clothing were also scarce and an appeal urged people to 'Take the coal off the fire before you go to bed ... The coal you save today, will start the fire tomorrow.'

With so many men in the armed forces, labour was in short supply and this led to a sharp increase in the earnings of both skilled and unskilled workers so that by 1918, some wages had doubled and in certain industries, even trebled. By mid-1915, food prices had risen by 30 per cent with some scarce foodstuffs more than doubling in price. Worse was to come when by late 1916 food prices had increased by 60 per cent compared with the 1914 level. Even so, wages rose more steeply than prices and generally people were better fed than ever before.

It has been estimated that the war cost the British people a staggering £75,077,000,000. This was paid for out of loans received from the United States and by increasing the money raised from taxation. High taxes were also levied on a wide range of luxury goods. In addition, a patriotic appeal was made to people to help the war effort by purchasing War Bonds.

Apart from providing many women with financial independence, their work in munitions factories and other industries meant that many households now enjoyed a very welcome additional income. In spite of the war, some trade-union leaders, usually those with left-wing views who regarded the conflict as a capitalist war, were prepared to take part in industrial action. Although strikes on Clydeside and in South Wales were settled through conciliation, bitterness remained and strikes in the munitions industry were declared crimes punishable in the courts. It was ironic that the areas that showed most union militancy were the very same areas that had produced the greatest numbers of volunteers for military service.

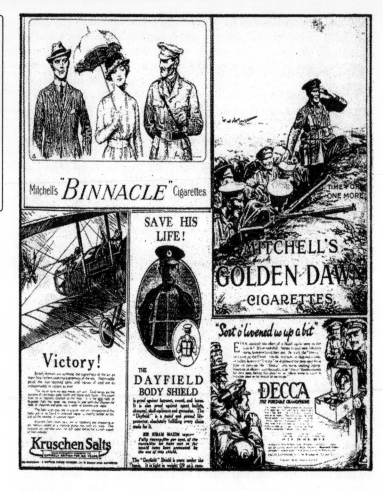

Many adverts showed a complete ignorance of the true nature of soldiering and life at the front. Top (left to right): rival cigarette companies show a young lady obviously preferring the attention of a soldier to that of a civilian; a sergeant treating his men to a final cigarette before going over the top. Bottom (left to right): the heroism of fliers is used to advertise a laxative, Krushen Salts; families were encouraged to buy serving men Dayfield Body Shields which, so the advert claims, will save their lives; an officer 'livens up' his men by playing them music on a Decca gramophone.

As the nation adapted to the needs of wartime production, areas became associated with new manufacturing industries. Whilst munitions factories were widely scattered across the land, the area around the Solent on the South Coast, the Home Counties and Glasgow in Scotland became centres for aircraft production. Whilst Warrington became noted for the production of barbed wire, poison gas was manufactured at Runcorn and the traditional shipbuilding areas in the north-east, north-west, Clydeside and Northern Ireland were called on to produce warships and merchant ships in even greater numbers. As thousands of wounded soldiers returned home to Southampton and other South Coast ports to be treated at Netley and many other hospitals so, for reasons of security, many German prisoners of war were sent to the Isle of Man.

A feature of the war was the speed with which manufacturers adjusted their advertising to embrace the patriotic fervour of the time.

Letters from soldiers serving at the front were often slow to reach home and were censored and often relatives had to make do with the very limited news included on a Field Postcard. News that a relative had been killed in action reached their next of kin by various means. Official notification might take months to arrive and relatives lived in dread of telegrams or letters in buff envelopes that began 'Deeply regret to inform you …' or 'It is my painful duty to inform you …'. Before this, such information might have already reached relatives in a letter from one of the soldier's comrades or from an army chaplain who had taken down his last words or attended his burial. It was usual for commanding officers to write personal letters to the wives and mothers of fellow officers who had fallen in battle. A *Weekly Casualty List* was published by the War Office and lists also appeared in local newspapers. Those informed that their relative was 'missing' continued to live in hope but only too often had to finally accept the inevitable. The Germans and the Allies kept each other informed of the details of men who had been taken prisoner.